Ministry
by the Book

Derek Tidball

Ministry
by the Book

New Testament patterns for pastoral leadership

APOLLOS

APOLLOS (an imprint of Inter-Varsity Press)
Norton Street, Nottingham NG7 3HR, England
Email: ivp@ivpbooks.com
Website: www.ivpbooks.com

First published 2008

British Library Cataloguing in Publication Data
A catalogue record for this book is available from the British Library.

ISBN: 978-1-84474-328-5

Set in Monotype Garamond 11/13pt
Typeset in Great Britain by Servis Filmsetting Ltd, Stockport, Cheshire
Printed and bound in Great Britain by Ashford Colour Press Ltd, Gosport, Hampshire

Inter-Varsity Press publishes Christian books that are true to the Bible and that communicate the gospel, develop discipleship and strengthen the church for its mission in the world.

Inter-Varsity Press is closely linked with the Universities and Colleges Christian Fellowship, a student movement connecting Christian Unions in universities and colleges throughout Great Britain, and a member movement of the International Fellowship of Evangelical Students. Website: www.uccf.org.uk.

Dedicated to
my friends

Sam Abramian, Simon Cragg, Andy Partington, Rhys Stenner

the next generation in ministry whom
it has been my privilege to mentor.

CONTENTS

ABBREVIATIONS

1QSa	*Rule of the Congregation*
AB	Anchor Bible
BibInt	*Biblical Interpretation*
BCL	Biblical Classics Library
BNTC	Black's New Testament Commentary
BST	The Bible Speaks Today
BTB	*Biblical Theology Bulletin*
DJG	*Dictionary of Jesus and the Gospels*, ed. J. B. Green and S. McKnight (Downers Grove: IVP; Leicester: IVP, 1992)
DLNT	*Dictionary of the Later New Testament and Its Developments*, ed. R. P. Martin and P. H. Davids (Downers Grove: IVP; Leicester: IVP, 1997)
DPL	*Dictionary of Paul and His Letters*, ed. G. F. Hawthorne and R. P. Martin (Downers Grove: IVP; Leicester: IVP, 1993)
ERT	*Evangelical Review of Theology*
EvQ	*Evangelical Quarterly*
ICC	International Critical Commentary
IVPNTC	InterVarsity Press New Testament Commentary
JBL	*Journal of Biblical Literature*
JPTSup	Journal of Pentecostal Theology: Supplement Series
JSNT	*Journal for the Study of the New Testament*

JSNTSup	Journal for the Study of the New Testament: Supplement Series
JSOT	Journal for the Study of the Old Testament
LNTS	Library of New Testament Studies
NCB	New Century Bible
NDCEPT	*New International Dictionary of Christian Ethics and Pastoral Theology*, ed. D. J. Atkinson and D. H. Field (Leicester: IVP; Downers Grove: IVP, 1995)
NIB	The New Interpreters' Bible
NICNT	New International Commentary on the New Testament
NIDNTT	*New International Dictionary of New Testament Theology*, ed. C. Brown, 3 vols. (Paternoster: Exeter, 1975, 1976, 1978)
NIGTC	New International Greek Testament Commentary
NLCNT	New London Commentary on the New Testament Series
NovT	*Novum Testamentum*
NovTSup	Novum Testamentum Supplements
NPNF[1]	*Nicene and Post-Nicene Fathers*, Series 1
NRSV	New Revised Standard Version
NSBT	New Studies in Biblical Theology
NT	New Testament
NTG	New Testament Guides
NTS	*New Testament Studies*
OBT	Overtures to Biblical Theology
PNTC	Pillar New Testament Commentary
SNTSMS	Society for New Testament Studies Monograph Series
SP	Sacra pagina
SPCK	Society for Promoting Christian Knowledge
TBC	Torch Bible Commentaries
TDNT	*Theological Dictionary of the New Testament*, ed. G. Kittel and G. Friedrich, tr. G. W. Bromiley, 10 vols. (Grand Rapids: Eerdmans, 1964–76)
TNIV	Today's New International Version
TNTC	Tyndale New Testament Commentary
TynBul	*Tyndale Bulletin*
WBC	Word Biblical Commentary

INTRODUCTION

'Oh no!' said a colleague when he asked me the title of this book. '*Ministry by the Book* sounds as if you are going to write a "how to" book on ministry; you know, like how to do ministry in six simple steps as if it's the same as cooking a McDonald's hamburger. And if that's not it, it sounds like you're wanting to tie people down and control them. The Book says . . . , so you must do it this way.' Ironically, neither of these is remotely true; quite the reverse, in fact. This book seeks to open up the imagination about ministry, not to close a discussion down. It seeks to sketch several models of ministry, all of which have their origin in the New Testament, and challenge the stunted understanding of ministry that so often characterizes our churches today. I hope it provides a number of 'models of permission' that enable a freer approach to ministry and the way it is conducted, and provides encouragement for those who don't fit the 'McDonaldized' version of ministry so common today.

The remarkable growth of the church is primarily to be accounted for in terms of the purposes of God and the power of his Spirit. These, however, were accomplished and channelled through the leaders he gave as gifts to his fledgling church (Eph. 4:11–13). Throughout history God has provided societies with leaders, even if they have fulfilled their calling in different ways and through various forms and structures of authority. To leave people without leadership is not, in the biblical world view, a sign of a mature democracy (for even a democracy needs to be led) but a symbol of anarchy (Judg. 17:6; 18:1;

19:1; 21:25). Within Israel there were a variety of people who led. There were prophets, priests and kings, together with wise men and elders, who provided each other with the necessary checks and balances to stem the temptations positions of status spawn. And what God has done for the good of Israel he equally does for the good of the church by providing her with a variety of ministers.

Those who read on will quickly grasp that I believe biblical ministry to be multicoloured, not monochrome. Even so, it is fair to say that this book does not use the term 'ministry' in its widest sense. By ministry I primarily have so-called, full-time or professional ministry in mind, although the substance of the book is far from irrelevant to others who exercise ministry on a more occasional basis. Ministry embraces more than we are concerned with here, but not less. I also tend to use the terms 'ministry', 'leadership' or 'pastoral leadership' as interchangeable. I recognize that there are other forms of leadership, such as 'mission leadership' (although pastoral leadership should be missional!), or 'organizational leadership'. But the aspects of the New Testament that concern us here are about pastoral leadership within local churches or groups of churches. And an appropriate word for that is 'ministry'.

My contention is that the New Testament writers set before us a number of models of ministry, each one of which is shaped by the needs of the church they were serving and, no doubt, by their own individual personalities and interests as well. Each New Testament book has a lot to say about pastoral leadership, even if it is not all transparent on the surface. Each book, with the exception of Paul's writings, will be examined in turn to see what form of ministry is advocated and why. (Rather than looking at each of Paul's letters separately, they will be considered in three groups where three different patterns of leadership are evident.) The needs Matthew was addressing were not the same as those addressed by Luke, nor Jude, nor John in Revelation. And Matthew and Luke, as well as Peter, James and Paul, were all wired up by God in different ways. They all bring to bear their own backgrounds, ambitions and passions to what they have to say about ministry. The context combined with the person of the writer gives rise to different conceptions of ministry, all under the inspiration of the Holy Spirit. As a result we discover the varying contours of New Testament pastoral leadership, a genuine diversity that finds its unity in Christ and his gospel.

It has long been popular in the field of New Testament studies to argue that the early church was not a tight, homogeneous organization where every church cloned every other church in its worship, doctrinal emphasis or structure. James Dunn, for example, gave a full exposition of this position when he argued that within the New Testament one can identify four separate strands of Jewish, Hellenistic or Apocalyptic Christianity and Early Catholicism.[1] Each of these gave rise to different forms of leadership, all of which found their unity in Christ, who serves as 'the essential focus of authority' and 'the pattern of ministry'.[2] Those who adopt this position also tend to argue that within the New Testament, ministry follows a trajectory, perhaps even an inevitable one, which largely results in a concern for proper order and doctrinal orthodoxy and that this leads to the concept of monarchical episcopacy developed by Ignatius.

While, on the one hand, I would want to argue that their unity was far more extensive than Dunn's conclusion would suggest, especially in terms of what they believed,[3] on the other hand, I would want to argue that the division of the early church into four strands short-circuits an understanding of ministry in the New Testament. There is much greater variety of style and focus in ministry than this scheme allows. All ministry is about continuing the work (and works) of Jesus and teaching people to live under his rule, in his kingdom, and in accordance with his truth. It is, in Dunn's words, 'Jesus pursuing his ministry by proxy'.[4] How that ministry is expressed, however, depends very much on the context in which ministry is exercised and who is exercising it. God gives appropriate leadership for the need of the hour. A best-fit approach is evident whereby the need of the church is matched by the particular gift and perspective of the leader.

An in-depth review of the books of the New Testament on ministry will lead to a far richer understanding of the multivaried forms of ministry than is customary among most churches today. It can prove a very releasing exercise for many pastors who struggle to fit into a current ecclesiastical mould even when they know their gifts do not quite match it, helping them to play to their strengths. It can prove a very salutary exercise for church authorities, whether national or local, who have attempted to compress the variety of God's gifts into a dull uniformity. It can demonstrate to us why some ministers are more

---

1. James D. G. Dunn, *Unity and Diversity in the New Testament* (Philadelphia: Westminster; London: SCM, 1977).

2. Ibid., p. 123; see pp. 103–123.

3. See D. A. Carson, 'Unity and Diversity in the New Testament: The Possibility of Systematic Theology', in D. A. Carson and J. D. Woodbridge (eds.), *Scripture and Truth* (Leicester: IVP, 1983), pp. 65–95. Carson argues that the diversity reflects different pastoral concerns rather than different creedal positions.

4. Dunn, *Unity and Diversity*, p. 106.

effective in some situations than in others. It can lead us to ask what the need of the hour is.

Recent years have witnessed ministry undergoing rapid changes and facing immense challenges. Various attempts to answer the discontent many feel about ministry in this period of change have been made. While the Lima Report of the World Council of Churches,[5] reasserted a classic view of ministry as priestly and a threefold order of bishops, priests and deacons, others have moved far away from such concerns. One group have emphasized the need for leadership that learns from and imitates the role of the Chief Executive Officer in business. Another group have stressed the need to be counsellors or spiritual directors. Yet another have essentially viewed leaders through a charismatic filter and stressed that leaders are a channel for the Holy Spirit. Yet others, feeling the barrenness of the spiritual desert, have put a premium on the cultivation of inner spirituality. Still others have argued that the primary problem of the church is its introversion and said that leaders should be looked to for a prophetic engagement with society.

To seek to address the current ills of ministry without anchoring our discussions within the New Testament runs the risk of the ship of the church being cast adrift on the tides of opposition that surround it even more than it is at present. Aspects of many of the above models may be seen in the various writings of the New Testament. But, far from merely endorsing our prejudged views of the need of ministry, the New Testament will correct our models, move us beyond superficial understandings of them, and introduce us to models we may not have thought about but that may prove essential to our situation. The New Testament must be normative in our thinking about ministry but, if we are true to it, it will not prove reactionary and restrictive.

Factions within the Corinthian church behaved in the way many of us find natural. Each championed a particular form of leadership and doubted the validity of the ministry of those who did not live up to their expectations. Paul denounced them for thinking according to the standards of their age, rather than as Christians should. He pointed out to them that they were making choices where choice was unnecessary. 'No more boasting', he wrote, 'about human leaders! All things are yours, whether Paul or Apollos or Cephas . . .' (1 Cor. 3:21–22). Similarly, we need not choose between the variety of models of ministry presented in the New Testament but rather rejoice that God has given

---

5. *Baptism, Eucharist and Ministry*, Faith and Order Paper 111 (Geneva: World Council of Churches, 1982).

such a rich diversity and look to encourage people who are different from us to use their calling to the full and as appropriate in different situations.

So, let us follow the contours of New Testament ministry rather than flatten everything out into a smooth path, which like a straight and uninteresting motorway runs the danger of the driver falling asleep through sheer boredom. And let us not worry about how it all fits together till our final chapter.

I want to thank so many people who have contributed to the writing of this book. It had its origins in the Swetland Lectures at Gordon-Conwell Theological Seminary I was privileged to give in 2004 under the title of 'Gospel Ministry'. I am grateful to Dr Ken Swetland for the invitation and to friends at Gordon-Conwell for their generous hospitality. The lectures were developed further for an intensive pastoral school in Malyon College, Brisbane, in 2005. I am grateful on that occasion not only for the welcome of the college but also for the warm hospitality of Brisbane Baptist Tabernacle as they celebrated their hundred and fiftieth Church Anniversary.

The Board of London School of Theology granted me sabbatical leave in 2007–8 during which this book was written. I have enjoyed discussions with a number of colleagues over lunch. Also the bookshop guys, Phil Groom and Nick Aston, as well as the librarian, Alan Linfield, are to be thanked for getting books at short notice. I owe a great debt to Jenny Aston, once again, who has been my personal assistant for several years, and particularly for her editorial skills. Dr Steve Walton and the Revd Ali Walton read the manuscript with their usual thoroughness and I am thankful for their comments. Simon Cragg similarly read the early chapters and offered helpful comments. I, of course, take full responsibility for what is published here. Nick Gatzke composed the indexes shortly after he had submitted his own PhD, which it was my delight to supervise – a work of extraordinary kindness indeed. I am also very glad to work with Phil Duce again, the editor responsible at IVP, and especially for his encouragement and swift responses.

As always, I am so grateful for the wonderful support of my wife, Dianne, and of my son, Richard, while I have been scribbling again.

Paul prayed for the Thessalonians that the Lord Jesus and God the Father would 'encourage your hearts and strengthen you in every good deed and word' (2 Thess. 2:17). My prayer is that the reading of this book will do the same, especially to those who labour hard daily in the tasks of ministry.

1. MATTHEW: MINISTRY IN A DIVIDED CHURCH

The ministry of wise instruction

The Gospel of Matthew can, according to R. T. France, 'appropriately be called the church's gospel'.[1] Matthew's interest in the church has long been recognized. He alone of the Gospel writers uses the word 'church' (16:18; 18:17) as if it already exists in a recognizable form and he alone mentions the significant role of Peter in the building of the church (16:13–20). But Matthew's interest in the church does not hang on these few brief references. Throughout his Gospel, Matthew demonstrates an obvious interest in addressing the needs of a newly founded and vulnerable community facing major questions about its own identity. In doing so, he gives evidence of being an excellent teacher and leaves a trail of clues about the nature of ministry as he practises it and as he encourages others to do so.

Matthew and his readers

Matthew's Gospel has provided scholars with some tantalizing material, so

---

1. R. T. France, *Matthew: Evangelist and Teacher* (Exeter: Paternoster, 1989), p. 251. He rightly qualifies it by saying that Matthew's ecclesiology is subordinate to his Christology.

that while currents ebb and flow there is no settled view as to the nature of the church he is addressing.[2] Most hold strongly that he was writing to a church of Jewish believers to answer the questions thrown up because the gospel was making such good progress among the Gentiles. In Donald Hagner's words:

> Matthew's original readers were . . . in a kind of 'no man's land' between their Jewish brothers and sisters on the one hand and gentile Christians, on the other, wanting to reach back for continuity with the old and at the same time to reach forward to the new work God was doing in the largely gentile church . . .[3]

What were they to make of this 'no man's land'? Others believe he was writing to a mixed church, where Jews and Gentiles rubbed shoulders with the result that questions about the continuing significance of the Jewish legacy of the gospel were uncomfortably posed. A minority argue it may even have been written to a Gentile church to explain to them the Jewish background of the faith.

The absence of certainty about the original readers is not a problem for us, since all are agreed about the sort of question Matthew is answering. Whether his readers were predominantly Jewish, predominantly Gentile, or a mixed audience, the question related to the divided nature of the church of which they were a part. The growth of the church had unexpectedly resulted in Gentiles being converted to Jesus Christ. The Great Commission of Matthew 28:19–20 was already being successfully pursued. While undoubtedly some of the converts would have been God-fearers, and therefore would have known something of the Jewish faith and been committed to identify with it in so far as they could, others would have been far from God-fearing. They would have had no tradition of monotheism, nor shared in the wider theological framework or moral commitments of the Jewish faith. Many would have brought baggage with them, both of a personal as well as a conceptual kind, which the Jewish converts would have preferred to do without. Since the movement was

---

2. For a recent survey, see Donald A. Hagner, 'The *Sitz im Leben* of the Gospel of Matthew', in D. R. Bauer and M. A. Powell (eds.), *Treasures Old and New: Recent Contributions to Matthean Studies* (Atlanta: Scholars Press, 1996), pp. 27–68; *Matthew 1–13*, WBC 33a (Dallas: Word, 1993), pp. lxiv–lxv; and Donald Senior, 'Directions in Matthean Studies', in David Aune (ed.), *The Gospel of Matthew in Current Study* (Grand Rapids: Eerdmans, 2001), pp. 5–21.

3. Hagner, *Matthew 1–13*, p. lxx.

finding success in this way, it is not difficult to imagine that concerns would have been expressed over the watering down of standards, or even, as Robert Gundry has suggested, over the inclusion of false disciples as well as true ones.[4]

This question makes Matthew's Gospel of immediate relevance to many in pastoral leadership today. There are strong tensions in many local congregations between those long schooled in the church and its culture and a new generation of incomers who are being converted without the benefits of a Sunday school upbringing, who are ignorant of the Bible and its contents, and often bring with them the effects of having lived a life without God until their conversion. The clash of cultures, lifestyles, family arrangements and moral frameworks can be all too apparent. Traditionalists seek to preserve patterns unchanged from the past. Legalists want to lay down the law to which all are expected to conform. Godly people fear the name of Christ will be dishonoured and want to guard the church from compromise, while others rejoice in the liberty they believe they have found in Christ and wonder why some fellow church members are so uptight about things. Hence, as Gundry has claimed:

> Wherever the church has grown large and mixed, wherever the church is polarized between the extremes of latitudinarianism and sectarianism, wherever the church feels drawn to accommodations with the forces that oppose the gospel, wherever the church loses its vision of worldwide evangelism, wherever the church lapses in smug religiosity with its attendant vices of ostentation, hypocrisy and haughty disdain for its underprivileged and correspondingly zealous members – the gospel of Matthew speaks with power and pertinence.[5]

The strategy Matthew adopts to guide the church in response to this is to carefully teach them their true identity and diligently expound the meaning of the gospel to them. One of the hallmarks of Matthew's Gospel is the thought that has been put into its arrangement. Its structure suggests he was a gifted teacher. Equally the style of his writing with its use of repetitions, catchphrases, numerical arrangement and clear markers betrays the marks of an educator. The way in which he selects and presents his material for its relevance further underlines his educational skills. He gives attention to a careful exposition of the relationship between the new work of God in Christ and the

---

4. Robert H. Gundry, *Matthew: A Commentary on his Literary and Theological Art* (Grand Rapids: Eerdmans, 1982), p. 9; and Hagner, '*Sitz im Leben*', pp. 58–59.

5. Gundry, *Matthew*, p. 10.

Jewish Scriptures, to the continuing place of the law, to the Jewish versus universal mission, and has a thread running through of 'us' versus 'them'. We may also note that when Matthew expands on the parallel passages and sayings in Mark, he does so for pastoral reasons.[6] Furthermore, he demonstrates pastoral sensitivity in the way he handles the tensions in this divided church. He enters into the *angst* of both sides seriously, neither denigrating one side of the argument or the other, nor parodying the position of any. In it all, he shows special care for the 'little ones' who are the most vulnerable members of the church (10:42; 18:2–14). So, here is a model pastor/teacher at work.

But, who was Matthew? Graham Stanton, commenting that he can be unsystematic as well as organized in his writing, concludes that 'his skills are those of a pastor and gifted communicator rather than those of a theologian'.[7] Some have been more specific and claimed that Matthew was probably a Jewish Christian who had received training as a rabbi. Years ago, Ernst von Dobschutz concluded that 'The Jewish rabbi had become a Christian teacher and now used his catechetical skills in the service of the gospel.'[8] While this may still be a matter of debate for some, it is fairly commonly accepted that Matthew had a scribal background but had come to devote his teaching gifts to the service of Jesus Christ.[9] It will become evident just how much Matthew's own background has shaped not only the way he wrote his Gospel but also his understanding of ministry, and just how much it matched the need of the church of his day.

The Gospel Matthew has written is not only written *by* a teacher but *for* teachers in order to provide them with a model of how to pass on and apply the ministry of Jesus to the practical questions of the day.[10] His unique

---

6. Ralph P. Martin, *New Testament Foundations* (Grand Rapids: Eerdmans, 1975), vol. 1, pp. 229–231. On the pastoral shape of Matthew, see Hagner, '*Sitz im Leben*'; Daniel J. Harrington, 'Matthew's Gospel: Pastoral Problems and Possibilities', in Aune, *Gospel of Matthew*, pp. 62–73; Mark Allan Powell, *God with Us: A Pastoral Theology of Matthew's Gospel* (Minneapolis: Fortress, 1995); Graham Stanton, *A Gospel for a New People: Studies in Matthew* (Edinburgh: T. & T. Clark, 1992), pp. 146–168; and Derek Tidball, *Skilful Shepherds: Explorations in Pastoral Theology*, 2nd ed. (Leicester: Apollos, 1997), pp. 56–67.

7. Stanton, *Gospel*, p. 4.

8. Ernst von Dobschutz, 'Matthew as Rabbi and Catechist', in G. Stanton (ed.), *The Interpretation of Matthew* (London: SPCK, 1983), p. 26.

9. See M. D. Goulder, *Midrash and Lection in Matthew* (London: SPCK, 1974).

10. P. S. Minear, *Matthew: The Teacher's Gospel* (London: Darton Longman & Todd, 1984), p. 3; cited by France, *Matthew*, p. 256.

contribution to our understanding of ministry is to introduce us to the wise or understanding scribe (*grammateus*) or teacher of the law as a positive role model for ministry.[11] But before exploring that role we should place the discussion in a broader context, and review, in summary form, some of the other features of Matthew's teaching about the church and ministry.

Church and ministry in Matthew: the wide perspective

Matthew's use of the word 'church' (16:18; 18:17) and his record of Jesus' response to Peter when he declared Jesus to be the Messiah, which appears to give Peter a prominent role in the founding of the church (16:13–20), has led some to believe that the church was well established by the time Matthew wrote his Gospel. It was, they believe, already in somewhat of a developed stage of organization and enjoying a structured, even hierarchical, form of ministry. But this is a misrepresentation of Matthew's view of both the church and ministry.

Matthew's favourite word for the followers of Jesus is disciple (*mathētēs*). Although he uses it of the twelve apostles (e.g. 10:1; 11:1) he does not restrict it to them and also uses it of all who follow Jesus. Indeed, in what has come to be called 'the Great Commission', Jesus instructs 'the eleven [remaining] disciples' to 'go and make disciples of all nations' (28:19). Closely allied to the language of discipleship is the language of followers and following (*akoloutheō*). Matthew himself might be seen as representative of others in this respect, for when Jesus called him he issued him with the brief invitation to 'Follow me' (9:9). Jesus had already taught others that following him was a decisive and lifelong act of commitment (8:18–22), which potential followers should weigh up carefully before embarking upon the journey with him.

The fellowship around Jesus is seen primarily as a community of disciples and from this a number of implications follow. First, disciples *follow a master* and, in using this concept, Matthew is encouraging us 'to see discipleship as essentially a matter of relationship with Jesus'[12] and through him with the trinitarian God (28:19). Disciples observed the life of their teachers closely as well as listening carefully to their teaching.

Secondly, the terminology stresses that the disciples were *learners*. They were a school of disciples. There was only one teacher (23:10). Their task was to

---

11. Key references are found in 13:52 and 23:34.
12. France, *Matthew*, p. 262. For further detailed argument on Matthew's view of the church, see pp. 242–278.

seek to understand his teaching and put it into practice. The five great dis-
courses of teaching Matthew records (5:1 – 7:29; 10:1 – 11:1; 13:1–58; 18:1–35;
21:1 – 25:46) are about the lifestyle expected of the community of disciples,
its mission and how its experience fits with the wider plan of God at work in
the world. The aim of learning was not the acquisition of theological information but obedience (7:21; 12:46–50). Embarking on the road of discipleship
meant embarking on a lifelong learning experience (10:22; 24:13) from which
the disciple should never turn back.

Thirdly, it is important to stress that this learning took place within a community and was not the individual learning experience that has characterized
so much of Western education. The community was not incidental to the
learning process; the learning took place both in it and because of it. Hence
Matthew is concerned to give guidance on a range of issues they would confront together, including how to handle relational problems when they arose
within the community (5:21–26; 18:15–20) and to ensure that the needs of
the 'little ones' were given special attention (10:42; 18:2–14; 21:14–16).
Matthew's portrait of the church is one where brothers and sisters work and
learn together. It is a community of equals, which can function well without
'teachers' or 'leaders' having to be given prominence (5:21–26, 47; 18:15–17,
35; 23:8; 25:40; 28:10), not an institution nor a hierarchically led organization.[13]

But what of the place of the Twelve, and especially of Peter, in the leadership of this community? Do they not have some priority and do they not
exercise authority within the church? Reviewing the evidence, Ulrich Luz
points out that the Twelve are not mentioned until 10:1 and Matthew never
really establishes them as a group apart; rather, he just assumes their existence.
Such factors led Luz to conclude that the Twelve are 'unimportant' to
Matthew.[14] Unlike Luke, Matthew does not refer to them as apostles, with one
exception (Matt. 10:2), and they are basically viewed 'as hearers of Jesus'
message'.[15] In one particularly significant passage (23:8–10), Jesus instructs
them to reject the status and title of 'Rabbi' or 'Teacher', because they were,
in reality, simply 'brothers' and any role they had in the church needed to be

---

13. James D. G. Dunn, *Unity and Diversity in the New Testament* (Philadelphia:
    Westminster; London: SCM, 1977), pp. 117–118. But see discussion in Richard
    Ascough, 'Matthew and Community Formation', in Aune, *Gospel of Matthew*, p. 99.
14. Ulrich Luz, 'The Disciples in the Gospel according to Matthew', in Stanton,
    Interpretation of Matthew, p. 99.
15. Ibid., p. 104.

played with humility as servants rather than masters. The spirit of their leadership, therefore, seems of far more importance to Jesus than their rights or position.

Peter's personal role is, of course, much more complex and controversial and this is not the place for a detailed discussion of it. In the light of the way Peter acts as a spokesperson for the disciples, in the light of Jesus' words in 16:18–19 and of his subsequent role in the Acts of the Apostles, it is not right to belittle Peter's role. If nothing else, he plays a foundational role as a historic witness to the Christ. Even so, Matthew's portrait of Peter is not uncritical. He points out Peter's lack of faith as he sought to walk on water like his master (14:28–31), and even at the moment of his great confession he earns a rebuke for misunderstanding the way of the cross and is called 'a stumbling block' to Jesus (16:21–23). Furthermore, the 'binding and loosing' authority given to Peter (16:19) does not, in the light of the wider context of Matthew (e.g. 18:15–20), appear to give Peter exclusive personal authority to exercise church discipline, as a successor to the Jewish rabbis, but gives him a role in doing so along with the wider church.[16] The 'binding and loosing' authority must not only refer to questions of church discipline but to the role of admitting people into the kingdom of God through the preaching of the gospel, or, indeed, preventing their admission as the gospel that is preached is rejected. Such a task is not exclusive to Peter but is committed to all disciples who are called to 'fish for people' (4:19) and 'make disciples of all nations' (28:19).[17] It is better, then, with Cullmann, to view Peter as 'a representative disciple' rather than as establishing his primacy or unique role within the early church.[18]

Although referring to the Synoptic Gospels as a whole, James Dunn's comment on the role of the disciples is an apt summary of Matthew's position:

> There is no evidence that they [the Twelve] were regarded or acted as functionaries, far less a hierarchy, constituting a community gathered around Jesus in Palestine (note Matt. 23:8; Mark 10:43f.). In particular there is no hint whatsoever of them playing 'priest' to the other disciples' 'laity'. What power and authority they did exercise was

---

16. See France, *Matthew*, pp. 244–249.

17. For a full discussion of these problematic verses, see D. A. Carson, 'Matthew', in F. E. Gaebelein (ed.), *The Expositor's Bible Commentary* (Grand Rapids: Zondervan, 1984), vol. 1, pp. 370–374.

18. Oscar Cullmann, *Peter: Disciple, Apostle, Martyr*, tr. F. V. Filson, 2nd ed. (London: SCM, 1962), p. 31.

within a community of discipleship for its upbuilding, but was given to them to share in Jesus' mission (Mark 3:14f.; 6:7 pars.; Luke 10:17ff.).[19]

Ministry in Matthew: his specific contribution

Within this broader context, Matthew has a particular contribution to make regarding our understanding of ministry.

In a saying unique to Matthew, Jesus says to the crowds who have suffered from the blind guides of Israel, 'Therefore I am sending you prophets and sages (*sophoi*) and teachers (*grammateis*)' (23:34). Earlier Jesus, using the same word *grammateus*, had referred to teachers of the law who had been instructed about the kingdom of heaven (13:52). These are very rare references in that they put a positive spin on the word *grammateus*, and commend the role as one of benefit to his disciples in contrast to the fairly negative use of the word, which is common throughout the Synoptic Gospels. They strike one as so unusual that they demand further exploration.

The model of the scribe
'Scribes' or 'teachers of the law' had their origins in the period of the monarchy when they served as secretaries and recorders of information (e.g. 1 Kgs 4:3; 2 Kgs 12:10; 1 Chr. 4:3). Their skills were valued in recording the wisdom of Israel and, in the case of Baruch, the words of the prophet Jeremiah (Jer. 36:4,18, 32). Hence they came to be associated with the wise men of Israel. After the exile their role became vital in copying, studying and teaching the law to the returnees. Ezra served as a model scribe of the time. It was said of him that he 'had devoted himself to the study and observance of the Law of the LORD, and to teaching its decrees and laws in Israel' (see esp. Ezra 7:10; also Neh. 8:1–18). Subsequently, they became 'a well-developed and distinct class of high social status alongside the priesthood', the scribes of the Pharisees forming a closed guild.[20] By the time of Jesus they were clearly an influential group, even if not necessarily a coherent one. They are sometimes mentioned in the same breath as the Pharisees, sometimes with the chief priests and sometimes on their own. By Jesus' day they were far more than copyists. The common thread was their devotion to the Scriptures, which

---

19. Dunn, *Unity and Diversity*, p. 106.
20. G. H Twelftree, 'Scribes', *DJG*, p. 732; and N. Hillyer, 'Scribe', *NIDNTT*, vol. 3, p. 480.

they handled variously as lawyers, teachers, interpreters or as custodians of the tradition.[21]

The Synoptic Gospels paint an almost wholly negative picture of the scribes, although Matthew tries to relieve it somewhat. His more sympathetic presentation of them involves a playing down of some of the negative comments found in Mark, the mention of one as at least a potential follower of Jesus (8:19), and the recognition that they did 'sit in Moses' seat' (23:2).[22] Even so, they are presented as in constant conflict with Jesus and a key component of the alliance of hostility against him. They are essentially 'blind guides' who fail to understand the truth (15:1–14), to whom revelation had not been given (11:25) and who could not teach with any persuasive authority (7:28–29). Their pattern of living was anything but commendable and Jesus could only warn his disciples against them (23:1–39).

The fact that there were so many poor representatives of the teachers of the law around did not render the model inherently unusable and Matthew seeks to rehabilitate it for the Christian church.

True scribes are people of understanding

As opposed to the blinkered scribes of the Jews who lacked insight and demonstrate spiritual ignorance, even obtuseness, the ideal scribe, called to exercise leadership in the church, demonstrates understanding. It is not an intellectual grasp they have, but a spiritual insight into the meaning of Jesus' teaching, especially his parables. In Matthew 13:51, after presenting a series of parables about the nature of his kingdom, Jesus asks his disciples if they have 'understood all these things?' and they reply 'Yes'. The question of their understanding occurs not only six times in chapter 13 but recurs in 15:15–16, 16:12 and 17:13.

Their understanding comes both through revelation (11:25–27; 13:11–13) and instruction (13:52). So a divine initiative is involved and God's gracious choice is at work in rejecting those whom mainstream society regarded as 'wise and learned', while he makes himself known to those regarded as insignificant, the 'little children'. But understanding is not simply a moment of illumination;

---

21. Good overviews are found in N. Hillyer, 'Scribe', pp. 477–482; and Twelftree, 'Scribes', pp. 732–735.

22. Hagner, perhaps with some justice, says this 'makes sense only if they [the difficult words about sitting in Moses' seat] are taken to indicate that Jesus agrees *in principle* with the Pharisees, i.e., insofar as they *truly* expound the meaning of the Mosaic Law' (*'Sitz im Leben'*, p. 55; his italics).

it is also a process of instruction, of learning what it means to be a disciple of Jesus. It is not a matter of learning facts but of learning both to see things from God's viewpoint and to live according to that viewpoint.

It goes without saying that the classic location for such teaching, but not the only one, is found in the Sermon on the Mount. There Jesus stands the conventional wisdom of the world on its head, stresses the importance of inner attitudes as well as outward behaviour and introduces shockingly radical ideas such as loving one's enemies, all within the context of saying that such behaviour would lead to a fulfilling of God's law and not a dispensing with it. True understanding should lead to living a life of righteousness that 'surpasses that of the Pharisees and the teachers of the law' (5:20). As David Bennett says, 'the teaching of Jesus changes life at the behavioural and ethical level. To be a disciple means not only to receive an infusion of knowledge but also to undergo a transformation of character.'[23]

True scribes are people of authority
There would appear to be a tension between the sense of community Matthew stresses and the recognition of authority accorded the true scribes in his Gospel. How can some exercise leadership and teach with authority, albeit under Christ, if all are equal? The resolution lies in the fact that within the church there is at one and the same time an equality of grace but a diversity of gifts.[24]

The notes of authority are unmistakably present. Scribes do 'sit in Moses' seat'. As a result, Jesus warns his disciples that although he has no wish for them to imitate their behaviour, 'you must obey them and do everything they tell you' (23:2–3). It follows that the scribes he commissions will have equal, if not more, authority. Their words are not to be dismissed lightly. Such authority is also implicit in the binding and loosing image of 16:19–20. So it is wrong, just because of the emphasis on an equality of grace, to draw the conclusion that the church needs no leadership and that its life will be inevitably harmonious and full of vitality without anyone giving direction, providing care and offering guidance about belief. To abandon any

---

23. David Bennett, *Biblical Images for Leaders and Followers* (Oxford: Regnum, 1993), p. 39.

24. David Bartlett, *Ministry in the New Testament*, OBT (Minneapolis: Fortress, 1993), p. 87. Bartlett comments, 'Matthew, in his own quite different way, wants to hold together what Paul wants to hold together: a diversity of gifts and equality of grace.'

leadership is a likely recipe for anarchy both in behaviour and belief, as history testifies.

The key question is not whether there is authority but what kind of authority it is. And there Matthew is clear. The only authority to be exercised is one that is in submission to the 'one Teacher, the Messiah' (23:10). He taught 'as one who had authority, and not as their teachers of the law' (7:29). I take this to mean that his teaching had the ring of authenticity about it. He was not so enmeshed in the documents of Scripture that he was removed from the real questions of life. He was able to distinguish between the key issue and the minutiae that often became a distraction or even a stumbling block to true obedience and righteousness. He spoke from the experience of knowing God and having been sent by him. His words carried life and grace and brought transforming freedom to people's lives. His was not the authority of position, of status, of title or of the right 'old school tie'. Nor should that of the scribes of the kingdom be. If they were in submission to the 'one Teacher', then even the greatest of them would be keen to imitate his example and adopt the position of a servant. Humility is the key. It is not a stepping stone to greatness; it is greatness.

The calling of the scribe

Matthew identifies several aspects of the role of the wise teacher in the new community called together by Christ. First and foremost is the task of teaching itself.

The calling to be a creative teacher

Just as the Jewish scribes taught and interpreted the law of Moses, so the primary task of the scribes of Jesus is to teach, explain and apply his new law, the law of his kingdom. This is a far more demanding responsibility than merely repeating his word, and requires skill, wisdom and creativity.

According to David Orton, the background to Jesus' commissioning of 'prophets and sages and teachers' (23:34) lies in Daniel 11 and 12. In an apocalyptic context of crisis and confusion, Daniel prophesies that there will emerge a group who are 'wise' in contrast to the majority who do not understand the times and are blind to the actions of God in them. Daniel says of the wise that they 'will instruct many' (Dan. 11:33) and that they 'will shine like the brightness of the heavens, and those who lead many to righteousness, like the stars for ever and ever' (Dan. 12:3). The wise ones have, Orton explains, 'a dual role: (1) to "understand" in the last days ([Dan.] 12:10), and (2) to exercise the missionary, or at least pastoral/didactic function of "causing many to understand" ([Dan.] 11:33) in a time of national and religious distress'.[25] The connection between wisdom and instruction, found in Daniel, is clearly made by Matthew. The 'wise' and the 'scribe' are virtually interchangeable terms.[26] Also common between Daniel and Matthew is the prediction that the wise will suffer, of which more later. As a result, Orton argues that Matthew sees what is happening as 'the eschatological fulfilment' of Daniel's prophecy and sees them as a harbinger of the judgment to come.[27]

Instructing others requires a great deal of skill, both in terms of making truth plain and also in making it appropriate for the listener. Good communication involves both elements. Job's comforters may have spoken a good deal of theological truth, although they were far from infallible, but they wielded their knowledge so inappropriately that they misrepresented God to the further and unnecessary hurt of God's servant, Job (Job 1:8). Truth is one thing, but an apt teaching gift is another.

The need for the teacher to be creative in handling truth is particularly highlighted in Matthew's other (earlier) key saying about the 'understanding scribes' in 13:51–52: Jesus 'said to them, "Therefore every teacher of the law who has been instructed about the kingdom of heaven is like the owner of a house who brings out of his storeroom new treasurers as well as old."' This somewhat enigmatic statement introduces two dimensions involved in teaching: new and old. It may be that this is a reference to the continuity of the Christian faith with its Jewish roots,[28] but it may have wider implications than this. The teacher has a responsibility not to neglect the old but rather to recognize its importance and use it. Yet the teacher also has a responsibility to bring out the new. The wise scribe is no antiquarian but the communicator of a living word, as Matthew himself had demonstrated. This means the old message of the gospel is not to be reinvented for every age, but it is to be re-expressed in relevant ways and its implications reapplied to the contemporary situation. Orton sets out the challenge like this:

> creativity . . . , the production of new parables, new wise sayings from the store of divinely granted insight, is precisely the role to which the disciples, as scribes, are enjoined in this passage. Of course, the old things are there too, for it is important

25. David E. Orton, *The Understanding Scribe: Matthew and the Apocalyptic Ideal*, JSNTSup 25 (Sheffield: Sheffield Academic Press, 1989), p. 148.

26. Ibid., p. 155.

27. Ibid., pp. 145, 157–158.

28. So, Hagner, *Matthew 1–13*, pp. 401–402; '*Sitz im Leben*', p. 68.

that the scribe be conservative as well as innovative – he is custodian and interpreter of a vast treasure in the scriptures; but the emphasis here is on the freshness of revelation and inspiration.[29]

The importance of this task is further underlined by the way Matthew himself instructs the church. It is evident that he does not give his readers a detailed set of instructions as to how to handle each specific question they face, but rather gives them 'the raw materials from which an answer can be constructed'.[30] Here is a further reason why Christian scribes are called to be creative in their teaching.

The calling to be a tender shepherd
The image of the shepherd does not feature large in Matthew's Gospel, but it is not altogether absent. Matthew, as I have mentioned, has a concern for the 'little ones' and this is especially mentioned in chapter 18. Here he calls for the church to exercise mutual pastoral care and ensure that none behave in such a way as to cause others to stumble in their discipleship (18:6–9). But he immediately goes on to include his version of the parable of the good shepherd, connecting it with his previous instructions by the words 'See that you do not look down on one of these little ones' (18:10). Even if the words still apply to the whole community, they have special pertinence for its leaders. Christian scribes were being warned that they 'need always to avoid the danger of despising the Christians whom they lead' – a temptation that may be more common than many pastors would like to admit.[31]

But there is another lesson to learn from this as well. Within the scribal groups various specialisms may have emerged, with some being especially committed to pastoral care and others exclusively to teaching. But even those scribes who majored on teaching are here enjoined to show pastoral care and sensitivity. Teaching does not take place in a vacuum. Good teachers are acutely aware of the needs of their students and know how and when to

---

29. Orton, *Understanding Scribe*, p. 152. For a dissenting interpretation of these verses and Matthew's interest in Christian scribes, see Sjef van Tilborg, *The Jewish Leaders in Matthew* (Leiden: Brill, 1972), pp. 131–134. Tilborg interprets 13:52 as meaning, 'such a scribe will fare as the lord of the house, who handles everything he possesses in a carefree manner, who does not save anything and even uses what is old' (p. 132).

30. France, *Matthew*, p. 259.

31. Bartlett, *Ministry*, p. 81.

deliver their instruction, how much should be taught, and what needs the student may have for individual support in the learning process. The writings of the early church fathers showed great perception about this and regularly returned to the theme. John Chrysostom wrote, for example, about church discipline, an issue to which Matthew will turn next (18:15–20):

> For we ought not to apply punishment, merely to proportion it to the scale of the offence, but rather to keep in view the disposition of the sinner lest, while wishing to mend what is torn, you make the rent worse, and in your zealous endeavours to restore what is fallen, you make the ruin greater.[32]

The character of the shepherd ideally goes hand in hand with the calling of the scribe.

The calling to be a suffering prophet

As mentioned, one of the clear connections between Matthew 23:34 and Daniel 11:33 is the prediction that the wise will suffer. Jesus is not sending his emissaries out to find a ready acceptance of their message and to become popular, but to face opposition and conflict, even if they do not deliberately court it. So Jesus says to the Jewish leaders whom he has been denouncing, 'Some of them you will kill and crucify; others you will flog in your synagogues and pursue from town to town' (Matt. 23:34). He then claims this is consistent with this previous history of Israel where the blood of the prophets has been shed. Previously, in the parable of the tenants (21:33–44), Jesus had drawn attention to the long record Israel had of killing the servants of the owner, until he sent his own son to them, whom they also killed. It seems, from these passages and from 5:11–12, that persecution was the anticipated lot of Jesus' followers, and especially the leaders among them.

The present-day image of the prophet, much spoken of in some sections of the church, tends to be somewhat distorted. The call for the church to be prophetic usually means that the church is being called to take a moral or political stand over those who have economic or political power. So often it is presented more as an image of confidence rather than courage. We do not hear much about the recurring biblical theme that prophets suffer for the stance they take. But here Jesus warns those whom he sends, not only as prophets but also as wise scribes, that they will suffer.

---

32. John Chrysostom, *On The Priesthood, NPNF*, vol. 9 (Grand Rapids: Eerdmans, 1889), 2.4.

The calling to be a global missionary

Careless talk in the contemporary church often opposes the maintenance of
the church with the mission of the church. There may be some truth in the
fact that pastors and evangelists/missionaries seem to be wired up differently,
with the former having a primary concern for preservation and the latter for
pioneering. But the New Testament will not let us easily drive a wedge between
the two. The role of the shepherd is, after all among other things, about going
out to search for the lost sheep.[33]

The work of the scribe, as Matthew envisages it, is evangelistic. Having sent
his disciples out on a mission that during his lifetime was restricted to Israel
(10:5–8), he releases them from that restraint as he leaves the earth and commissions them to engage in a worldwide task. Given Matthew's particular commitments, it is unsurprising to hear the spin he puts on the Great Commission.
They are to '*make disciples* of all nations, baptizing them in the name of the
Father and of the Son and of the Holy Spirit, and *teaching them* to obey everything I have commanded you' (28:19–20; my italics). The commission cannot
be expressed more aptly for those who were to be the scribes of the new age.
Scribes are not called to teach merely within the cosy confines of church or
seminary walls, but to go where the instructions of the one who has all authority have not yet been heard, and recruit new learners there as well.

David Bartlett tentatively suggests that Matthew may have envisaged a
difference in function between scribes, shepherds, prophets and missionaries,
although he acknowledges that 'what is more striking than the distinction
among Christians' is their unity.[34] But I would doubt that we are intended to
draw strong distinctions between the various roles. In so far as Matthew has
an image of the 'minister', it is that of the scribe and, although there will be
variations of emphasis mirroring our individuality, all scribes are called to exercise their teaching function as shepherds and missionaries, and to be aware that
they may well reap the rewards of the prophet for doing so.

The challenge of the scribe

Assuming we have understood the background to Matthew's Gospel rightly,

---

33. I am also always struck by the fact that the clearest instruction in the New
     Testament to do the work of an evangelist is found in 2 Tim. 4:5 in what we call
     the 'pastoral epistles', and addressed to 'Pastor' Timothy.
34. Bartlett, *Ministry*, p. 85.

we have an opportunity of seeing how Matthew himself exercises his ministry as a model of a wise scribe. We can do this in reference to the way in which he reports Jesus fulfilling the Old Testament, bringing new out of old. We can also do it with the example chosen here of his account of the place of the law in the new age of the Christ.

Strong views would have been expressed in the church, giving rise to tensions with Jew and Gentile, legalist and libertine, traditionalist and innovator, strong and weak, all taking a different, even contradictory, stance on issues. Matthew's approach is not to steer a course of compromise, offering a pragmatic solution that papers over the cracks and patches up a temporary peace between the warring factions, but to remind them of the teaching of Jesus. Matthew, like Jesus, is a teacher not a politician, a principled truth-teller, not a lowest-common-denominator diplomat. So he places the contemporary situation in the context of the fulfilment of prophecy, gives them understanding about their identity, and sets out principles with regard to ethics and moral lifestyle that can be reworked time and again, long after the particular discussions of his day have been forgotten. In doing so, he rejects both legalism and laxity with regard to the law and presents its positive ongoing relevance for Christian disciples.

We can identify four aspects of the teaching of Jesus that Matthew emphasizes for his readers. First, *Jesus affirms the continuing relevance of the law*. He explicitly states that he has not come to abolish the law and the prophets (5:17) but rather to fulfil them. While what it means for Jesus to 'fulfil' the law may be a matter for discussion, his statement that he is not abolishing it is abundantly clear. His fulfilment of the law may well be intended to point to the way in which he fulfils the Old Testament law within himself, but even if this is so it is also likely to mean that he is 'showing the direction in which it points, on the basis of his own authority'.[35] Since in the Sermon on the Mount Jesus immediately goes on to explain the meaning of the law and to intensify it by internalizing it, it seems that by 'fulfilling the law' he means to draw people back to its real meaning. This gives the law an added depth and relevance that were missing when its interpretation was in the hands of the scribes and Pharisees. There is no going back on the law, which by nature is good because it reflects the very character of God himself.

Secondly, *Jesus reinterprets the law*. In quoting 'You have heard that it was said . . . But I tell you' (5:21–22, 27–28, 31–32, 33–34, 38–39, 43–44), Matthew

---

35. Carson, 'Matthew', p. 144. For a wide discussion on the interpretation of Matt. 5:17, see pp. 141–145.

gives a prime example of the 'something old, something new' technique of the wise scribe. Jesus connects with what has been said but builds on it, contradicting the interpretations of the blind scribes of Israel. So he takes the familiar and gives his listeners a new insight into its meaning by either driving it deeper (murder becomes anger, adultery becomes lust) or by reapplying it into the different circumstances they face ('an eye for an eye' becomes turning the other cheek and loving your neighbour becomes loving your enemy). None of this goes back on the essence of the law, which remains in force.

Thirdly, *Jesus rejects the way of legalism.* It is evident from the last paragraph that although the law had a continuing part to play, there was to be no encouragement given to legalists in Matthew's church. It was precisely their narrow and literal interpretations that Jesus rejected in the Sermon on the Mount. Such interpretations were characteristic of the blind scribe, not the wise scribe of the new age.

In reporting various incidents and parables later in his Gospel (21:8 – 22:40), Matthew makes clear that nationalistic Israel's time is over, and with it the way she has handled God's law. It is to be supplanted by a new kingdom, the true Israel, and with it a new way of handling the law. This section ends with Jesus commissioning his disciples to fulfil a great commandment (22:34–40), as important in its way as the Great Commission with which the Gospel concludes (28:19–20). Here, using the explicit terminology of teaching, law and commandment, Jesus stresses that the priorities that mark his rule are love of God and love of neighbour 'as yourself'.

Fourthly, *Jesus advocates discipline within the community.* The stress on love does not mean that Jesus leaves his community with a woolly ethic, which implies, in effect, that anything goes. From elsewhere in the Gospel we see the church as a disciplined community where high moral standards are expected (5:20, 48), and offences need to be confronted and corrected (5:23–26; 18:15–20), and where uncorrected behaviour ultimately leads to expulsion (18:17). Yet the savoury diet of discipline is always heavily laced with the sweet fare of forgiveness and restoration. The lost sheep that wanders off is sought and found (18:12–14), the servant who fails to show mercy is shown no mercy (18:21–35), and the apostle who wants to limit forgiveness is taught to forgive to a totally unreasonable extent (18:21–22). He lays a yoke on the neck of his followers, but his 'yoke is easy and [his] burden is light' (11:30).

Here, then, is a classic example of a wise scribe at work. Mathew treats all sides of an argument with respect. He grounds his teaching clearly in the revelation of the past, but refuses to be imprisoned within it. He sets out clear principles none can miss. Yet he carefully nuances his teaching so that he avoids being simplistic. His vision is to teach the church in such a way that they can go on living out the law of the new kingdom, not just in their immediate circumstances but also in whatever future circumstances they face.

The temptations of the scribe

Jesus, in the most forthright terms, denounces both the teachers of the law and the Pharisees they served, pronounces seven curses on them ('Woe to you': 23:13, 15, 16, 23, 25, 27 and 29) and identifies nine temptations to which they have succumbed wholesale. It is at the end of his denunciations that Jesus speaks of sending out an alternative group of 'prophets, sages and teachers' (23:34). Although his denunciations do not apply to this alternative group, it is unwise of them to think they are immune from the temptations of the scribes they are replacing. Jesus' words, then, serve as a perceptive warning to the scribes of the kingdom about the pitfalls they should avoid. Here is not only radical surgery that removes a cancer, but also preventive medicine that guards against a regrowth of such destructive cells.

The temptations are as follows.

Ostentation (23:5). 'Everything they do is done for others to see'. Ministry too easily degenerates into an outward show whereby we parade our piety and spiritual achievements in public for others to acknowledge, long after the private reality of life with God has been spent.

Status-seeking (23:6–12). How easy it is to fall into the trap of loving the respect ministers receive and expecting the courtesy titles to be used of us. The 'top-table' syndrome can creep up on us unawares until the day we are not invited to join it and are rudely awakened as we jostle for a seat with the ordinary folk who are without privileges. Being saluted and using titles are marks of status the scribe of the new age should avoid.

Authoritarianism (23:13–14). The scribes and Pharisees acted as the gatekeepers of the kingdom, ruling on who measured up sufficiently to enter and who, because of their failure, should be kept out. Ministry seduces one into a position of control if we do not remain vigilant.

Fanaticism (23:15). Their enthusiasm to make converts knew no bounds. But rather than being commendable it was reprehensible, because they were making converts in their own distorted image. Pastors face a constant pressure to increase numbers in their church, but too often do so by winning people to themselves rather than to Christ.

Casuistry (23:16–22). The scribes of the old covenant were masters at fine-tuning their interpretation of the law in such a way that its real purpose was subverted. Some pastors are so zealous at ensuring their members conform outwardly to certain interpretations of what it means to be holy that they have long traded the positive beauty of God's wisdom for the dead husk of legal minutiae.

Legalism (23:23–24). Closely allied to casuistry is legalism, the insistence on slavishly obeying the petty details of the law while failing to fulfil its spirit altogether. In a memorable phrase that uncomfortably describes too many pastoral practices where pastors have a genuine motive in urging their flock to high standards, at least on the surface, Jesus accuses the scribes and Pharisees of straining out a gnat but swallowing a camel.

Hypocrisy (23:25–26). The blind guides of Israel consider outward appearances more important than inner realities. Jesus looks to his scribes to be people of integrity, where there is consistency between the outer and the inner, the surface and the depth, what we show to others and what we are when alone or in private.

Professionalism (23:27–28). One failing leads to another: they are all of a piece. This sixth 'woe' continues the theme of the contradiction between the outside appearance and the inside reality. Bluntly, the outside looks attractive but the inside is dead. Ministers can fall into the trap of ministering in a way that looks so acceptable on the surface, always having the right word to say and always offering the right pastoral encouragement, and yet the truth is their own relationship with God has long since died and they are merely 'professional' in the worst sense of that word.

Inconsistency (23:29–30). It all added up to one massive life of inconsistency, where they honoured the prophets their ancestors murdered and claimed they would have treated them differently, while repeating the same mistake in their own generation. How easy it is to pronounce wrong judgments on the very people through whom God would long to speak.

The scribes of the new age are not automatically exempted from falling into the same errors the scribes of the old era had turned into an art form. Only as they stay close to their Master and learn his teaching for themselves before passing it on to others will they avoid the pitfalls of ministry.

Conclusion

Matthew sets before us the wise scribe as a model of ministry. For these ministers the teaching gift is uppermost. But before being teachers, they must be learners who understand his radical message, instructed by the one Teacher himself. They must prove that they will not be blind guides. They function alongside members of the community, rather than above them, faithfully applying old truths to new situations, guiding them into a truer understanding of their identity and navigating them through the winds of division. Their teaching necessarily involves them in both pastoral care and evangelistic mission. They can neither shelter behind their books, nor their chapel walls. They have authority, but their very position renders them vulnerable to temptation. That is why David Bennett's advice in respect of leadership generally is advice of which Matthew would have approved:

> The single most important lesson for the leader to learn is that he/she is first a sheep and not a shepherd; first a child and not a father or mother; first an imitator, not a model. Rather than thinking only about those biblical images that set him/her apart, the leader should reflect on the many more images that apply to him/her as fully as to any other believer.[36]

---

36. Bennett, *Biblical Images*, pp. 193–194.

2. MARK: MINISTRY IN AN OPPRESSED CULTURE

The ministry of kingdom emissaries

At first sight the possibility of developing any concept of ministry from the Gospel of Mark does not seem promising, especially if one accepts Ernest Best's judgment:

> There is no trace of a ministry within the community. That is not to say there was no ministry. We do not know to what stage ministry had developed in the time Mark was writing; he is not interested in it. In so far as he depicts the Twelve as exercising a ministry it is toward the outside world; they are sent to teach and to exorcise; they are not given authority over others.[1]

---

1. Ernest Best, *Mark: The Gospel as Story* (Edinburgh: T. & T. Clark, 1983), p. 91. Best believes that Mark's Gospel has a pastoral purpose, namely the desire to build up the faith of the disciples facing persecution (pp. 51–54). But his purpose is a different question to the one we are discussing here. Mark's advocacy of a form of ministry and his own pastoral writing are not so closely bound together as they are in Matthew. Interestingly, David Bartlett's work *Ministry in the New Testament*, OBT (Minneapolis: Fortress, 1993), omits Mark altogether and has only a few references to it in the index, all included because of their significance for other parts of the New Testament.

It is true Mark shows little interest in the church as such, especially when compared to Matthew. But that will only prove a stumbling block to developing an understanding of ministry from his Gospel if we adopt too narrow a definition of 'ministry'. Mark has an immense amount to say about ministering in a culture where people feel oppressed. It leads to a concept of ministry as a powerful encounter with the forces and agents of tyranny on the frontiers of the believing community.

The oppression that dominates his Gospel is the oppression of Satan at loose in the world. However, the subtext of the Gospel addresses the oppression that will be experienced too by the church. Mark may chiefly have had theological reasons for writing his Gospel, namely to reveal Christ and his kingdom, but many have concluded that Mark also had a pastoral motivation and was writing to encourage the church to remain strong in the face of the persecution, even martyrdom, they were experiencing as disciples of Jesus.[2] Oppression, then, both broods over and is found deep within the Gospel from the opening scenes, where John the Baptist is imprisoned, to the penultimate scene of the darkness that covers the face of the earth when Jesus is crucified.

Mark includes detailed reports of the calling of the disciples and commissioning of the Twelve, which has significance for our quest in exploring what model of ministry he portrays. Jesus, saying, 'I will send you out to fish for people', first calls Simon and Andrew to follow him (1:17). Next he calls Levi to leave his work and follow him (2:14). Then we read, Jesus 'appointed' the Twelve so that 'they might be with him and that he might send them out to preach and to have authority to drive out demons' (3:14–15). Later he sends them out 'two by two and gave them authority over evil spirits' (6:7). Underlying each of these calls is the idea that the ministry of the disciples is a continuation of the ministry of Jesus himself. So to understand the ministry of the Twelve, as presented by Mark, and of other disciples whom they represent, we must first consider the ministry of Jesus himself.

---

2. William L. Lane, *The Gospel of Mark*, NICNT (London: Marshall, Morgan & Scott, 1974), pp. 12–17. For a survey of views, see Ralph P. Martin, *Mark: Evangelist and Theologian* (Exeter: Paternoster, 1979), *passim*; or the more recent, cautious comment by R. T. France, *The Gospel of Mark*, NIGTC (Grand Rapids: Eerdmans, 2002), p. 23. Note should be taken of Richard Bauckham's argument that we should not concern ourselves with the specific audiences addressed by the Gospels, which inevitably involves a great deal of speculation because they were written as encyclicals. See Richard Bauckham (ed.), *The Gospel for All Christians: Rethinking the Gospel Audiences* (Grand Rapids: Eerdmans, 1998), pp. 9–48.

The ministry of Jesus

Within the total picture of Jesus' ministry, four major elements have special relevance to the ongoing ministry of the disciples.

It was a liberating ministry

Jesus himself announces the purpose of his mission. ' "The time has come," he said, "The Kingdom of God is near. Repent and believe the good news!" ' (1:15). The Gospel then proceeds to catalogue the various ways in which people are oppressed because they are living under the alien authority of Satan and to detail the power of Jesus to release them from his grip and bring them under the rule of God.

The presence of sickness is pervasive and Jesus heals many, so much so that he is in danger of becoming known solely as a mass healer (1:32–39). The illnesses are of various kinds, but underneath them all lies the thinly disguised activity of demons (1:34; 9:14–29). Demon infestation leads to uncontrollable behaviour; it is not only disruptive of family and community (1:21–26) but also destructive of the afflicted person (5:1–20). Some illnesses are aided and abetted by the religious purity rules of the day that demand the removal of the impure from any social contact and leave them isolated and vulnerable (5:25–34). Disease, of whatever kind, leaves people unable to enjoy the fullness of life as God intends it.

Another form of oppression is the way people are rendered powerless in the face of natural disasters and hunger (4:35–41; 6:30–44; 8:1–13), and made to live in fear of hostile forces they cannot control. The ultimate oppression (the final enemy), of course, is death itself, not yet defeated by Jesus' resurrection. But the raising of Jairus' daughter is an early sign of God's kingdom breaking in (5:22–42). The revolution against Satan has begun and, although not without cost, will one day inevitably triumph.

In miraculously overcoming all these forms of oppression, Jesus reveals himself not only to be 'an exceptionally powerful miracle worker',[3] though he is that, but also the Lord of creation, as he masters natural forces; the conqueror of evil, as he expels the forces of Satan; the healer of sickness, as he restores the broken to wholeness; and, the victor over death, as he brings the dead to life again.[4]

---

3. Graham H. Twelftree, *Jesus: The Miracle Worker* (Downers Grove: IVP, 1999), p. 92.

4. See G. R. Beasley-Murray, *Preaching the Gospel from the Gospels* (Peabody: Hendrickson, 1996), pp. 67–105, for a full exposition of this theme.

One form of oppression not explicitly confronted, except at the cross, is the oppression of Rome. But it is implicit in the recording of many of Mark's stories. One illustration of this is to be found in the exorcism of the tomb-dweller of the Gerasenes. Not for nothing are the demons who inhabit him and are causing his disintegration known as 'Legion'. As Ched Myers points out, once alerted by this clue, we discover the rest of the story is filled with military allusions, including terms like 'herd' (5:11) (*agelē*, used for a band of military recruits) and 'he dismissed them' (*epetrepsen*, a military command, loosely translated in TNIV as 'he gave them permission'). The herd's immersion in the lake, he adds, would invoke an important memory:

> Enemy soldiers being swallowed by hostile waters of course brings to mind the narrative of Israel's liberation from Egypt (Ex 14), as Moses' victory hymn sings: 'Pharaoh's chariots and his army Yahweh cast into the sea; his elite officers are sunk in the Red Sea' (Ex 15:4).[5]

In another crucial statement, Jesus, speaking of the strong opposition between the kingdom of Satan and the kingdom of God, uses the image of tying up the strong man before plundering his house (3:27). His mission is to bind Satan and then 'release' those he holds prisoner within his domain. Time and again Mark's Gospel illustrates Jesus doing this successfully, leading Robert Gundry to conclude that 'the Jesus of Mark is overpowering'.[6] He is 'the strong one': a man of authority, a worker of miracles, a performer of exorcisms, a teacher of wonders, and the one who even provokes nature to hide itself in shame when darkness covers the earth during the hours of his dying (15:33).

It was a teaching ministry

It is unbalanced to conclude, as some have done, that the Jesus of Mark's Gospel is nothing more than an action man. It is true that he includes less teaching than the other Gospel writers. For example, he includes only eleven parables compared with Matthew's twenty-seven and Luke's thirty-three, and it may be, as Ernest Best has claimed, that Mark is less interested in the content

---

5. Ched Myers, *Binding the Strong Man: A Political Reading of Mark's Story of Jesus* (Maryknoll: Orbis, 1995), p. 191. Myers's commentary provides the most thorough and consistent exposition of the political dimension of Mark's Gospel.

6. Robert H. Gundry, *Mark: A Commentary on His Apology for the Cross* (Grand Rapids: Eerdmans, 1993), p. 1026.

of Jesus' teaching than his activity as a teacher.[7] Even so, Mark stresses the teaching ministry of Jesus and regularly sets it on a par with his ministry of healing and exorcism. It has been estimated that 40% of the verses of Jesus contain teaching.[8] The initial response of the crowd, having witnessed his first exorcism at Capernaum, was to ask, 'Who is this? A new teaching – and with authority!' (1:27). When Peter seeks to persuade him to return to Capernaum to conduct more healings, Jesus determinedly goes to 'preach' in other villages, saying, 'That is why I have come' (1:38). Mark includes plenty of teaching in his Gospel (4:1–34; 7:1–23; 9:30–50; 10:17–31: 11:27 – 12:44; and 13:1–37). He records Jesus as teaching his disciples in private (4:10; 7:17; 9:28; 10:10) and is especially concerned to show him instructing them in the art of discipleship.

True, the teaching is interwoven with the action stories and often arises from them.[9] In this way, Jesus' teaching is presented as an indispensable partner to his miracles. A review of 8:27 – 10:45 demonstrates this. There he covers issues of suffering, prayer, humility, tolerance, holiness, divorce, wealth and his own identity. But his expositions are prefaced by the feeding of the four thousand, 'interrupted' by the transfiguration and healing of the boy possessed by an evil spirit, and immediately followed by the healing of blind Bartimaeus. As here, Jesus' teaching seems always to arise on the job and take place on the way, rather than being unrelated abstract teaching merely of a bookish kind.

Far from parroting conventional platitudes, his teaching is always radical; calling people to carry the cross, pray and fast to drive out demons, be inclusive of others, care for those whom many would regard as insignificant, remain faithful in marriage rather than be concerned about divorce, leave riches behind for the sake of total commitment to the kingdom of God and, as leaders, become servants, shunning the normal concerns about status and authority. In the light of this, it is unsurprising that even the Pharisees and Herodians are forced grudgingly to admit that he is 'a man of integrity . . . [not] swayed by others but [who teaches] the way of God in accordance with the truth' (12:14).

It was a strategic ministry
More briefly, we should note that Jesus does not conduct his ministry in a haphazard way, but, arising from prayer with his Father, conducts it according to

---

7. Best, *Mark*, pp. 62–63.

8. R. T. France cited by ibid., p. 62.

9. Twelftree, *Jesus*, pp. 95–96.

a strategic plan that leads to the cross. When, as mentioned above, early one morning, Peter wants to entice him back to Capernaum to build on the success of the previous evening's healing ministry, Jesus refuses. It is obviously a worthwhile thing to do and a compassionate response to a genuine need. Many remain sick in Capernaum and would have benefited from his healing power. Yet Jesus turns his back on them, shunning the road to popularity to preach in other villages, and says, 'That is why I have come' (1:35–39). It is not that he is unfeeling in the face of need. How can he ever be accused of that? It is not that he is being arrogant, reserving the right to spend his energies as he determines. Rather, his priorities are shaped by the early hours he has spent with his father in prayer. His direction is determined by his need to minister first in Galilee and then to make his way towards Jerusalem, knowing all that it will hold for him.

This strikes me as being in sharp contrast to the way many undertake their ministry today. Many have no sense of strategic focus but merely respond to who or what crosses their path each day with the result that little is accomplished. While Jesus had time for interruptions and was on occasions responsive to the immediate needs of people, as the healing of the woman with internal bleeding shows (5:24–34), he could permit such interruptions because it was consistent with his strategy. His strategy enabled him to discern priorities, and we today need a similar sense of God's particular calling and direction for our work if we are to be worthy of being Jesus' emissaries.

It was a cruciform ministry

Mark's Gospel is dominated by the cross. The opposition to Jesus begins from the moment he heals a paralysed man in the synagogue at Capernaum (2:1–12) and threads its way through the Gospel, coming centre stage from 8:31 onwards[10] until he is crucified. Robert Gundry has said, with some justification, that Mark's Gospel is 'a straightforward apology for the cross'.[11]

Even where the cross is not evident, it is implicit, for it is always at the heart of the Gospel. So discerning readers, when they read of Jesus quietening the storm (4:35–41), cannot but recall the story of Jonah who also fell asleep during a storm on a boat and brought about peace by throwing himself to certain death in the raging sea, only to experience resurrection after three days. It all points forward to Jesus' death and resurrection. Equally, when they read of the demon-possessed man of the Gerasenes being exorcized by Jesus,

---

10. Note the three predictions of the cross in 8:31; 9:31; 10:45.
11. Gundry, *Mark*, p. 1.

discerning readers can see the way in which later Jesus is going to the cross to take his place, thus enabling him to be released in anticipation. On the cross, Jesus is bound, tormented, stripped naked, wounded and dwells among death. When the woman whom the law considers unclean because of her long-standing haemorrhaging of blood is healed (5:24–34), we see how Jesus, the pure one, exchanges places with her and becomes unclean on the cross. And in raising Jairus' daughter from the dead (5:21–24, 35–43), we see Jesus already in conflict with our last enemy, death, and how through his own death he will overcome it.[12]

Cross-bearing was, as we shall see, to mark the ministry not only of Jesus but also of his disciples. As they sought to bring liberty to people in an oppressed culture, they would themselves experience the oppression of rejection and persecution.

The ministry of the disciples

In Mark's Gospel, there are close parallels between the ministry of Jesus and that of his disciples. Although not exhaustive, three passages set out the crucial aspects of his understanding of ministry. They relate to the *creation, commissioning* and *cross-bearing* of the apostles, who are to serve as emissaries of his kingdom.

The creation of the Twelve (3:13–18)
The brief report Mark gives of the appointment of the Twelve is packed full of meaning. Their appointment takes place on a mountain. As with Sinai, Tabor and Golgotha, mountains are places where God reveals himself, and this mountain, whichever it was, is to serve as the venue for another significant revelation of God. The Twelve are 'called to him'. Usually, disciples made the decision as to which master they would follow, but here it is the Master who chooses his disciples. The verb *proskaleitai* often has overtones of 'summoning' and here of 'selecting', which stresses the note of Jesus' authority. This is further underlined by the next phrase, which speaks of the Twelve as 'those he wanted'. None was forced on him. He sovereignly chose them. But the sovereign who called them also took delight in them as friends and brothers. Having come to him, 'he appointed' them. Again Mark uses interesting vocabulary. The word 'appointed' (*epoiēsen*) is often translated 'made' or 'created', and

---

12. See further, Tom Wright, *Mark for Everyone* (London: SPCK, 2001), pp. 54–57, 65.

some see in its use a subtle indication that they are being made a new creation to serve the new age of the kingdom that had drawn near in the coming of Jesus.[13]

The way in which the purpose of their appointment is expressed stops us from passing over it as if it were predictable, since it involves a curious tension, if not an outright conflict. The disciples are appointed to 'be with him' but at the same time 'that he might send them out'. Here is the twofold movement that should be at the heart of all Christian ministry. Ministry must arise from intimacy with Christ and yet consists of involvement in the world. How can one be in two places at once? It is, of course, possible for the Christian worker, because the Christ whose closeness we must experience is the Christ who is simultaneously on the loose and at work in his world. He is to be found among the oppressed, broken and marginalized who are in need of liberation and healing.

His desire 'that they may be with him' plainly teaches that ministry 'is a relationship before it is a task' – a matter of *being* as well as of *being sent*.[14] To be with Jesus involves more than just learning his teaching in order to repeat it, or even discovering his strategy for mission in order to follow it. It involves learning from his person. Part of the background to this saying lies in the apprenticeship model of training that disciples undertook in Jesus' day. Such a method of training inevitably left its mark on the apprentice. Although apprentices, when they had served their time, were free to develop their trade in their own way, they would undoubtedly have been moulded in ways far beyond the mechanics of how to ply their trade or accomplish a task. The sayings, passions, values and even the eccentricities of their masters would have rubbed off on them. So it should be with disciples of Jesus. We should not let the undoubted busyness of the task crowd out time spent in cultivating our relationship with our master. Spending time in his company in prayer and study of his word are not optional extras but the very bedrock of ministry. In doing so, we learn to imitate what Michael Griffiths has called 'the beautiful lifestyle of Jesus'.[15] And that can prove as powerful a weapon for the kingdom as can any words or actions, which Jesus addresses next.

---

13. James R. Edwards, *The Gospel of Mark*, PNTC (Grand Rapids: Eerdmans; Leicester: Apollos, 2002), p. 112.

14. Ibid., p. 113.

15. Michael Griffiths, *The Example of Jesus*, The Jesus Library (London: Hodder & Stoughton, 1985), p. 104.

Although we are called to an intimate relationship with Jesus, we are not called to twist it into a cosy relationship that feeds our personal need for security and warmth at the expense of cutting us off from the real world in all its need. The disciples who were chosen to 'be with him' were also chosen to be sent on a mission. Their task was to be twofold: 'to preach and to have authority to drive out demons' (Mark 3:14–15). Words and wonders, saying and doing, preaching and working were to go hand in hand. Each would complement the other. The teaching they were to undertake was not to be undertaken within the Christian community, as in Matthew's Gospel, so much as more widely in the world.

The chief substance of Jesus' teaching was the announcement that 'the kingdom of God has come near' in his own person. From his clear-cut announcement all else would flow and the preaching of the disciples would amplify it. The re-establishment of God's kingdom would raise the question of how it was he overthrew the tyranny of Satan and would lead to speaking the message of the cross and resurrection. The claims about this kingdom would necessitate evidence being produced about its reality and call forth teaching about the deeds of Jesus. The existence of this kingdom would raise questions as to how its subjects were to live and relate to one another. The opposition experienced by his kingdom would require an explanation regarding its future success and the nature of its citizens as an eschatological community. We have seen how Jesus spent time as a teacher. Now his disciples were to pass on his teaching and make it widely known.

The Twelve, however, were about more than words. They were also to imitate Jesus' powerful actions and, like him, release people from bondage to demons. To do so was to give people a tangible sign of the kingdom, an illustration of what it was to live under God's rule rather than that of Satan. They were 'parables of the kingdom', actualizing it for people to see and for those who had 'the eye of faith' pointing beyond the miracles themselves to the true identity of Jesus.[16] They continued to demonstrate that Satan was being defeated. True, not everyone would be exorcized or healed. But then neither had Jesus healed everyone who sought his salvation (see 1:35–39). When the kingdom reached its fulfilment, then all who followed him would be liberated and restored. In the meantime, a foretaste of that day was to be made visible to the world.

The emphasis on exorcism is not because Mark has a particular curiosity about 'deliverance ministry' but because, in the culture of the day, demon possession was the most specific evidence of Satan's control of someone's life and

_____

16. Twelftree, *Jesus*, p. 98.

their deliverance from demons was the most specific sign of God's liberating rule. Its prominence was a kingdom issue. This calling of the Twelve to 'drive out demons' should save us from two opposite errors. On the one hand, it should prevent us from seeing the call as merely a call to engage in good works or social work, or even faith healing, no matter who undertakes it. No doubt good works are a good thing and a biblical foundation could be made for engaging in such activity. But something more precise is happening here. The disciples are being invited to encounter the reality of evil powers (demons) in the world and release people from them by using the authority they have been given by the King himself. Here, as Tom Wright has put it, is 'not simply a healing mission. This isn't simply a time of spiritual renewal. This is the restoration we've all been waiting for.'[17] It is the restoration of the rule of God again in his world.

If, on the one hand, a careful understanding of this commission prevents us from baptizing any good deed as kingdom work, on the other hand, it should not restrict us to seeing demon-possession as the only sign of the presence of evil powers, nor press us into thinking that unless we engage in deliverance ministry we cannot be doing the work of the kingdom. The way in which evil powers express themselves will vary at different times and in different cultures. Exorcism is one powerful and, in Jesus' day, highly relevant manifestation of evil powers at work. The commission makes it incumbent on the disciples of Jesus to release people from the forces of evil however they express themselves and to do so with the authority of the King. Indeed, Jesus later puts exorcism in the same bracket as offering a cup of cold water to someone who is thirsty, providing it is done in his name (9:38–41).

For many, exorcism remains a vital issue. Rationalists in the West are probably too tempted to dismiss the direct expression of evil as revealed in the presence of demons. But they may equally fail to perceive the less direct ways oppressing forces of evil are at work: through society's values or its institutions. Elsewhere in the world the forces of evil, as encountered in Mark, are all too real and those in ministry need no persuasion of the immediate relevance of Jesus' commission. Either way, the commission holds. We are called to be emissaries of the kingdom.

The commissioning of the Twelve (6:6–13)
An illustration of the way in which Jesus multiplies his ministry like this is seen

---

17. Wright, *Mark*, pp. 34–35.

in his sending out of the Twelve 'two by two' to liberate people from evil spirits 'in regions that Jesus had not yet visited or wanted to visit later'.[18] Although the initial instructions about their mission only mentions their authority to exorcize people, the report ends with a fuller account of their activity, which involved preaching and healing alongside exorcisms. They preached that people 'should repent', which picks up on the first words of Jesus Mark records (1:15). Given this, the invitation to repentance is not for Mark about wallowing mournfully and expressing sorrow for sin but of choosing a change of direction and a new management for one's life. It is a matter of aligning one's self with the dawning and revolutionary work God is doing in Jesus. This is consistent with Matthew's fuller account, where we are told that the content of their proclamation is to be that 'The kingdom of heaven has come near' (Matt. 10:7).

From the fuller version of these instructions found in Matthew, Mark chooses only briefly to report a minimum of detail. He makes the point that they are sent out without the usual means of support: 'no bread, no bag, no money in your belts. Wear sandals but not an extra shirt.' The point of these instructions, in R. T. France's view, 'is not so much to encourage asceticism as such (they are after all to expect and accept hospitality), but to emphasise that their loyalty to the kingdom of God leaves no room for a prior attachment to material security'.[19] Hengel more pointedly explains, 'If the disciple in following Jesus was to share the same mission and authority as Jesus himself, he likewise needed to be free for service, unrestrictedly ready to share the total insecurity, exposure to danger, and slander which were the fate of his master.'[20] Mark then briefly alludes to the way in which they are to respond to the varying receptions they will meet, again without going into the detail of Matthew or Luke.[21]

It may be asked whether this commissioning, and the previous discussion of the calling of the Twelve, apply only to them or whether it is legitimate to claim them as a model for subsequent ministry. Clearly, the Twelve have

---

18. Eckhard J. Schnabel, *Early Christian Mission*. Vol. 1: *Jesus and the Twelve* (Downers Grove: IVP; Leicester: Apollos, 2004), p. 290.

19. France, *Mark*, pp. 249–250.

20. Martin Hengel, *The Charismatic Leader and his Followers* (Edinburgh: T. & T. Clark, 1981), p. 78.

21. The parallels are found in Matt. 10:1–15 and Luke 9:1–6. Luke 10:1–24 records very similar instructions to the larger group of seventy-two whom Jesus subsequently sends out on mission.

a significance for Mark that does set them apart from others. It is not hard to see the symbolism of twelve apostles as corresponding to the twelve tribes of Israel. In Schnabel's words, 'they represent symbolically the restoration of the people of God in the last days'.[22] They do have a fundamental shaping role in the church as witnesses to the life, death and resurrection of Jesus. And yet it is plain that their calling and commission is not to be theirs alone.

While Mark does not refer to the mission of a wider group of seventy-two disciples, as Luke does, it is clear that Mark is aware of a wider group of disciples in addition to the Twelve to whom the challenge of mission applies. In 10:17–31, for example, Jesus moves from talking to a potential disciple who is not one of the Twelve, to making a general reference to the demands and rewards of those who would follow him.

Furthermore the insight contained in the window of 9:38–41 would be enough on its own to argue that Mark does not envisage the commission to be fulfilled by the Twelve alone. When John, suffering from a sense of 'inflated self-importance',[23] wants to control who should engage in exorcism, and restrict the exercise of the power of the kingdom to the chosen few ('one of us'), Jesus rebukes him. Providing people are operating 'in my name', he says, all acts, however simple, will be owned and rewarded by God. Again, the precise form of words proves important. John was protesting that the independent exorcist he had seen was 'not one of us'. Jesus tells him that allegiance to the body of disciples is not an important issue. It is allegiance to Jesus, the one through whom the miracles are performed, that matters. James Edwards perceptively entitles this section of his commentary, 'The Kingdom of God is larger than our experience of it'.[24]

The commissioning, then, of kingdom emissaries is the way in which Jesus intends to multiply his ministry, extend the reach of his kingdom and exercise

---

22. Schnabel, *Mission*, vol. 1, p. 270. See also pp. 263–271.

23. Edwards, *Mark*, p. 289.

24. Ibid., p. 288. Edwards suggests this explains what is often considered to be a contradiction between this passage and Matt. 12:30 and its parallel in Luke 11:23. In Matt. 12:30 Jesus says, 'Whoever is not with me is against me' (NRSV). In Matthew the issue is whether people were with Jesus. In Mark the issue is that the independent exorcists are not with the disciples, but are with Jesus. 'Thus, whereas there can be no neutrality with regard to the person of Jesus, the disciples must be tolerant of those who differ from them' (*Mark*, p. 291).

his authority in the world he is reclaiming from Satan.[25] Mark is providing a model for others subsequently to imitate.[26]

The cross-bearing of the Twelve (10:35–45)

As we have seen, the cross hovered over Jesus' ministry and it was going to be no different for his disciples. Their ministry was to be cross-shaped. They had witnessed Jesus facing hostility enough to take his warnings seriously that they too would face hardship and persecution (6:8–10; 8:34–38; 10:17–31; 13:9–13), even if they did not always understand them. Denying oneself, taking up one's cross and following Jesus on the road to Golgotha was a basic mark of all discipleship (8:34), not just of leadership. Losing their lives for Jesus was the only way to gain a life (8:35), whether one was a leader or not. Leaders could not be leaders unless first they were followers. The only leadership in the church was one that led people in the way of Jesus, which inevitably meant in the way of death before resurrection.

Mark was nothing other than totally realistic about the prospects of being a disciple of Jesus, even to the extent of laying down one's life, as Jesus himself had, in a Godforsaken death. Writing about Jesus' cry of desolation from the cross (15:34), Ralph Martin has commented:

> This is Mark's way of encouraging the church. He provides no props for a weak faith and extends no crutch on which the persecuted believers may lean. He is realistic in admitting that Christians may have to tread a lonely path in darkness, with no last-minute dénouement to save them from death. Some Christians may even die in the anguish of God's withdrawn face, when he fails to comfort and cheer his own, The sole support the Markan church is offered is Jesus' own promise to return to them after death.[27]

Although these principles apply to all disciples, the conversation between Jesus and James and John, in 10:35–43, brings them into sharp focus as far as

---

25. Gundry, *Mark*, p. 164; Colin G. Kruse, *New Testament Foundations of Ministry* (London: Marshall, Morgan & Scott, 1983), p. 32.

26. Twelftree, *Jesus*, pp. 97–98, 336, argues this specifically with regard to miracles. But see the more qualified view of Keith Warrington, *Jesus the Healer: Paradigm or Unique Phenomenon?* (Carlisle: Paternoster, 2000), pp. 141–163. Howard Kee, in *The Community of the New Age* (London: SCM, 1977), p. 176, widens the discussion beyond miracles and argues that Mark was designed as a handbook for itinerant evangelists.

27. Martin, *Mark*, p. 219.

leadership is concerned. James and John want to ensure they have the best ringside seats when Jesus comes to reign in glory. They seek position and status and want to be marked out as worthy of special honour. But Jesus promises them nothing other than that they will drink the cup he drinks from and will be baptized with the baptism he will undergo, which are both images of the suffering he will shortly face.[28] He then broadened the conversation to teach all the Twelve that leadership in the church was about servanthood, not lordship, as his own life proved.

No one in recent years has expressed this more powerfully than Martin Luther King in his sermon on 'The Drum Major Instinct'. Speaking on this very passage, King explained:

> And so Jesus gave us a new norm of greatness. If you want to be important –
> wonderful. If you want to be recognized – wonderful. But recognize that he who is
> greatest among you shall be your servant. That's your new definition of greatness.
> And this morning, the thing I like about it . . . by giving that definition of greatness, it
> means everybody can be great. Because everybody can serve. You don't have to have
> a college degree to serve. You don't have to make your subject and your verb agree to
> serve. You don't have to know about Plato and Aristotle to serve. You don't have to
> know Einstein's theory of relativity to serve. You don't have to know the second
> theory of thermodynamics in physics to serve. You only need a heart full of grace.
> A soul generated by love. And you can be that servant.[29]

How easy it is to agree with this in principle; how hard it is to live by it in practice. Nietzsche taught that all of us are driven by a will to power. The temptation to it is often subtle and, because we know it to be so contrary to the spirit of leadership as Jesus taught it, we often deny its existence. The servant can exercise control while pretending to serve, as Jeeves, Bertie Wooster's valet in the stories of P. G. Woodhouse, illustrates and as many of us have experienced at first hand from caretakers and janitors (mercifully not all of them!). Satan can cunningly twist our desire for the best into an attitude of control over

---

28. For the cup as a symbol of God's judgment on wickedness, see Isa. 51:17–23;
    Lam. 4:21. There is no similar precedent for the use of baptism in this way,
    although, as France points out, it soon came to be used by the early Christians as a
    symbol of 'death leading to new life' and of uniting with the death of Jesus (*Mark*,
    p. 416).

29. Martin Luther King, *A Testament of Hope: The Essential Writings and Speeches of Martin
    Luther King Jr.*, ed. J. M. Washington (New York: HarperCollins, 1991), pp. 265–266.

those to whom we minister. And instead of preserving their freedom in Christ we subject them to our lordship.

The temptation stalks us in every area of our ministry. Pastorally, we can be overdirective and sometimes fail to see legitimate options that face weak or struggling Christians. Organizationally, we can drive a strong programme and manipulate people's commitment to 'our programme'. Even in the pulpit, which John Stott has described as an 'exceedingly dangerous place for any child of Adam to occupy',[30] we can assume an authority beyond what either the Holy Spirit or the text of Scripture warrants. Our intentions are so often right but the expression of them can sometimes be very clumsy, as I know from my personal experiences and mistakes in ministry.

So, as servants of Jesus, we need constantly to be on our guard against the spirit of authoritarianism and status-seeking. We must never be power mad control-freaks, and never anything other than servants. This inevitably involves taking the lowest place, not thinking of our own interests and ambitions and daily dying to self that others may live.

We should not miss the importance of this theme when juxtaposed with the nature of ministry as Mark envisages it. As kingdom emissaries, the servants of Christ are involved in the battle for the control of our world and of people's lives. Their preaching, like his, should be 'with authority' (1:27). Their deeds, like his, will sometimes be dramatically powerful as people are released from the control of Satan. Given the powerful Christ presented by Mark and the powerful ministry to which his emissaries are commissioned,[31] it is of vital importance that we do not let that power seduce us. The only context in which to exercise a 'powerful ministry' is in the context of self-denying, cross-carrying, life-losing servanthood. That was the 'powerful ministry' modelled by the King himself.

Conclusion

The implications of Mark's Gospel for ministry are wider than has been detailed above. David deSilva also lists the way it encourages us to rethink

---

30. The theme was developed by John R. W. Stott at the Keswick Convention in 2000 and is published in *Calling Christian Leaders: Biblical Models of Church, Gospel and Ministry* (Leicester: IVP, 2002), pp. 37–58.

31. This powerful commissioning is evident enough in the body of Mark's Gospel without referring to the longer ending and the 'signs following' to which Mark 16:17–18 draws attention.

purity codes in the church, to see ministry as needing to be shaped by prayer, and how all of it is placed 'against an eschatological horizon'.[32] But at the heart of the matter is the calling to be emissaries of the new kingdom God is bringing to birth through Christ. 'The conscious goal', wrote Martin Hengel, 'after which the disciples who "followed" Jesus strove was simply not, as with the rabbis, to carry on the tradition or to create a new tradition, but to prepare for the service of the approaching rule of God.'[33] They prepared by teaching people about Jesus and liberating them, as he had done, from the bondage of Satan.

Discussing a contemporary theology of evangelism, William Abraham has argued that models of evangelism that stress proclamation, church growth and witness have their weaknesses. Instead, he proposes we should see evangelism as engaging in a 'set of intentional activities which is governed by the goal of initiating people into the kingdom of God for the first time'.[34] While I am unsure it is necessary to choose between these, and while I might want to argue that all four models of evangelism Abraham has identified should ideally contribute to a balanced model that embraces them all, the model of initiating people into God's kingdom is exactly the pattern of ministry Mark advocates, except that he has an eye to helping people persevere within the kingdom too.

In cultures where people are burdened and oppressed by the activity of Satan, however it manifests itself, the vision of ministry Mark sets out, that of the kingdom emissary, is an ideal form of service for the Christ who proved himself and still proves himself to be the powerful King.

---

32. David deSilva, *An Introduction to the New Testament: Contexts, Methods and Ministry Formation* (Downers Grove: IVP; Leicester: Apollos, 2004), pp. 229–233.

33. Hengel, *Charismatic Leader*, p. 81.

34. W. Abraham, *The Logic of Evangelism* (London: Hodder & Stoughton, 1989), p. 95. For his discussion of this model, see pp. 92–116.

3. LUKE: MINISTRY IN A GRACELESS WORLD

The ministry of apostolic compassion

We live in a world almost totally devoid of grace. Philip Yancey has summed it up well:

> From nursery school onward we are taught how to succeed in the world of ungrace. The early bird catches the worm. No pain, no gain. There is no such thing as a free lunch. Demand your rights. Get what you pay for. I know these rules well because I live by them. I work for what I earn; I like to win; I insist on my rights. I want people to get what they deserve – nothing more, nothing less.[1]

Luke's Gospel seems to have been written for just such a world and consequently it views ministry as a ministry of mercy and compassion. Mary introduces the theme of God's compassion towards his people early on, as she rejoices in the angelic announcement of Jesus' birth. Her song is echoed by Zechariah's. So in Luke's opening chapter the note of God's mercy is sounded five times in addition to other melodies in the music of grace.[2] In Luke's

---

1. Philip Yancey, *What's So Amazing About Grace?* (Grand Rapids: Zondervan, 1997), p. 64.
2. 'His mercy extends', v. 50; 'remembering to be merciful', v. 54; 'the Lord had shown her great mercy', v. 58; 'to show mercy', v. 72; 'because of the tender mercy of our God', v. 78.

version of the Sermon on the Mount, the Sermon 'on a level place' (Luke 6:17), Jesus instructed his disciples to love their enemies and those from whom they would not receive love in return. He gives a number of reasons for doing so, but the deepest reason he gives is, 'Then . . . you will be the children of the Most High, *because he is kind to the ungrateful and the wicked. Be merciful, just as you Father is merciful'* (6:35–36; my italics). It is the nearest thing to a definition of God that the Gospel gives. For Luke, as we shall see, God's mercy is conveyed not only by words but by kind actions to the most unlikely of people. His Gospel presents us with a portrait of Jesus ministering on a constantly crowded stage, populated by people who are poor, marginalized, insignificant no-hopers, who don't measure up. His cast of characters seems mostly to be composed of the great unwashed and the great unwanted.

Luke stresses that it is into this culture devoid of grace that he sends his apostles with good news. 'The prophet' is an important feature of Luke's writing (Luke 1:76; 4:24; 7:16, 26, 39; 13:33; 20:6; 24:19),[3] but his favourite term for disciples is that of 'apostles', sent ones. Luke's version of the calling of the Twelve puts the stress on their apostleship. 'When morning came, he [Jesus] called his disciples to him and chose twelve of them, *whom he designated apostles'* (6:13; my italics). This title is used only once each by the other Gospels (Matt. 10:2; Mark 6:30; John 13:16), whereas Luke uses it six times in his Gospel (6:13; 9:10; 9:52; 17:5; 22:14; 24:10) and many more times in Acts. Only on two occasions does he use it to refer to disciples more widely than the Twelve (Luke 11:49; Acts 14:14). As apostles they are witnesses to the life, death, and especially resurrection of Jesus. As his 'fully authorised representatives'[4] they play a primary and authoritative role in explaining the significance of Jesus and in proclaiming and defining the Christian gospel. Paul may subsequently use the term more inclusively on occasions, but for Luke the term is restricted.[5] Yet even in Luke, although the Twelve have a special role, they do not act exclusively. Jesus sends the Twelve out on mission (9:1–9) but not long afterwards

---

3. See Paul Minear, *To Heal and to Reveal: The Prophetic Vocation according to Luke* (New York: Crossroad, 1976); and Max Turner, *Power from on High: The Spirit in Israel's Restoration and Witness in Luke-Acts*, JPTSup 9 (Sheffield: Sheffield Academic Press, 1996).

4. John Nolland, *Luke 1:1–9:20*, WBC 35a (Dallas: Word, 1989), p. 270. There is quite a debate about the background of the word *apostolos* and exactly what authority the role implied; see ibid., pp. 265–269, and F. H. Agnew, 'The Origin of the NT Apostle-Concept: A Review of Research', *JBL* 105 (1986), pp. 75–96.

5. See p. 129.

he commissions[6] seventy-two others 'and sent (*apesteilen*) them two by two ahead of him to every town and place where he was about to go' (10:1). They may not have a foundational role in the teaching of the church but their function in mission is identical to that of the apostles. The 'sent ones' therefore cannot be limited to the Twelve. Whatever the nuances of the differences between these two groups, there can be no escaping the stress on being sent. Both groups, and subsequently others, are called to go and minister grace in a graceless world, preaching in the name of Jesus to all nations (24:47). The grace they channel is the grace of peace, of forgiveness, of deliverance, of healing and the good news that the kingdom of God has come near (9:1–2; 10:5, 9).

Since these disciples are 'chosen by Jesus to participate with him in his own work',[7] it is reasonable to ask first what sort of ministry Jesus conducted before reviewing the ministry of the apostles themselves.

Jesus: the model

The mission of Jesus

Luke 4:14–30

Luke mentions the mission of Jesus explicitly on a number of occasions. The fullest account of his mission is found in 'the Nazareth Manifesto' in Luke 4:14–30. Reading Isaiah 61:1–2 in the synagogue at Nazareth, Jesus reinterprets it and makes it his own in a special way. Joel Green has pointed out that the version Jesus uses (the Septuagint) lays emphasis on the words 'me' and 'release' or 'freedom'.[8] Jesus is clearly claiming that he is the fulfilment of Isaiah's prophecy (4:21). Chosen by God and anointed with the Spirit, his mission is to bring 'good news to the poor' and bring release to those held in some form of bondage. The omission of the phrase 'the day of vengeance of our God' from Isaiah 61:2 and the inclusion of 'to set the oppressed free' from Isaiah 58:6, further lays emphasis on the positive mission of liberation that

---

6. There is a variation in the Greek, which means the verb could be either 'commissioned' or 'appointed'. In practice there is little difference in meaning. See I. Howard Marshall, *The Gospel of Luke*, NIGTC (Exeter: Paternoster, 1978), p. 414.

7. Nolland, *Luke 1:1–9:20*, p. 268.

8. Joel B. Green, *The Theology of the Gospel of Luke*, New Testament Theology (Cambridge: Cambridge University Press, 1995), p. 77.

Jesus came to accomplish rather than the negative element of judgment. It was to restore freedom and wholeness to people's lives that he came.

Jesus concludes his exposition by referring to the widow of Zarephath and to Naaman, the Syrian general, as recipients of God's grace, though neither was a member of the chosen people. Thus he puts down a marker about the inclusiveness of his mission and sends out a signal they cannot fail to miss (as their hostile reaction shows), that God's grace is to be channelled to the Gentiles as well.

Much discussion has taken place on the identity of 'the poor', to whom Jesus has come to proclaim good news.[9] Though today we might naturally assume the word was primarily an economic term, it meant something much wider in Luke's day. Luke uses the word 'poor' seven times either as a headline or as a summary for lists of people who were normally thought to be undeserving of God's grace and who were excluded from the community of God's people (Luke 4:18; 6:20; 7:22; 14:13; 14:21; 16:20, 22). It is reasonable to believe that these lists explained what being poor meant. They included the prisoners, blind, oppressed, hungry, mournful, persecuted, lame, lepers, deaf, disabled, the diseased and even, on a different level, the dead. These were the people whom society cast aside as insignificant, even an embarrassment, the unclean who were of low status and no consequence. They were those shunned by the Pharisees, including people in despised trades, as those who were unable or unwilling to keep the social and religious codes of the day. For whatever reason, they lacked purity.[10]

The label 'sinner' is also relevant to this discussion. Luke uses the word seventeen times in contrast to Matthew and Mark's sparing use of the term (Luke 5:8, 30, 32; 6:32, 33, 34 [twice]; 7:34, 39; 13:2; 15:1, 2, 7, 10; 18:13; 19:7; 24:7). 'Sinners' were the people who were despised by the religious leaders of the day (the tax collector and harlot type of individual), but Jesus loved to eat with them and obviously enjoyed their company. Because they had no meaningful relationship with the Pharisees, they were assumed to be out of fellowship with God.[11]

---

9. Ibid., pp. 79–84; and Joel B. Green, 'Good News to Whom? Jesus and the "Poor" in the Gospel of Luke', in Joel B. Green and Max Turner (eds.), *Jesus of Nazareth: Lord and Christ: Essays on the Historical Jesus and New Testament Christology* (Grand Rapids: Eerdmans, 1994), pp. 59–74.

10. R. Alan Culpepper, 'The Gospel of Luke', NIB 9 (Nashville: Abingdon, 1995), p. 23. On the despised trades, see Joachim Jeremias, *Jerusalem in the Time of Jesus* (London: SCM, 1967), pp. 303–317.

11. Culpepper, 'Gospel of Luke', p. 23.

So to the oppressed who need releasing, the sick who need healing, the lost who need finding, the outcasts who need restoring and the impure who need cleansing, we must also add the sinners who need forgiving. In fact, it is unwise to define any of these terms too precisely. They run into one another and often simply provide a different perspective on the same experience of being unacceptable. It was to these people, however defined, that Jesus came to make God's mercy known.

In all this, Jesus not only rides roughshod over these customary ways of assessing a person's worth and status but also insists on turning conventional measurements upside down. His commitment to reversing society's understanding of status is encapsulated in his saying, 'There are those who are last who will be first, and first who will be last' (13:30).[12]

Luke 5:31–32

The two other explicit references to the purpose of his mission bear out the Nazareth Manifesto. Responding to criticism from the Pharisees about the company he kept, Jesus said, 'It is not the healthy who need a doctor, but the sick. I have come not to call the righteous, but sinners to repentance' (5:31–32). Jesus had already alluded to himself as a physician when in Nazareth (4:23) but here explicitly develops the image.

In this saying, Jesus is claiming to fulfil another Old Testament prophecy. Ezekiel 34:16 had envisaged the time when the false shepherds of Israel would be overthrown and God himself would act as their shepherd. In doing so, God says, 'I will search for the lost and bring back the strays. *I will bind up the injured* and strengthen the weak' (my italics). That is exactly what Jesus says he came to do. Setting it against this background explains why the Pharisees reacted so negatively to Jesus. Their theology had a place for sinners to repent, but in alluding to Ezekiel they heard Jesus say that he was indicting them for failing in their responsibilities as Israel's leaders. God himself had now come in the person of Jesus to take over the responsibility of being a shepherd to Israel, and beyond its borders too.[13]

The Old Testament background is not the only one against which to understand Jesus' saying. The image of the doctor was a common way in Hellenistic culture of talking about the philosophers who saw vice as a sickness and virtue

---

12. John O. York, *The Last Shall Be First: The Rhetoric of Reversal in Luke*, JSNTSup 46 (Sheffield: Sheffield Academic Press, 1991).

13. David A. Neale, *'None but the Sinners': Religious Categories in the Gospel of Luke*, JSNTSup 58 (Sheffield: JSOT Press, 1991).

as health. Here Jesus presents himself as a doctor, sin as the sickness and right-eousness as health.[14] But the key question is how those who are unhealthy sinners (the poor) can be made healthy. For that Jesus prescribes 'repentance', which turns people from themselves to receive the mercy of God in their lives. The forgiveness spoken of here is the same as the release spoken of at Nazareth. As Joel Green explains, they relate because Jesus

> portrays both forgiveness and healing in social terms to match their more evident spiritual and physical overtones. What is forgiveness but removing the barrier (sin) that had previously excluded one from one's community? And what is healing, if not at least the removal of the barrier (sickness, uncleanness) that kept one from one's community? 'Release' for Luke signifies wholeness, freedom from diabolic and social chains, acceptance.[15]

Luke 19:10

The third explicit reference by Jesus to his mission, found in 19:10, is not dis-similar. Here he says, 'For the Son of Man came to seek and to save what was lost.' Again, the background may be found in Ezekiel 34:15. It is important to note that no reason as to why they are lost is given and no blame is attached to them for being lost. Sometimes people get lost through their own stupid fault. They have refused to listen to advice or failed to take the necessary steps to prepare themselves. But not all who are lost are lost because they have been wilful or stupid. Sometimes people get lost through no fault of their own. They have been misdirected, the information has been inadequate, or the fog has descended. To all such people, whatever the cause, Jesus came on a search-and-rescue mission and proved to be an unfailing guide out of trouble.

So the primary focus of Jesus' ministry is to release the oppressed, to heal the sick, to rescue the lost and to forgive the sinner. The words 'oppressed', 'sick', 'lost' and 'sinners' describe Jesus' target group, with the word 'poor' as an inclusive catch-all sort of word.

The actions of Jesus

The actions of Jesus are perfect demonstrations of his mission. Virtually any of his actions (his calling of disciples, his contact with women and children, or his miracles) can be summoned to witness to the authenticity of his mission. We examine just four as prime examples.

---

14. Luke T. Johnson, *The Gospel of Luke*, SP 3 (Collegeville: Liturgical, 1991), p. 97.

15. J. B. Green, *Theology*, p. 79.

First, there is *the raising of the widow of Nain's son (7:11–17)*. Although our interest might properly lie in seeing Jesus as the conqueror of death, Luke's focus seems to be more on the grieving mother than on the dead son.[16] Here is a woman who is already a widow and this is her only son. His death then is calamitous for her since she will lose her only means of support. Seeing her, 'his heart went out to her' and in an act of compassion, reminiscent of Elijah's action at Zarephath, to which Jesus has referred in his Nazareth address, he restores her son to her (1 Kgs 17:17–24).

Secondly, we choose *the healing of the man with dropsy (14:1–6)*. One sabbath, perhaps after Jesus speaks at the synagogue service, and while eating in the house of a prominent Pharisee, a man with dropsy provides a great diversion from the meal. How the man comes to be in the house is unclear. He may have gatecrashed the occasion, but since Luke tells us Jesus is under minute scrutiny it may even have been a set-up to test Jesus. If so, it would have been extreme behaviour on the Pharisee's part. The man's body is bloated, while at the same time craving for water; therefore he is considered unclean. Dropsy was thought to be a punishment from God. His presence in the house would have done nothing for the Pharisees' religious street cred! One chose one's guests with an eye to improving one's social and religious standing and he would have done anything but that. But Jesus, in spite of being under suspicion, does not hesitate. He heals the man immediately and sends him away whole. People matter more than religious niceties and what better day is there for ministering wholeness than on the sabbath? The healing, in this case, is a prelude to some important teaching, of which more in a moment.

Thirdly, we might look at *the healing of the ten lepers (17:11–19)*, a third miracle unique to Luke but also one that, as a mass healing, is the only miracle of its kind. Jesus heals ten lepers on the boundary line between Samaria and Galilee while on the outskirts of a village (17:11–12). Their very location emphasizes their marginalization, while their number testifies to the fact that they are a whole colony of despair. They ask for 'pity' and he shows them mercy by healing them and commanding them to fulfil the law so that they can resume their place in the community. Only one, realizing what has happened, comes back to express gratitude, and Luke adds 'and he was a Samaritan', an outsider. Luke's vocabulary indicates that this man knew full salvation as opposed to the other nine who knew only physical healing.[17] For our purposes we might note

---

16. Joel B. Green, *The Gospel of Luke*, NICNT (Grand Rapids: Eerdmans, 1997), pp. 289–291.

17. G. H. Twelftree, *Jesus: The Miracle Worker* (Downers Grove: IVP, 1999), p. 163.

Jesus' commitment to heal both Jew and Samaritan, both body and soul, both God's created people and his covenant people, both the one and the many. It is a classic expression of his compassion to those who are forced to live on the borders of community and to use his powers for their wholeness and restoration.

Fourthly, as an illustration of Jesus' actions other than that of a miracle, there is *the salvation of Zacchaeus (19:1–10)*. Zacchaeus may have been wealthy but, as the story amusingly hints, as a tax collector he was not tolerable company. He was among those who by their profession had crossed unacceptable boundaries and placed themselves among the impure. Yet Jesus takes an initiative of grace and invites himself to the house of this 'sinner'. It results in Zacchaeus' repentance, as demonstrated by the way he restores the monies he has stolen, to a much greater degree than the law requires.[18] It also results in the remarkable absolution of Jesus who now pronounces him a recipient of salvation and 'a son of Abraham'. This miracle, coming at the end of the phase of Jesus' ministry in Galilee has been described as 'the climax of the ministry of Jesus' and 'the epitome of the message of the gospel'.[19] While David Neale has commented about it that 'The initial declaration of ministry to the "sinners" (Lk 5:32) has now found its fulfilment and fullest expression in the person of Zacchaeus. The policy of inclusion and seeking the lost is fully vindicated.'[20]

The teaching of Jesus

Two passages, among many, might be selected to illustrate the coherence between his teaching and the purpose of his mission.

We have already seen that Jesus used the healing of the man with dropsy on the sabbath to raise important issues (14:1–6). The healer quickly became the teacher. The meal became a seminar. The dining room becomes a classroom, giving rise to Fred Craddock's delightful and perceptive comment that 'nothing can be for Luke more serious than a dining table'.[21] So much of Jesus' most important teaching takes place over the meal table (5:27–32; 7:36–50; 10:38–42; 14:1–24; 19:1–9; 22:7–38; 24:13–35).

First, there is *the teaching in the Pharisee's House (14:1–24)*. Jesus begins by

---

18. Compare his fourfold restoration with the law's requirement that one-fifth should be added to the sum originally defrauded (Lev. 6:1–7).

19. Marshall, *Luke*, pp. 694–695.

20. Neale, *'None but the Sinners'*, p. 180.

21. Fred B. Craddock, *Luke*, Interpretation (Louisville: John Knox, 1990), p. 175.

tackling the question of status and invites them to behave in a way most would consider unreasonable (14:7–11). The Pharisees may be watching him carefully but he, no less, has been noticing their behaviour. They have jockeyed for position and recognition at the meal table. Jesus tells them to forget issues of status because the law of reversal operates in his kingdom. Not only will the first be last but the honoured will be humbled, while the humble will be exalted.

Then he instructs them to invite to their feasts those considered undesirable (14:12–14). The 'poor, crippled, lame and blind' should be on the guest list, rather than the normal hangers-on like family and friends. Joel Green explains that, for three reasons, no one would dream of doing this: (1) it would undermine one's social standing; (2) it would be a waste, because these people could not reciprocate the invitation; and (3) it would only embarrass the poor who were not in a position to repay.[22]

Then Jesus instructs them to think the unthinkable. In response to a remark by one of the guests, Jesus tells a parable about a banquet as a means of instructing them about the messianic banquet to come, as foreseen in Isaiah 25:6–8. In this story, the guests normally considered to qualify for a seat at the table refuse to attend, while 'the poor, the crippled, the blind and the lame' (again!) sit down to enjoy the feast. These are the very people excluded elsewhere as unfit. Leviticus 21:7–13 states that these conditions would prevent a person from becoming a priest and so entering into God's presence, while the teaching of the community at Qumran states:

> Let no person smitten with any human impurity whatever enter the Assembly of God. And every person smitten with these impurities, unfit to occupy a place in the midst of the Congregation, and every person smitten in the flesh, paralysed in the feet or hands, lame or blind or deaf, or dumb or smitten in the flesh with a blemish visible to the eye, or an aged person that totters and is unable to stand firm in the midst of the Congregation: let these persons not enter.[23]

But these are the very people welcomed to the table by Jesus who, in a world devoid of grace, brings grace to those who otherwise have no hope.

The second passage that brings Jesus' teaching into sharp focus is *the parable of the Good Samaritan* (10:25–37). There is a danger that we reduce this parable to being mere encouragement to being a good neighbour, but its import is altogether more significant than that.

---

22. J. B. Green, *Luke*, p. 550.

23. Dead Sea Scroll 1QSa 2:3–8, cited by Culpepper, 'Gospel of Luke', p. 287.

Here is another instance of Jesus commending the ministry of compassion. The ministry of compassion to the victim in need of healing and his need of a good neighbour is obvious. But there is an added and unexpected element in this parable. The one who proves to be the good neighbour and comes to the rescue is not from among the leadership of Israel, as might be expected, but a Samaritan, a member of a nation to which the Jews showed nothing but hatred and hostility. So here Jesus gives us a double whammy. There are two 'poor' people in this story: a Jewish victim who is sick and a Samaritan saviour who, from a Jewish viewpoint, is lost. The irony is, that in line with the upside down kingdom of Jesus, where conventional measurements and values are turned on their head, the people in the parable who are truly lost are the priest and the Levite, the accepted 'insiders' in the religion of Israel. Jesus, then, makes his point in this parable, not once but twice. God's heart is a heart of compassion for the lost.

In a plea for holistic mission, John Stott has insightfully contrasted the story of the man on the road from Jerusalem to Jericho with that of the prodigal son:

> Both depict tragic situations which, it is implied, are displeasing to God. God does not want human beings made in his image either to become demoralized and lost in a far country or to be assaulted and abandoned half-dead in the gutter. His desire is that both the lost and the battered be brought home.[24]

Yet there are contrasts in the stories that, in summary form, might be presented like this:[25]

In the good Samaritan, there is	In the prodigal son, there is
a victim of a 'desperate plight'	a victim of his own sin
social sin	personal sin
a rescue of a helpless victim	a rescue of a repentant victim
a love of one's neighbour	a love of the father
a resistance by priest and Levite	a resistance by the older brother

God has a concern for both the victims and the villains, who are often victims by another name, of the world.

---

24. John R. W. Stott, *The Contemporary Christian* (Leicester: IVP, 1992), p. 346.
25. Ibid., pp. 346–347.

Jesus' teaching, then, is a perfect fit with his actions and his stated mission to minister the compassion of a merciful God to a graceless world. As John Stott says, 'Jesus' works made his words visible; his words made his works intelligible.'[26]

The disciples: the sent ones

As we have seen from his use of language, Luke views the disciples primarily as apostles, that is as those commissioned with the authority of the sender to act in his name and continue his mission.[27] This we see them doing not only in the vignettes of mission Luke records in his Gospel but as their mission is extended beyond Jerusalem, as recorded in the Acts of the Apostles. Time and again the sick are healed, the marginalized are included and the oppressed are delivered.

This perspective on ministry raises major questions for the way many churches conduct ministry today in succession to the apostles.

The focus of our ministry

Much contemporary ministry focuses on the insiders, whereas the focus of Jesus' ministry was on the outsiders.[28] Many pastors have become chaplains to religious clubs, or managers of a religious supermarket, and their primary focus has been on satisfying the needs of its members or keeping the loyalty of its customers. Truth to tell, there is some pressure on them to do so because often those members are paying the pastor's salary and therefore, even if unconsciously, tend to view the pastor as an employee and subtly send out signals to that effect. But many insiders, not all, are already quite comfortable and their needs really quite trivial. By virtue of belonging to a church they have friendship and support, have some sense of self-worth and significance and are probably from the more respectable and better-off sections of society.

Given that this is the context in which many will minister, William Willimon has recently fired off a challenge that is spot on target. We need not just to be satisfying the needs of the insiders but helping them to learn whether those needs are even legitimate ones to have or not. He writes:

---

26. Ibid., p. 345.

27. On the origin of the concept of apostle, see p. 129.

28. For the Old Testament roots of ministering to outsiders, see Walter Brueggemann, *Biblical Perspectives on Evangelism* (Nashville: Abingdon, 1993), pp. 48–70.

Our culture tends to be a vast supermarket of desire. Anyone who goes out to meet my needs is going to be working full time!

I believe this is one reason many pastors are so fatigued. They are expending their lives, running about in such busyness, attempting to service the needs of essentially selfish, self-centred consumers, without critique or limit of those needs. Flannery O'Connor mocked a clergyman of her acquaintance, whom she called 'one part minister and three parts masseuse'.

He adds, 'The gospel is not simply about meeting people's needs. The gospel is also a critique of our needs, an attempt to give us needs worth having.'[29]

Yet Jesus would call us to be more radical still and not only critique the trivial needs of many insiders but call us to serve the real needs of the outsiders: the poor, the sick and the lost. These are the ones who stand in true need. They have not encountered grace in the world. Rather, they have encountered its hard, demanding and unforgiving edge. Having found no mercy in their situation they, of all people, stand in need of God's grace.

All this seems very individualistic. It raises the question as to whether our calling is exclusively to care for the victims of society but not do anything to change the circumstances that have made them victims. In terms of Luke's Gospel, we might ask, is it only right to pick up wounded Samaritans on the road from Jerusalem to Jericho or is it equally right to police the road, clean it up and remove the bandits who prey on others from it? Is it right to heal the lepers but not engage in preventative medicine that reduces the incidence of leprosy in the first place?

The answer is, of course, that we are called to both. Luke's ethical stance is radical in its challenge to the existing structures of society as much as in its call to care for individuals, as the Song of Mary (1:46–56) alone is enough to demonstrate. But if part of Luke's purpose is to commend the gospel to the Roman authorities, as many have argued, it is unsurprising that he does not overstress this aspect of the gospel.[30] His treatment of the nonentities of society is radical enough by implication to sow seeds that eventually even brought down the massive institution of slavery in the Roman Empire.

It might be added, however, that there are certain dangers, as well as many benefits, in the emphasis on social action. First, there is the danger that while

29. William Willimon, *Pastor: The Theology and Practice of Ordained Ministry* (Nashville: Abingdon, 2002), pp. 95–96.

30. David deSilva, *An Introduction to the New Testament: Contexts, Methods and Ministry Formation* (Downers Grove: IVP; Leicester: Apollos, 2004), pp. 328–329.

structures are being challenged, individuals who could be helped are left struggling. There is a whole army of social reformers who jet around the world to
professional conferences, talking to each other, who have substituted their
own rhetoric for offering practical help to victims on their doorsteps. And,
while it is right to improve our political, social and economic arrangements, we
must never fall into the trap of thinking that doing so will turn our present
world into a new paradise. Our world is fallen and 'subjected to frustration' by
God's will until it is to be fully restored by him (Rom. 8:20). The problems of
sin and the need for forgiveness and release (see below) will always be with us.

   Furthermore, Luke's writings are not trapped in individualism, because the
church has a vital role to play in his thinking. Luke teaches us that the church
is 'a community of restoration'.[31] The church is God's agent of bringing
people to new life and their growth towards wholeness. For Matthew the
church is a schoolroom of learning. For Mark it is a charismatic powerhouse.
But for Luke it is 'a therapeutic community', not essentially of a psychological
but of a spiritual kind,[32] through which healing takes place, the poor are
valued, not for their status and wealth but as children of Abraham, and the lost
find their way back home. Without the tangible modelling of this in the community, grace would remain an abstract ideal rather than an authentic reality
that those in need can actually experience. That is why, fellowship around the
meal table, where forgiveness and acceptance are served up generously, is such
an important theme for Luke.

The purpose of our ministry

The danger inherent in the above picture is that we interpret the calling too
superficially and forsake true ministry for social work (valuable though social
work is), and gospel ministry becomes supplanted by social action. To understand Luke's portrait of ministry to the poor we must go deeper, without
falling into the trap of spiritualizing people's problems, which he will not
permit us to do. People's problems and their release from them are always presented by Luke both as actual physical or social realities and actual spiritual
realities at one and the same time.[33] But the underlying problem is always one
of sin, and the underlying solution is always one of forgiveness. So when Jesus
uses the image of the doctor about his mission, he immediately explains
its meaning by saying he has come to 'call sinners to repentance' (5:32). The

---

31. Ibid., pp. 323–324, 343–344.

32. Derek Tidball, 'Practical and Pastoral Theology', *NDCEPT*, pp. 46–47.

33. J. B. Green, *Theology*, p. 79.

alleviation of the symptoms of sickness are valuable, as we saw in the healing of the ten lepers (17:11–19), but true salvation goes further than this.

The real problem is the problem of sin and of alienation from God. But at the heart of our universe stands one who is 'The Waiting Father',[34] waiting to receive us, his prodigal children, back home. He does so because of the sheer miracle of his love. Forgiveness flows freely from the Father to release us from all our sins and debts and provoke a corresponding love in return (7:36–50).

Luke stresses that two elements are necessary to enable people to receive the forgiveness that is so freely available, namely repentance and faith. Jesus came to call 'sinners to repentance' (5:32), warned people that they would perish unless they repented (13:5) and commissioned his disciples to preach 'repentance for the forgiveness of sins . . . in his name to all nations' (24:47). The prodigal son would not have known the father's forgiveness unless he came to his senses and returned home. Even when Jesus instructs his disciples to forgive those who have offended them, Luke alone adds the phrase 'if they repent' to the command to forgive frequently (17:3–4). Repentance will express itself in many ways. For Levi it meant following Jesus on the road literally. For a sinful woman it meant worshipping Jesus extravagantly. For the prodigal son it meant going home. For Zacchaeus it meant restoring what he had stolen. In each case, however, though the expression varied, there was a tangible and appropriate action that expressed the new direction in which people were determined to go in life.

The second essential element in experiencing the forgiveness of God is that of faith. In working his miracles, Jesus repeatedly makes the same point: 'your faith' has saved you. He says it to the sinful woman (7:50), to a sick woman in a crowd (8:48), to the lone, returning leper on the border between Samaria and Galilee (17:19) and to the blind beggar outside Jericho (18:35–43). Faith is not the decision of a moment but the response to their long-standing desperation that drives them to cast themselves on God's mercy alone, and then becomes the commitment of a lifetime that grows and matures as they follow Jesus.

All this challenges us not to be satisfied with alleviating people's problems at a superficial level, however beneficial that may be for the persons concerned. Some who see ministry through the lens of social activism are in danger of falling short of their calling and merely improving people's economic or social situation. Others who see ministry through the lens of personal counselling

---

34. This is the title of Helmut Thielicke's expositions of the parables, *The Waiting Father* (Cambridge: James Clarke, 1960), where the first two chapters expound the parable of the prodigal son superbly.

are equally in danger of falling short by merely improving a person's psychological health. Tim Yates has rightly stated the challenge: 'If, as counsellors (or social activists), we do not cooperate with God in bringing men and women to evangelical repentance then we must question in what sense our counselling (or social activism) is authentically Christian.'[35] This, he explains, is because 'a change of heart . . . affects the total disposition of a person' and has an impact in changing the intellectual, emotional and volitional dimensions of the person's life.[36] Ministry is about going to the heart of the matter and reconnecting people who are poor and lost to God who alone can offer forgiveness and bring about wholeness.

The qualifications needed for our ministry

Luke draws out three factors, consistent with his general emphases, of special relevance for those in ministry. Those who exercise the ministry of apostolic compassion will soon find themselves discouraged and become exhausted except for these. They are *faith*, *prayer* and the *Holy Spirit*.

When confronted with the difficult teaching of Jesus, the apostles pray, 'Increase our faith!' (17:5). The word, especially given the context, might be translated 'faithfulness'.[37] Either way, the disciples know their need to keep their eyes fixed on the Master. It is only by trusting to him, who alone can give them the strength to keep going when they are tempted to give up, that they will persevere.

Secondly, Luke stresses the importance of prayer. Luke records nine of the prayers of Jesus, but for our purposes his parable about the friend at midnight (11:5–13) and the parable of the unjust judge (18:1–8) are particularly significant. Both are unique to Luke and both have the disciples as his intended audience. Both are designed to encourage the disciples to pray to a God who, in contrast to the way humans behave, will prove generous in his response to their requests. Add to these Luke's report of Jesus praying for Peter (22:32) and his exhortation to the disciples in the Garden of Gethsemane to 'Get up and pray' (22:46), and one cannot mistake the importance of prayer if ministry is to be sustained and fruitful.

Thirdly, throughout Luke's Gospel he stresses the work of the Holy Spirit. The Spirit plays an important part in Jesus' own ministry, descending on him at his baptism (3:22) and leading him, when 'full of the Holy Spirit' into the

---

35. Tim Yates, 'The Importance of Repentance', *Care and Counsellor* 4.2 (1994), p. 23.

36. Ibid., p. 22.

37. J. B. Green, *Luke*, p. 613.

wilderness temptations (4:1). This same Spirit gives the seventy-two joy as they return from their mission (10:21). Jesus is described as the one who will baptize 'with the Holy Spirit and fire' (3:16), while he himself teaches that God will 'give the Holy Spirit to those who ask him' (11:13). Furthermore, the disciples are assured that when they face persecution, 'the Holy Spirit will teach you at that time what you should say' (12:12). And it is in line with all this that, in a clear anticipation of the day of Pentecost, Jesus, in his last instruction to his disciples, commands them to 'stay in the city until you have been clothed with power from on high' (24:49). While we may argue about the nature of how we are to experience the Holy Spirit, there can be no argument about his absolute indispensability if we are to engage in a ministry of compassion in a graceless world. No one has the resources within themselves to do so. It takes the supernatural grace and energy of the Spirit to minister in this way.

Conclusion

Luke emphasizes pastoral ministry as one of ministering grace to needy individuals: the oppressed, poor, sick and lost, all of whom are sinners, leading them to turn their lives around, and discover the mercy of God that brings them to a new beginning. It is a ministry that calls for faith and repentance as their means of receiving forgiveness and release. This ministry operates on a different plane from much contemporary therapeutic counselling or social action, both of which have the laudable aim of improving people's situations in life. This ministry is one that connects people to their Maker and Redeemer apart from whom there can be no ultimate change in life. It does not merely improve their social lot, nor their mental health, but sets them free from their spiritual enemy, Satan, and ministers grace in the deepest recesses of their being, assuring them that although there may be little grace in the world in which they live, there is abundant grace to be found in God himself, who transcends this graceless world with the gift of his Son.

4. JOHN: MINISTRY IN A SPIRITUAL DESERT

The ministry of the good shepherd

Among the Gospels, John's provides the most varied imagery about ministry, so much so that it may be unwise to select a single focus for consideration. Even so, one image is more explicit than others and one recurring theme provides a good context for our understanding of how it functions. The image is that of the *good shepherd* and the theme is that of the *spiritual desert*. Before exploring this further, however, it would be wise briefly to acknowledge the question often raised as to whether John has any place for the church in his Gospel and then to survey the wider images of ministry in John.

John and the church

John's Gospel is often said to be the Gospel of individualism. C. F. D. Moule spoke for many when he wrote, 'This is the gospel, *par excellence*, of the approach of a single soul to God: this is the part of scripture to which one turns first when trying to direct an enquirer to his own personal appreciation of salvation.'[1] Stress is laid on the individual believer coming to faith, being

---

1. C. F. D. Moule, 'The Individualism of the Fourth Gospel', in *Essays in New Testament Interpretation* (Cambridge: Cambridge University Press, 1982), p. 104.

loved by the Father and being in union with the Son. This has led many to argue that he has little concept of the church and even less concept of ministry, certainly as anything organized into a structure.[2] Those who take this position concede that there is something of a community around Jesus, but they view it as more incidental than central. The disciples seem to have no special place and are never given the term 'apostles' or 'the twelve' but 'are most likely intended to represent all (including future disciples) in their common responsibility of mutual love and mission (14–16; 20:22)'.[3] The beloved disciple (see below) is often considered to be the model of an individual believer.

Such an argument has self-evident merit. On the surface John seems to have little interest in the church. Why should he? He is concerned primarily with the revelation of who Jesus is. But the argument as it is often presented both overstates the truth and is, I believe, based on a wrong presupposition. It overstates the truth because Jesus uses collective imagery in teaching his disciples. No flock consists of a single sheep and it would be a very poor vine indeed that had only a single branch! Furthermore, the emphasis on mutual love and service presupposes that the individual believer belongs to a community. It is not a call to love or serve one's self. Howard Marshall rightly comments, 'Although John does not use the word *church*, the concept of mutual love is indicative of an organic unity binding believers to God and to one another.'[4] John's Gospel makes no sense apart from the church, which is 'the *sine qua non* of Johannine theology, the indispensable ground or background'.[5]

The wrong presupposition lies in the fixed nature of church that many have in mind when they overstress John's individualism. Those who say that John does not have a concept of the church really mean he has no concept of a developed or institutional church in his Gospel. It is this that leads Dunn, and others, to conclude that therefore John has 'no real concept of ministry, let

---

2. James D. G. Dunn, *Unity and Diversity in the New Testament* (Philadelphia: Westminster; London: SCM, 1977), pp. 118–119. Such an argument is ironic in view of the way in which many have also argued that John alludes to the sacrament of the Holy Communion in his writing.

3. Ibid., p. 119.

4. I. Howard Marshall, *New Testament Theology* (Downers Grove: IVP, 2004), p. 523.

5. D. Moody Smith, *The Theology of the Gospel of John* (Cambridge: Cambridge University Press, 1995), p. 137. Elsewhere he writes of John's ecclesiology as 'implicit' ('Theology and Ministry in John', in E. E. Shelp and R. Sunderland [eds.], *A Biblical Basis for Ministry* [Philadelphia: Westminster, 1981], p. 217).

alone office'.[6] But this is to presuppose one form of church and to judge everything from that perspective. Both within the New Testament, down through
history and around the world today, many 'churches' take or have taken the
form of small face-to-face communities, more akin to the 'two or three gath-
ering in Jesus' name' than to the complex organized denominations with which
we are familiar. Perhaps this idea of church 'is that of a community with no
hierarchy, formal organization, or sacraments and inspired by the Spirit',[7] but
even such communities need ministry and leadership. And John is not silent
on the issue. There is much that, at the least, we can infer.

John's varied imagery

The three most important images regarding ministry, other than the good
shepherd, to which John alludes are those of *witness*, *beloved disciple* and *fruit-
bearer*.

Witness

The burden of John's Gospel is that the invisible God has revealed himself in
the visible presence of Jesus (1:14). But for him, this revelation is inextricably
bound up with those who witness to it.[8] The frequency with which John uses
the language of witness compels us to take notice of it. The verb 'to witness'
(*martyrein*) is used thirty-three times in John's Gospel, plus a further fourteen
times in the other documents that bear his name, as opposed to a total of thirty
times elsewhere in the New Testament.[9] The imagined setting is that of a
courtroom where various witnesses are called to give evidence that Jesus is the
Christ.[10] The parade of witnesses include John the Baptist, human witnesses,
the Father himself, the signs Jesus performs, the Holy Spirit and even Christ
himself.[11] Believing means to accept the truth of what these witnesses say.[12]

6. Dunn, *Unity and Diversity*, p. 119.
7. D. M. Smith, *Theology*, p. 136.
8. James Montgomery Boice, *Witness and Revelation in the Gospel of John* (Exeter:
   Paternoster, 1970), pp. 14–15.
9. Ibid., p. 24.
10. The most recent thorough examination of this motif is found in Andrew Lincoln,
   Truth on Trial: The Lawsuit Motif in the Fourth Gospel (Peabody: Hendrickson, 2000).
11. See Boice, *Witness and Revelation*, pp. 25–29.
12. Lincoln, *Truth on Trial*, p. 242.

As the Gospel plot unfolds, it becomes obvious that the disciples occupy a special and ongoing role as witnesses to Jesus. They are sent into the world (17:18; 20:21) to testify to what they have seen and heard (15:27). They are the 'link' between the life of Jesus on earth and the people yet to come to faith in Jesus (17:6–26). To fulfil that commission they will need the help of a divine advocate. Only the continual presence of the Holy Spirit with them will enable them to make sense of all they have seen and heard and to proclaim it with courage and effectiveness in a hostile world (14:15–31; 15:26–27). The manner of their witness, as Lincoln has pointed out, was to be modelled on the manner of Jesus' service, who took his place as a servant and washed his disciples' feet (13:1–17).[13] 'By this,' Jesus said, 'everyone will know that you are my disciples, if you love one another' (13:35). The word *martys* came to have a more particular meaning as it came to be associated with being a martyr, of witnessing by laying down one's life. Jesus had made no secret in his teaching of the element of cost that would be involved for those who were to witness for him. To be his witness would necessarily involve losing one's life and following Jesus on the road that would lead to the cross (12:25–26). It would mean facing a hostile world (15:18–25) and even imprisonment and death (21:18–19).

Contemporary ministry follows in the footsteps of these original witnesses, just as they stood in the footsteps of Jesus. We are called to bear testimony, often at cost, in humble and loving ways, to what we have seen and heard concerning Jesus, with a view to persuading people of the truth of our account.

Beloved disciple

A second and puzzling model for ministry in John's Gospel is that of the beloved disciple (1:35–40; 13:23–26; 18:15–16; 19:25–27, 35; 20:2–10; 21:2, 7, 24). The identity of the disciple has long been a matter of debate and continues to be so. So too has been the role he plays within the Gospel. Many regard

---

13. It might be objected that the image of servant merits treatment in its own right, but since John's Gospel is so rich in relevant material I decided, perhaps unwisely, to refer to the servant under the overall theme of *witness*. D. Moody Smith, acknowledging that 'Jesus does not speak of himself as performing a ministry or ministering in the Fourth Gospel', argues for the importance of 'servanthood' as exemplified in John 13 as portraying the ministry of Jesus ('Theology and Ministry in John', in E. E. Shelp and R. Sunderland [eds.], *A Biblical Basis for Ministry* [Philadelphia: Westminster, 1981], p. 219).

him as a picture of an ideal disciple,[14] although Richard Bauckham has recently questioned this saying that although he may sometimes function in this way in 'the only undisputed references to him, we find an emphasis on an exclusive privilege which is precisely not representative'.[15] Granting the point, it surely does not rule out the possibility that he might also serve as a model subsequently. If so, he models several things. In 'reclining' next to Jesus, he models the intimacy of a disciple with his master (13:23–25). It is out of this close relationship of love that his other qualities flow. In lingering near the cross, he models the need for faithfulness, of being a witness to the last (19:25–27). In witnessing to Jesus' death, he models the courage required and content of the testimony we should give (19:35). In approaching the empty tomb, he models the spiritual perception and faith we need (20:2–10). When fishing on the lake, he demonstrates that same spiritual perception that eludes others (21:7).

The beloved disciple is also often contrasted with other disciples, such as the traitor Judas,[16] or the less than ideal Peter.[17] But Bauckham helpfully argues that rather than seeing the beloved disciple as superior to Peter, we should see them as representing 'two different kinds of discipleship: active service and perceptive witness'.[18] This, he says, makes the beloved disciple an ideal author of the Gospel, while Peter's qualities make him 'better qualified to be the chief undershepherd of Jesus' sheep'. He adds:

> It is worth noticing that whereas in Peter's case, the Gospel emphasizes his love for Jesus, in the Beloved Disciple's case it emphasizes Jesus' love for him. The former emphasis is appropriate for the active role of discipleship as participation in Jesus' activity and sacrificing: it corresponds to Jesus' love for his disciples. The latter emphasis is appropriate for the more receptive role of discipleship as witness and corresponds to Jesus' enjoyment of his Father's love.[19]

---

14. E.g. Stephen Barton calls him 'the epitome of the true believer' (*The Spirituality of the Gospels* [London: SPCK, 1992], p. 129). For fuller documentation, see Richard Bauckham, *Jesus and the Eyewitnesses: The Gospel as Eyewitness Testimony* (Grand Rapids: Eerdmans, 2006), p. 394, n. 16.

15. Ibid., p. 395.

16. Barton, *Spirituality*, p. 192.

17. Bauckham, *Jesus*, p. 395. See also Kevin Quast, *Peter and the Beloved Disciple: Figures for a Community in Crisis*, JSNTSup 32 (Sheffield: Sheffield Academic Press, 1989). Quast takes the view that they represented two streams in the early church (pp. 159–167).

18. Bauckham, *Jesus*, p. 395.

19. Ibid., pp. 399–400.

He concludes that these are not rivals but two complementary ways of ministering for Christ: one more active and the other more contemplative.

We might add that just as camels are ideally suited to desert conditions because they have the means to sustain themselves for long barren journeys, so those who imitate the model of the beloved disciple are ideally suited to serve in the spiritual desert because of the rich reserves of faith that have been filled through their intimate relationships with Jesus and their contemplation of his life and work.

Fruit-bearer

Two of the 'I am' sayings of Jesus that John includes, and the teaching that surrounds them, are of immediate relevance to those called to ministry, even if the lessons of both are not confined to leaders but have implications for all disciples. They are 'I am the good shepherd' (10:1–21), which we shall deal with later, and 'I am the vine' (15:1–17).

We begin with the way Jesus expands on the metaphor of the vine. In using it, the destination to which he seems to be heading is found in 15:16, where he says to his disciples, 'You did not choose me, but I chose you and appointed you so that you might go and bear fruit – fruit that will last'. The disciples have been chosen for a purpose. Their election is not to do with their status in eternity, nor to do with their personal security on earth, but to do with a job that needs to be done, that of fruit-bearing. Israel had been expected to undertake that task but had only managed to produce bad fruit (Isa. 5:2).[20] The disciples are now commissioned to do what Israel had failed to do.

It is interesting that Jesus defines the fruit for which he looks as 'fruit that will last' (15:16). He is obviously more concerned about the quality of the fruit the disciples will produce than its quantity. He encourages his disciples to bear 'much fruit' (15:8), so he values quantity. But he is also looking for converts who will both mature and endure, rather than the zealous respondents who show great enthusiasm for a time but then quickly perish because they become too ripe too soon. In a culture where success is measured by numbers, we may easily succumb to the temptation to mass produce fruit by forcing it to ripen

---

20. The metaphor of 'the vine' is, in David Gooding's words, 'a metaphor with a history' (*In the School of Christ: A Study of Christ's Teaching on Holiness, John 13–17* [Port Colbourne, Ont.: Gospel Folio, 1995], p. 137). It was an image used of Israel, who had been given the most advantageous of conditions to produce good fruit but did not do so (see Ps. 80:8–9; Isa. 5:1–2; Ezek. 17:8; Hos. 10:1).

too quickly. So we may well mistakenly put our energies into producing a following of enthusiastic converts whose loyalty is maintained by one exciting event after another, rather than producing deep converts who have counted the cost of discipleship.

Jesus sets out four essentials if such fruit is to be produced. First, good fruit is a result of *pruning (15:2)*. The gardener's knife may be unpleasant and hurtful but it produces strong trees and better fruit. So, in our lives, much fruit is borne not because of the easy times but as a result of God's correcting ministry in our lives, his chastening when we sin and his challenging of us concerning our true ambitions. Secondly, good fruit is a result of *remaining (15:4–6)*. 'No branch can bear fruit on its own'. It is essential that it is connected to the vine. So, with us, we must stay connected to Jesus to minister effectively, just as the beloved disciple did. But it is obvious that Jesus did not just have the idea of intimate fellowship in mind. He clearly means that to remain in him is to have his instructions in our minds and hearts and therefore to obey as well. Thirdly, good fruit is the result of *praying*. Twice Jesus encourages his disciples to pray, asking the Father 'whatever you wish', as long as it is in his name (15:7, 16). This qualification somewhat limits what we can write on the blank cheque of asking. If we ask in his name, we shall not only ask with his authority and support but also ask for what is consistent with him and for that which will please him. The multiplication of good fruit will certainly do so. The fourth and final secret of effective fruit-bearing is *loving*, which Jesus stresses in verses 9–17. Fruit-bearing is not a matter of adopting the right marketing technique but the right spiritual strategy. We may pour all the resources we have into mission and drain all the wisdom the world has to offer about winning customers, and fail. God's strategy is simpler: we should love one another.

All this, says Jesus, 'is to my Father's glory' (15:8), not our own. His glory is always our most urgent objective and our deepest obligation. As John Stott has pointed out, this means that

> The highest of all missionary motives is neither obedience to the Great Commission (important though that is), nor love for sinners who are alienated and perishing (strong as that incentive is . . .) but rather zeal – burning and passionate zeal – for the glory of Jesus Christ [and so of his Father].[21]

---

21. John R. W. Stott, *The Message of Romans*, BST (Leicester: IVP, 1994), p. 53.

The spiritual desert

In spite of the diversity, a case can be made for the theme of shepherding in the wilderness as a major motif in John's understanding of ministry. Israel's experience of the Passover and the wilderness wanderings form the background to much that John recounts, and Jesus himself is compared, or contrasted, to Moses, not only as lawgiver but as the one who guides people through the wilderness.

John has a special interest in the Passover, mentioning it by name eleven times and alluding to it more widely (2:13, 23; 4:45; 6:4; 11:55 [twice]; 12:1; 13:1; 18:28, 39; 19:14). John refers to Jesus as 'the Lamb of God, who takes away the sin of the world', which is probably a reference to the Passover lamb, especially since John strongly identifies Jesus' death with the celebration of the Passover (19:14).[22]

The allusions to the wilderness in John's Gospel are frequent.[23] Jesus is said to dwell 'among us' (1:14). In using the word eskēnōsen, 'tabernacled', John is recalling God's presence in the tabernacle in the Israelite camp. Jesus compares his own death to the incident when Moses erected a serpent in the wilderness (3:14; Num. 21:1–9). When Jesus fed the five thousand, he not only was clearly imitating the provision of manna to Israel in the wilderness but said as much while claiming himself to be 'the bread of life' (6:1–15, 25–58, esp. 32–35; Exod. 16:1–36). A further clear allusion occurs as Jesus goes to the feast of Tabernacles and invites the thirsty to him so they may receive living water, recalling the desperate need for water Israel experienced in their desert wanderings (7:37–39; Exod. 15:22–27; 17:1–7). Jesus' claim to be the light of the world alludes both to the lights that perpetually burned in the tabernacle and to the pillar of fire that guided Israel through the dark nights of the wilderness (8:12; Exod. 13:20–22).

While, in reading these passages, we might immediately relate them to the story of Israel in the Sinai desert, we should not forget that the wilderness imagery was taken up and used by the prophets, especially Isaiah, in reference to Israel's later and future experience. To take but one example, the need for water, Isaiah had looked forward to the time when Israel would be restored in the golden age of the Messiah. About that time he wrote:

---

22. See Derek Tidball, *The Message of the Cross*, BST (Leicester: IVP, 2001), pp. 177–180.
23. For a fuller discussion, see T. Francis Glasson, *Moses in the Fourth Gospel* (London: SCM, 1963).

> The desert and the parched land will be glad;
>> the wilderness will rejoice and blossom.
> (Isa. 35:1)

> The poor and needy search for water,
>> but there is none;
>> their tongues are parched with thirst.
> But I the LORD will answer them . . .
> I will make rivers flow on barren heights,
>> and springs within the valleys.
> (41:17–18)

God had said:

> See, I am doing a new thing!
>> Now it springs up; do you not perceive it?
> I am making a way in the desert
>> and streams in the wasteland . . . to give drink to my people, my chosen.
> (43:19, 20)

And:

> I will pour water on the thirsty land,
>> and streams on the dry ground;
> I will pour out my Spirit on your offspring,
>> and my blessing on your descendants.
> (44:3)

All this came to fulfilment when Jesus exercised his ministry to those who found themselves in the desert.

John also presented the person of Jesus as the new Moses, the shepherd who led Israel through their wilderness wanderings to the brink of the Promised Land.[24] The relationship is flagged up as early as 1:17 and there is a frequent correspondence between Moses and Jesus after that (1:45; 3:13; 5:45–46; 6:32; 7:19, 22–23; [8:5]; 9:28–29). But perhaps the clearest indication of Jesus as the new Moses comes not when Moses' name creeps into the text

---

24. M.-E. Boismard, *Moses or Jesus: An Essay in Johannine Christology*, tr. B. T. Vivano (Minneapolis: Fortress, 1993); and Glasson, *Moses*, pp. 20–32.

but when Jesus is acclaimed as *the* Prophet. God had promised Moses, 'I will raise up for them a prophet like you from among their people, and I will put my words in his mouth' (Deut. 18:18). When people encountered Jesus they were driven to ask, 'Are you the Prophet?' (1:21), with many concluding that he was (6:14; 7:40). Timothy Laniak amplifies the comparison like this:

> Like Moses, Jesus is 'sent' to his own people who reject him (Exod 2:11, 14; John 1:11). Both perform miraculous signs to reveal God's glory and gather believers (Exod 4:8–9; John 20:8). While Moses' miracles were primarily acts of judgment on Egypt (which also revealed God's mercy on Israel), Jesus' miracles were primarily acts of mercy for his followers (accompanied by words of judgment on their false leaders). Moses turned water into blood (a symbol of death); Jesus turned water into wine (a symbol of abundant life). Moses brought disease to people and destruction to Egypt's crops; Jesus brought healing to the lame and multiplied their bread. Moses brought darkness to the Egyptians (like blindness; Exod 10:23); Jesus brought light to the blind. Moses brought death to the firstborn; Jesus raised the dead back to life.[25]

Wilderness imagery is, of course, ambiguous in Scripture. It is at one and the same time the place of close reliance on God where he guides his people and provides for them miraculously, constantly attending to their need of protection. But it is also a barren place. It is a dry, inhospitable desert where people are condemned to wander and where no progress appears to be made towards a better land.

If we take the negative aspect of the imagery, John's Gospel is full of people who live in a spiritual desert, as do many today. Their encounters with Jesus reveal the emptiness inside and their longing for spiritual satisfaction. The crowded worlds in which they live, or even the busy lives they lead, do little to disguise that their true location is the desert. Nicodemus exhibits his emptiness in coming to Jesus at night, and searching out how one can begin life anew (3:1–15). The Samaritan woman demonstrates the barrenness of broken relationships and an intense inner thirst (4:1–26). The Roman official shows the barrenness that comes as one faces loss and grief (4:43–54). The man at the pool of Bethesda displays the barrenness of bitterness that may arise from loneliness (5:1–14). And so we could go on. The desert is created in people's lives for many different reasons but it has a common cause, namely a lack of

---

25. Timothy S. Laniak, *Shepherds after My own Heart: Pastoral Traditions and Leadership in the Bible*, NSBT 20 (Downers Grove: IVP; Leicester: Apollos, 2006), p. 209.

living relationship with God. It is by entering into a relationship with him through believing in his Son that the desert is transformed and the gift of eternal life is experienced. And that is where the presence of the shepherd is so important.

The good shepherd

The most obvious and direct image John uses concerning pastoral ministry is the metaphor of the good shepherd (10:1–21). Although he does not devote great space to it and although he refers only twice to shepherding imagery in the Gospel (10:1–21; 21:15–19), the metaphor is developed in some depth and has an importance because it resonates with earlier and later Scriptures. It is also an image most appropriate for the setting of the desert. What people need in a desert is a shepherd to guide, protect and feed them. It was while serving as a shepherd in the desert that Moses received the call of God to deliver Israel from Egypt (Exod. 3:1–22). And, although the title is not applied to him in Scripture,[26] Moses spent years after the exodus shepherding Israel through the wilderness.[27] It was natural to him, when asking God about his successor, to ask him to send someone who would 'lead them out and bring them in, so that the LORD's people will not be like sheep without a shepherd' (Num. 27:17). Subsequent leaders like David also served their apprenticeship as leaders as shepherds in the wilderness.

The model as it relates to Jesus
When Jesus uses the metaphor of the good shepherd he does so in an extended and complex parable. He first presents himself as the gatekeeper (10:3) and then the gate itself (10:7), before speaking of himself as the good shepherd (10:11, 14). For all the complexities, the meaning is clear. Jesus presents himself as 'the good shepherd' in contrast to foolish shepherds. In his day, shepherds were not greatly respected. Their lifestyle often took them a long way from the conventional society that revolved around the home, the family, the community and its synagogue, and the festivals at the temple. Their contact with these groups was at best occasional and they hung loose to much that ordinary people valued. Their lifestyle bred suspicion and they had the

---

26. It is used as a title in later Judaism; see Joachim Jeremias, *'poimēn'*, *TDNT*, vol. 6, p. 489.

27. Laniak, *Shepherds*, pp. 77–93, 131–134.

reputation of being scoundrels.[28] In contrast to the shepherds of his day, Jesus was declaring himself to be authentic, genuine, trustworthy and morally good.

He was also, more significantly, contrasting himself with the false shepherds of Israel, who had served themselves instead of their flocks. The background to this metaphor is found in Ezekiel 34. There God prophesies that he is going to remove 'the shepherds of Israel', that is, the rulers and priests, because, instead of caring for their flock, they only care about themselves. To put it starkly: they are butchers, not shepherds. He promises that he himself will step in and assume the role. He says:

> I myself will tend my sheep and make them lie down, declares the Sovereign LORD. I will search for the lost and bring back the strays. I will bind up the injured and strengthen the weak, but the sleek and the strong I will destroy.[29] I will shepherd the flock with justice. (Ezek. 34:15–16)

Here is the perfect outline of the shepherd's responsibilities. Not only is he to feed, guide and protect the flock but also to understand that there are individual sheep to which he must give special attention. The lost must be found, the wandering restored, the injured tended, the weak strengthened and the strong disciplined. Here so many aspects of ministry come together. We are called to be evangelists who bring the lost home, pastors who go after those tempted to drift and slide backwards in discipleship, nurses and doctors who bring healing to the wounded, educators who build up the young and encourage the vulnerable, and disciplinarians who admonish the arrogant.

The burden of John 10, however, is not so much on the task of the shepherd as on the manner in which the shepherd undertakes his role. Unlike the 'false shepherds',[30] the good shepherd has a close and caring relationship with his flock. They follow him, because they know him, know the sound of his

---

28. Jeremias, '*poimēn*', vol. 6, p. 489; *Jerusalem in the Time of Jesus* (London: SCM, 1967), pp. 302–305.

29. There is an alternative reading for 'the sleek and the strong I will destroy', which takes it to mean, 'the sleek and the strong I will watch over'. Although the alternative reading reminds us that even those who seem strong in our churches need pastoral care, it does not enjoy strong textual support. The word 'shepherd' was regularly used in the ancient Near East for rulers and here there is recognition of the judicial function the shepherd exercises.

30. I am using this as a generic title for all the forms of false shepherd Jesus refers to, namely 'strangers', 'thieves and robbers' and 'hired hands'.

voice and have confidence in him. His own interests are secondary to those of the sheep and he does not run away when difficulty comes. The task calls for someone to be courageous as well as caring. The image is not, as Alastair V. Campbell has said, that of the contemporary, settled farmer, but more of the Wild West cowboy, trekking miles from civilization through barren territory and facing all sorts of dangers as he goes.[31]

The climax of the metaphor takes this exercise of courage to the ultimate degree. The shepherd does not put the interests of the sheep first only when it is reasonable to do so, but also when it requires more than might be expected. Raymond Brown states that 'the unique feature in the Johannine picture of the shepherd is his willingness to die for the sheep'.[32] Yet this was not just 'willingness' but actuality; not a theory but a practice; not an abstract principle but a personal commitment. Jesus says, 'I know my sheep and my sheep know me . . . and I lay down my life for the sheep. . . . The reason my Father loves me is that I lay down my life – only to take it up again. No-one takes it from me, but I lay it down of my own accord' (10:14, 17, 18).

Again, there is a background to these statements of Jesus – found in Isaiah 53 and in the prophet Zechariah. Here the image of the good shepherd merges with that of the suffering servant. Zechariah's prophecy may, in fact, have influenced Jesus' thinking about the shepherd more than any other Old Testament passage.[33]

Zechariah's prophecy regarding the shepherd bears the same message as Ezekiel to start with. God has a concern for his people who 'wander like sheep / oppressed for lack of a shepherd', and so he will step in to judge the false leaders of Israel and care for his flock himself (Zech. 10:2–3). As shepherd, one of God's prime tasks is to bring home the scattered flock and, destroying their enemies, create a safe and secure environment for them (Zech. 10:10–12). But then Zechariah develops the image in fresh directions. First, in chapter 11, Zechariah is called to shepherd the flock and assume the role of a good shepherd. He does so conscientiously at first but then 'breaks under the pressure' of the flock's hostility and seeks to give up.[34] God then calls him to act himself as a foolish shepherd, doing the reverse of

31. Alastair V. Campbell, *Rediscovering Pastoral Care* (London: Darton Longman & Todd, 1981), p. 27.

32. Raymond E. Brown, *The Gospel according to John I–XII*, AB (New York: Doubleday, 1966), p. 398.

33. R. T. France, cited by Laniak, *Shepherds*, p. 170.

34. Laniak, *Shepherds*, p. 167.

all that Ezekiel 34:16 had said was good. The chapter provides a rigorous critique of worthless shepherds.

So is there any hope? Can the flock ever be gathered in safety and will they ever respond to the wise leading of a good shepherd? Yes, but it does not come in the way expected. Paradoxically, hope comes through the striking of the Shepherd who is close to God (Zech. 13:7). Two things will follow from such a tragedy. The people will be refined and cleansed and the flock will be scattered again. But these results will herald a change in their relationship with God. They will call on him and he will remember his covenant with them and be to them once more their God. There are obvious echoes of this in the account of the events of the crucifixion and in the words of Jesus who, in laying down his life, will bring other sheep 'that are not of this sheep pen' so that there would be 'one flock and one shepherd' (John 10:16). The striking of the shepherd is essential to the salvation of the sheep.

Put together, the picture of the good shepherd presents a model of pastoring that blends care with courage, tenderness with toughness, attention to the one and the many, concern for those within and without the sheepfold. But the bottom line is that the good shepherd is one who sacrifices himself and always puts the interests of the sheep ahead of his own, even to an unreasonable degree.[35]

The model as it relates to us

The parable of the good shepherd is primarily a claim about Jesus himself. He is the messianic shepherd through whom God will rule his flock. He is the shepherd who will be struck, at first scattering and then reuniting his sheep. The prophecies of Isaiah, Jeremiah, Ezekiel and Zechariah find their fulfilment in him.[36] But since these words are Christological, in what sense can we claim them as applicable to us? Is it not an 'I am' saying rather than a guidebook for pastoral ministry?

Laniak has argued that the use of the word *kalos*, 'good' (10:14, 17), points to our using the parable as a pattern. If Jesus had wanted merely to comment that the shepherd was morally virtuous, there were other words he could have used. But, Laniak writes, '*Kalos* implies an attractive quality, something noble or ideal. "Model" captures these connotations.'[37] So, he concludes, Jesus is

---

35. I have developed this paragraph in D. Tidball, *Builders and Fools: Leadership the Bible Way* (Leicester: IVP, 1999), pp. 133–149.

36. See Laniak, *Shepherds*, pp. 117–170.

37. Ibid., p. 211.

putting forward the model of the good shepherd as something his followers are to seek to imitate. Most commentators would not take this view, even while acknowledging that *kalos* means 'noble' or 'worthy'.[38] Most take this to be a variation on John's theme of truth (as in 'the true bread' and 'I am the true vine') and hence to mean 'authentic' or 'genuine' as opposed to 'false'. Westcott, however, lends some support to the view when he writes, 'Christ is not only the true shepherd, who fulfils the idea of the shepherd, but the good shepherd who fulfils the idea in its *attractive loveliness*.'[39]

But we do not need to rely on a vague hint to establish that Jesus intended this to be the model for others. Jesus uses the vocabulary of shepherding when, following breakfast on the shore of Lake Galilee after the resurrection, he recommissions Peter, who has so spectacularly failed him. He tells Peter to 'Feed my lambs', 'Take care of my sheep' and 'Feed my sheep' (21:15–17). In doing so, he is clearly passing on the task of the shepherd into Peter's hands. The conversation, as well as the metaphor of the good shepherd, marks Peter deeply. When Peter writes to the church leaders of his day, he naturally uses the term 'elders' to address them, but his thought is governed by the shepherd motif. 'Be shepherds of God's flock that is under your care, watching over them – not because you must, but because you are willing, as God wants you to be . . .' (1 Pet. 5:2). All the work they undertake is done under the watchful eye of 'the Chief Shepherd' (v. 4), who will reward them for their service and example in due course.

Conclusion

The metaphor of the good shepherd, although first and foremost a revelation of Jesus himself, does indeed set before us a model of ministry. We are called to accompany many who walk through the spiritual wastelands of their lives, guiding them, feeding them and protecting them. We are called to

- seek out those who cannot find their way and bring them into the safety of the fold
- go after those meandering away and restore them

---

38. E.g. G. R. Beasley-Murray, *John*, WBC 36 (Waco: Word, 1987), p. 170; and D. A. Carson, *The Gospel according to John*, PNTC (Grand Rapids: Eerdmans; Leicester: IVP, 1991), p. 386.

39. B. F. Westcott, *The Gospel according to St. John* (London: James Clarke, 1958), p. 154.

- take up the wounded victims and minister healing
- instruct the ignorant and the young so that they can grow in strength
- exercise discipline on those whose presence is detrimental to the flock

To do this calls for personal skills that enable us to build trusting relationships. It requires sensitivity to the needs of others. But it calls just as much for courage as we journey with people through the dark valleys of suffering, walk with them under the shadow of doubts and encounter the wild animals of temptation and satanic attack. Above all, it requires us to put the needs of others before our own, however demanding that may be.

To journey, like this, through the desert means that the shepherd must be well equipped so that he can sustain himself through tracks of barren territory. It is here that the other features of John's Gospel that speak of ministry come in. We shall only be equipped for the journey if we are witnesses to what Jesus has said and done both in history and within our own lives. We shall only have enough sustenance to sustain us if, like the beloved disciple, we stay close to Jesus. And we shall survive only if, as a mere branch, we constantly draw nutrients from the vine to which we must stay attached.

5. ACTS: MINISTRY IN AN EMERGING CHURCH

The ministry of community formation

The Acts of the Apostles was written to record the remarkable progress of the gospel in the ancient world and the growth of the church. It was not written as an instruction manual for church leaders or a blueprint for leadership structures. The opening verse tells us clearly that Luke is writing about the continuing story of Jesus and the spread of his message, while many have also thought that he was writing to commend the Christian faith to the Roman authorities. But this leaves us with a puzzle that has provoked many a debate. To what extent was Acts intended to be merely descriptive and how much was it intended to be prescriptive? Or, to put the question from a slightly different angle, how much of its story was unique and so by definition unrepeatable and how much was intended to set out the recurring pattern for the life of the church. These questions relate as much to leadership in the church as to the work of the Holy Spirit, where the storm clouds of debate have often gathered, and to other matters like methods of mission.[1]

There are passages in Acts that are clearly meant to be teaching for the

---

1. On these questions, see Gordon D. Fee and Douglas Stuart, *How to Read the Bible for All Its Worth*, 3rd ed. (Grand Rapids: Zondervan, 2003), pp. 107–126; and I. Howard Marshall, *The Acts of the Apostles*, NTG (Sheffied: JSOT Press, 1982), pp. 101–115.

church for all time. For our purposes, Paul's farewell address to the elders at Ephesus (20:13–38) is one such. The intention of other passages is clear and some indicate that what is being said sets a precedent for the church to come. But much may be unclear and where this is so we can at least learn how the early Christians responded to the challenges they faced as the church not only spread rapidly but did so in unexpected ways.

The early church was an imperfect church. It faced all the challenges of an emerging church without any experience or precedence to fall back on. It is evident that it did not always get things right, at least initially. But it was a church remarkably guided by the Holy Spirit and witnessed the remarkable spread of the word. So in terms of leadership there is wisdom from which we can benefit, even if it does not present a blueprint we should automatically adopt.

The nature of church

Since leadership is shaped by one's understanding of the church, we must ask first about the nature of the church as portrayed in Acts. And since Acts uses the word *ekklēsia* nineteen times of the church, this is a reasonable thing to do (5:11; 8:1, 3; 9:31; 11:22, 26; 12:1, 5; 13:1; 14:23, 27; 15:3, 4, 22, 30; 18:22; 20:17, 28).[2] In virtually all cases, it refers to a specific local expression of church, with the exception of the editorial comment in 9:31 and Paul's reference in his address to the Ephesian elders (20:28), where it stands for a wider reality.[3] But what meaning does he invest in this word?

The church is above all else a community of the Spirit. It is he who brings it to birth on the day of Pentecost (2:1–4) after the long period of gestation during the ministry of Jesus, and a further period of confinement after the resurrection and ascension. It is he who initiates people into the church (2:38). All members receive the Holy Spirit (4:31; 9:31; 13:52) but special emphasis is laid on leaders being 'full of the Holy Spirit' and directed by him (4:8; 6:3, 5; 7:55; 9:17; 11:24; 13:2, 4, 9; 16:6–7; 20:22–23). He is the Spirit of power (6:8) but his power is not the brute force that mighty secular figures would recognize, for everything he does is coloured by the fact that before anything else he is the Spirit of Jesus (16:7). He will act only in the way Jesus would and will work only in complete harmony with him.

----

2. *Ekklēsia* is also used in reference to the people of Israel in the wilderness (7:38) and to 'secular' assemblies in 19:32, 39, 41; 23:7.
3. Kevin N. Giles, *What on Earth Is the Church?* (London: SPCK, 1995), pp. 83–86.

Each stage of advance in the church's mission is marked by the confirmation of the Spirit. So the unexpected turns that lead to the incorporation of those other than Jews into the church, such as the Samaritans (8:14–17), Gentiles (10:44–46) and even Ephesians, who may have been disciples of John the Baptist rather than Jesus (19:1–7)[4] is authenticated by his unmistakable presence.[5] The incorporation of the Gentiles into the church caused tensions and divisions that led them to debate the issue at a meeting in Jerusalem, which included representatives of all sides of the argument. Here, too, the legitimacy of the Gentile mission was authenticated by the Holy Spirit (15:28), yet this time not through immediate dramatic signs but rather by testimony as to what God had done, listening to one another, considering the meaning of Scripture together and through the influence of the Spirit on their discussion. He did not always work through the dramatic, neither did they always find the way forward as easy as we sometimes assume it should be if the Spirit is in it.

Throughout Acts we read of a church energized by the dynamic Holy Spirit with the purpose of continuing the mission that Jesus began. Its missionary complexion and strategic advance is inseparable from the work of the Spirit among them. This is no settled community but a constantly expanding one whose forward path is directed by the Holy Spirit and that constantly has to adapt to new cultural and changing political contexts.

It is also a community of 'brothers'.[6] Luke's earlier portrait of the church

---

4. I recognize that this is not a universally agreed interpretation. Others see it as possibly 'an incomplete initiations process' (James D. G. Dunn, *The Acts of the Apostles*, Epworth Commentaries [Peterborough: Epworth, 1996], p. 256). See also the discussion in I. Howard Marshall, *Acts*, TNTC (Leicester: IVP, 1980), pp. 305–308.

5. Some would want to build a case from these passages that all new believers should be 'baptized in the Spirit' subsequent to conversion and be initiated into discipleship by supernatural signs. But the word 'baptism' is not explicitly used of these episodes in reference to the work of the Spirit and they do seem to be especially significant advances rather than about the more regular making of converts. Acts seems largely to present a picture of repentance, baptism and reception of the spirit as a unity: Max Turner, *Baptism in the Holy Spirit*, Renewal Series 2 (Cambridge: Grove, 2000).

6. Fuller information on the terms used can be found in Giles, *What on Earth?* pp. 83–94; and Howard Clark Kee, *Good News to the Ends of the Earth: The Theology of Acts* (Philadelphia: Trinity; London: SCM, 1990), pp. 81–86.

in his Gospel as a community where the poor can find restoration and acceptance continues in Acts, yet with inevitable differences as it spreads in different
cultures. But the sense of belonging together and of family, where all are
valued, rather than the church as a hierarchical institution, is hard to miss
because of the frequency with which Luke refers to the church as a group of
brothers and sisters. He uses the term *adelphoi* over forty times in his sequel to
the Gospel. Admittedly, he does not use the term exclusively of Christians,[7]
but it is used frequently of the believers who formed the church. It stresses
the family nature of the church, which David Bartlett has commented is better
seen as patriarchal than hierarchical.[8]

Next in frequency as a description of church members comes Luke's use of
the word 'disciples'. It occurs twenty-five times. The frequency with which it
occurs indicates something of how Luke viewed the church and here the
accent falls on being followers of Jesus Christ and learners together about him.
It is normally taken for granted that they are disciples of Jesus, but in 9:1 they
are explicitly referred to as 'the Lord's disciples' and the connection to Christ
is also made obvious in 11:26, where we read that 'The disciples were called
Christians first at Antioch.'

The early Christians were also described as 'saints' (9:13, 32; 26:10)[9] and
followers of 'the Way' (19:9, 23; 22:4; 24:14, 22). The former is used only in
the context of their being persecuted and marks them out as people who
belong to God. The latter stresses they were on the journey with Jesus but
had not yet arrived. 'The Way' also indicated they were on a *purposeful journey*,
and not merely meandering through the variety of religious opinions in the
ancient world. Hence we read of Apollos being 'instructed in the way of the
Lord' (18:25).

Who were the leaders?

The above suggests that the church did not see itself as a settled institution
with a hierarchically structured pattern of leadership. It is not without
leaders but is primarily a community where there is an equality of grace and

---

7. E.g. Stephen uses it in addressing the Sanhedrin (7:2), and Paul uses it of a
   synagogue congregation in Antioch (13:15).
8. David Bartlett, *Ministry in the New Testament*, OBT (Minneapolis: Fortress, 1993),
   p. 145.
9. TNIV loses the word 'saints' in favour of 'the Lord's people'.

discipleship. Care needs to be exercised in saying, in an unqualified way, that 'spiritual egalitarianism' is evident.[10] It is in some respects, but not others. It is essential that we have the right model of community in mind if we are to understand what is going on. And it is more accurate to say that the nature of the church's community evident throughout the New Testament is that of a family. Within families there is a great deal of acceptance, openness and equality. No one needs to dress up or, indeed, no one is able to dress up and pretend they are other than they are. It is the first place where love is experienced but also the first place where members who get above themselves will be put down. And yet families have structure and parents are leaders within them. This seems to make the best sense of the description of the community of Jesus' disciples from the Gospels on.[11] It also provides the best understanding of how certain tensions between leadership and servanthood, authority and equality, adaptability and structure, cohere.

It is this model of the church (combined with its devotion to mission and consequent continual expansion) that had an impact on the shape of the leadership it enjoyed. Its leadership fitted an expanding movement that was seeing the formation of many new Christian communities. Hence it was responsive and marked by flexibility.

James Dunn confessed that it is possible to draw up two pictures of ministry from a reading of Acts. The first is where the apostles are in effect bishops, elders are priests and the Seven are the prototype of deacons. So we come to the historical threefold order of bishops, priests and deacons, which the universal church largely acknowledges today.[12] But, he rightly comments, this scheme may appear 'more straightforward but [it] is probably more contrived'. The second pattern is 'less obvious but probably more historical'.[13] This recognizes that ministry was 'much more spontaneous and charismatic in nature, and leadership took several diverse forms before' settling down to

10. Kevin N. Giles, 'Is Luke an Exponent of "Early Protestantism"? Church Order in the Lukan Writings', *EvQ* 55 (1983), p. 3.

11. For a detailed justification of this position, see John H. Elliott, 'Jesus Was Not an Egalitarian: A Critique of an Anachronistic and Idealist Theory', *BTB* 32 (2002), pp. 75–91; 'The Jesus Movement Was Not Egalitarian but Family-Oriented', *BibInt* 11 (2003), pp. 173–210.

12. *Baptism, Eucharist and Ministry*, Faith and Order Paper 111 (Geneva: World Council of Churches, 1982), pp. 20–32.

13. James D. G. Dunn, *Unity and Diversity in the New Testament* (Philadelphia: Westminster; London: SCM, 1977), p. 106.

reflect the pattern of leadership found in the Jewish synagogue.[14] A review of the evidence seems to support this view.

The chief terms for leaders are 'apostles', 'the Seven', 'elders', 'prophets' and 'evangelists'. In addition, it is necessary to explore the role of James and of women in the leadership of Acts.

The Twelve

Luke limits his use of the word 'apostle' to the Twelve, with the exception of 14:4 and 14, which refer to Paul and Barnabas. But he essentially has no wider concept of apostleship along the lines that will later become evident in the writings of Paul. The number 'Twelve' is important; hence the election of Matthias (1:15–26) to replace Judas.[15] They have a unique place and their number clearly signifies that they are the counterparts of the twelve patriarchs and have a foundational role in this new move of God.

The apostles' role is presented as being witnesses to Christ's ministry and resurrection (1:22; 4:33) and as having a fundamental place in determining the church's belief as those who teach and devote themselves to 'prayer and the ministry of the word' (6:4). Their personal ministry includes the exercise of miraculous gifts of healing (2:43; 3:1–10; 5:12–16). Strategically, they ensure the church is 'managed' well (6:1–7). They engage primarily in mission to Israel but legitimize the church's expansion beyond Israel by engaging in cross-cultural mission themselves (10:1 – 11:18) and authenticating the mission work of others (8:14–17; 11:19–30; 15:1–35). Andrew Clark has captured their role in four phrases: 'the nucleus of a restored Israel', 'witnesses to Jesus' resurrection', 'authoritative teachers' and 'missionaries to Israel'.[16]

It is as important to see what they did not do, as much as what they did. They are not shown to be congregational leaders except in the sense of leading the first congregations in Jerusalem for a brief time. Nor are they the ones who initiate all the developments in mission. That role belongs to the Spirit and to irrepressible individuals who feel compelled to share the gospel with others. The apostles often appear to be 'after the event' people rather than the sorts of proactive strategic leaders so prized today. Furthermore, they are not shown as holders of an office that has to be transmitted to succeeding generations.

---

14. Ibid., p. 108.

15. Giles, 'Is Luke?', p. 5.

16. Andrew Clark, 'The Role of the Apostles', in I. Howard Marshall and David Peterson (eds.), *Witness to the Gospel: The Theology of Acts* (Grand Rapids: Eerdmans, 1998), pp. 173–181.

Bartlett is right in commenting that 'There are important issues of succession in the way leaders are chosen . . . but the succession is the succession of true teaching rather than that of office or ordination.'[17]

James

Once the initial work has been established and the direction set, the apostles seem to disappear from view and other leaders take over. James, for example, came to prominence in the leadership of the church at Jerusalem (12:17; 15:13; 21:18; Gal. 1:19; 2:9, 12), probably after the apostles left Jerusalem.[18] The oldest (step)brother of Jesus (Mark 6:3), he had a reputation for piety and became known for his wisdom. For a decade he led the Jerusalem church but, given its significance as the mother church, his personal influence stretched far beyond it.[19] He appears just to emerge on to the scene. We read of no election, appointment or ordination. We do not know how he came to be respected as the Jerusalem church's leader, except, of course, that his close relationship with Jesus would have meant he was naturally looked to in a Jewish culture to further his brother's interests.[20] It would seem that his leadership was one of a natural progression or simple emergence.

The Seven

The leadership structure in Jerusalem obviously took a step forward on the appointment of 'seven men' chosen to take responsibility for the distribution of food to the widows who were Hellenistic, as distinct from Hebraic, Jews (6:1–7). The church was expanding and old leadership patterns were insufficient to cope with it. The revised form of leadership they adopted was one that would have been recognized in a local synagogue, and so it was not particularly a departure from Jewish custom.[21]

---

17. Bartlett, *Ministry*, p. 129.

18. Richard Bauckham, 'James and the Jerusalem Church', in Richard Bauckham (ed.), *The Book of Acts in its Palestinian Setting* (Grand Rapids: Eerdmans, 1995), pp. 427–441.

19. See the addressees of James's letter in Jas 1:1.

20. It would seem that he was not a convinced disciple of Jesus during Jesus' lifetime. Perhaps his conversion took place because Jesus appeared to him after the resurrection (1 Cor. 15:7). However his conversion took place, he was pleased to announce himself as 'a servant of God and of the Lord Jesus Christ' when he wrote his letter (Jas 1:1).

21. Roger W. Gehring, *House Church and Mission: The Importance of Household Structures in Early Christianity* (Peabody: Hendrickson, 2004), p. 97.

Much has been built on this episode, but a careful examination of what the text claims quickly reveals that many of the accepted superstructures are built on a very flimsy foundation. On the one hand, many have looked to their election as the origin of a second order of ministry, under the apostles. But their appointment seems much more like a pragmatic response to a particular need. Nothing is said about their continuing accountability to the apostles and even less about their subsequently graduating from this tier of ministry into another. The fact is that the only two people listed of whom we know anything afterwards are known because they do not go on serving tables but rather preach Jesus. On the other hand, other churches have looked to this passage as providing evidence of a lay diaconate whose responsibilities are to do with the administration of the church as opposed to the pastoral and teaching responsibility of the church. But while the verb *diakoneō* (I serve) is used, the noun is not used as a title for these people. And although the title is used later in the New Testament, it is used rarely and with little insight as to the role (Phil. 1:1; 1 Tim. 3:8, 10). To argue that this is the basis for a lay diaconate is to build on a very slender foundation.

The method by which the men were chosen is unspecified. It might have been an election by a show of hands (common in Greek city states) or the reaching of a consensus after discussion. The men chosen were to be 'known to be full of the Spirit and wisdom' (6:3).[22] Luke is more concerned about personal qualification than procedural regularities. Their later ministries only briefly seem to be concerned with distributing food before at least two of them engaged in apologetic and evangelistic ministry. As mentioned, fluidity and response to a changing situation seems to have been the order of the day.

Elders

The term 'elders' is used frequently in Acts but of different groups. Seven times Luke uses it to speak of the elders of Israel who are associated with the chief priest and teachers of the law (Acts 4:5, 8; 5:21; 6:12; 23:14; 24:1; 25:15). Seven times it refers to the elders of the church in Jerusalem, mostly in connection with the so-called 'Council of Jerusalem', and it is not used before the Twelve have begun to recede into the background (11:30; 15:2, 4, 6, 22, 23; 16:4). Three times it is used of leaders appointed by Paul and Barnabas in the churches they found (14:23; 20:13, 18). No particular responsibilities are

---

22. Gehring also speculates they may have been homeowners who had proven their leadership/teaching skills in the house churches before being appointed to this responsibility (ibid., pp. 97–98).

assigned to them by Luke, although the pastoral epistles speak of them as those who 'direct the affairs of the church' (1 Tim. 5:17; 3:5) and are 'able to teach' (1 Tim. 3:2).[23]

A great deal of discussion has recently taken place about the significance of elders, both here and elsewhere in the New Testament. Kevin Giles has reminded us that within Palestinian Judaism two types of elders were known: those in the Sanhedrin and those in local communities. The former primarily acted as judges and the latter as wise men recognized for their age and social standing. In both cases, they were laymen and neither group was set apart for a spiritual ministry by means of ordination.[24] He further argues, rightly, that Acts neither prescribes 'any specific function to Christian elders' nor does it give any indication of their being a class set apart by ordination.[25] When Paul and Barnabas 'appointed' elders (14:23), the verb *cheirotoneō* is used. Bruce explains that the origin of the word may lie in to '"stretch out the hand(s)," hence "elect by a show of hands" or "ordain by the laying on of hands"' but 'its regular sense in the New Testament is simply to appoint or designate'.[26]

The fact that so little is said about them here and elsewhere, apart from the pastoral epistles, which we shall consider later, means we are limited in what we can claim about them by way of normative practice or historical precedence. There seems great wisdom in the growing consensus that rather than occupying an office, elders were simply those older men in the congregation who were respected and recognized for their experience and wisdom.[27] This is especially so if one accepts the argument that the 'church' in Jerusalem, as elsewhere, was composed of a number of house churches, all of which would need leadership. If it is right that the earliest Christians met in homes, and there

---

23. Even this is problematic, for the term in 1 Tim. 3 is *episkopos* rather than *presbyteros* (see Titus 1:5, 7). I would argue that they are synonymous. Some have suggested that 1 Tim. 5:17 indicates that only some elders 'direct the affairs of the church' and that these are distinct from teaching elders, but I believe this to be unsubstantiated. See chapter 8 in this book.

24. Giles, 'Is Luke?', pp. 10–11.

25. Ibid., p. 12.

26. F. F. Bruce, *The Acts of the Apostles: Greek Text with Introduction and Commentary*, 3rd ed. (Grand Rapids: Eerdmans; Leicester: Apollos, 1990), p. 326.

27. R. Alastair Campbell, *The Elders: Seniority within Earliest Christianity* (Edinburgh: T. & T. Clark, 1994). For partial agreement and a sympathetic critique, see Gehring, *House Church*, pp. 101–105.

is little doubt about it, then leaders would be provided quite naturally by the household structure itself. And those leaders might well include women as well as men (see Lydia in Philippi in 16:13–15). Collectively, the leaders of the various house churches would be called 'the elders'. But what they are not is holders of an office, set apart by some official act of ordination and they are not to be equated with the contemporary minister of a church.[28] Nor are they a second generation of leader destined to replace the apostles.[29] The early church takes up and makes use of a common leadership pattern of its day, albeit investing it with a new spirit, as we shall see when we discuss Paul's concepts of ministry.

Prophets

Prophets are also mentioned in continuation of the interest Luke has shown in prophecy in his Gospel. The pouring out of the Holy Spirit on the day of Pentecost led to a new age in which prophecy would be restored (2:17). Some people and groups are specifically identified as prophets. These are Agabus and the group in Jerusalem (11:27; 21:10), those in Antioch (13:1) and the daughters of Philip (21:9). The gift is exercised more widely than by those named as 'prophets'. Inspired preaching, courageous testimony, exhortation and encouragement, and individual guidance all take place under the prophetic inspiration of the Holy Spirit.[30] It outruns the evidence to claim, as some do, that prophets were 'the main "ministers of the word"'.[31] It is certainly not always easy to distinguish the role of the prophets from that of others, partly because of the wide variety of functions they perform, and there certainly seems nothing fixed in stone about it.[32] With Giles, I agree, 'Their authorisation and ministry is Spirit-given. There is no mention of prophets being commissioned or ordained and their ministry is not said to be legitimized by the twelve apostles.'[33]

---

28. Giles, *What on Earth?* p. 94.

29. For a full discussion of these issues, see R. A. Campbell, *Elders*, pp. 151–175.

30. Giles, 'Is Luke?', p. 13.

31. Giles, *What on Earth?* p. 97; and E. Earle Ellis, 'The Role of the Christian Prophet in Acts', in W. Ward Gasque and Ralph P. Martin (eds.), *Apostolic History and the Gospel* (Exeter: Paternoster, 1970), pp. 58–62. For the case against, see Max Turner, *The Holy Spirit and Spiritual Gifts: Then and Now* (Carlisle: Paternoster, 1996), pp. 206–212.

32. Ellis, 'Role', pp. 64–66.

33. Giles, 'Is Luke?', p. 14.

Evangelists and teachers

Briefer mention may be made, for the sake of completeness, of evangelists and teachers. Although the practice of evangelism is evident throughout Acts, the term 'evangelist' is used only once of Philip (21:8).[34] This is consistent with its extremely rare use in the New Testament and seems to indicate that Philip's primary gift was that of announcing the gospel and provoking a response to it.[35] Likewise, 'teachers' are mentioned only in Acts 13:1, where the word is coupled with 'prophets' but, as with the practice of evangelism, the practice of teaching is evident throughout. The absence of any stress on these titles or roles indicates that no firm offices are in place and ministry is being exercised in a fluid and responsive manner, consistent with the demands of a rapidly expanding church.

Women in Acts

From a different perspective, attention should be drawn to the important role of women in Acts. Those named are Dorcas, who 'was always doing good and helping the poor' (9:36); Mary, the mother of John Mark, who hosted a house church in Jerusalem (12:12); Lydia, who provided hospitality for Paul and his team in Philippi (16:15); Priscilla who, with her husband Aquila, is acknowledged as the hostess and teacher of Apollos (18:26); and, the prophetically gifted daughters of Philip (21:8–9). Each of these is important.

Dorcas has been described as a leader 'in relief work' and it has been suggested that her 'example may have been instrumental in the development of church offices that focused on service'.[36] The suggestion, however, seems to stretch beyond the evidence. The description of Mary's house clearly indicates it was a wealthy one, substantial enough to accommodate a group of disciples to meet in and, Bruce comments, 'probably one of the houses indicated in 2:46'. He adds, with some legitimacy, 'The group that met here was evidently that to which Peter belonged.'[37] We do not know what had happened to John Mark's father, although he was probably dead. Mary was acting as a woman of independent means and would naturally have played something of a leading

---

34. See F. Scott Spencer, *The Portrait of Philip in Acts: A Study of Roles and Relations*, JSNTSup 67 (Sheffield: Sheffield Academic Press, 1982).

35. It is used again only in 2 Tim. 4:5 and in the plural in Eph. 4:11.

36. Stanley J. Grenz and Denise Muir Kjesbo, *Women in the Church: A Biblical Theology of Women in Ministry* (Downers Grove: IVP, 1995), p. 80.

37. Bruce, *Acts*, p. 285.

role in the group, even if not a teaching role, in view of the presence still of the apostles. Lydia plays a similar role in Paul's ministry at Philippi. She is clearly a businesswoman who is the head of her household. Given Paul's Jewish background it is extraordinary that he should want to establish a church in her house, but this he seems to have done, working out the principle of Galatians 3:28.[38]

More attention has been paid to Priscilla and Aquila than to others. They are an unusual, if not unique, example of a couple functioning together in serving the church.[39] Most would accept that the mention of Priscilla's name before that of her husband Aquila in 18:18 and 26 is significant. It may imply that she was of a higher social status than him[40] but it also implies that Priscilla took a leading role in instructing Apollos 'more adequately' in the faith. As Grenz and Kjesbo point out, since Apollos already had 'a thorough knowledge of the scriptures' this required some depth and it 'must have been of sufficient expertise to warrant his acceptance'.[41] Some have tried to downplay the importance of their role by arguing that this was unofficial teaching offered in private. But Luke gives no hint that this is an issue and Paul draws attention to both public and private teaching in his address at Miletus without suggesting that one was superior to the other (20:20). Others have perhaps overestimated their role, and seeking to relate it too eagerly to contemporary debates, have spoken of them as the first example of a couple in ministry. Care needs to be exercised or the language becomes anachronistic, and requires us to read back contemporary structures of ministry into the early church in an unwarranted fashion.[42]

Acts shows no inhibition about reporting the contribution of women to the leadership of the early church. Although the weight of reporting is heavily in favour of men, the amount of consideration given to women is remarkable given the patriarchal context in which the early church was emerging.

---

38. Gehring, *House Church*, p. 212. See the discussion about the role of women in leadership in Paul's writings in Robert Banks, *Paul's Idea of Community* (Exeter: Paternoster, 1980), pp. 126–128.

39. It has been suggested that Andronicus and Junia (Rom. 16:7) were another couple, but we cannot be sure.

40. Bruce, *Acts*, p. 390.

41. Grenz and Kjesbo, *Women*, p. 83.

42. Joy Tetley, 'Ordained Married Couples: A Theological Reflection', *Anvil* 9 (1992), pp. 151–152.

The appointment of leaders

It is evident that a variety of leaders were recognized within the communities of equal grace that formed the early church. And just as there was variety in their 'titles' and roles, so there was variety in the way in which they were appointed to, or recognized for, their leadership responsibilities. No single pattern is evident and nothing like the contemporary practice of ordination, as practiced by most denominations, can be derived from Acts. Jesus Christ chose and commissioned the Twelve. To these we might add that James and Paul, although not among the Twelve, were also commissioned directly by the Lord (1 Cor. 15:7; Acts 9:1–19; 26:12–19). Both of these may subsequently have had their call confirmed in other ways. James's role seems to have been a natural outworking of Jewish custom since he was the next oldest (step)brother of Jesus or as a result of his charismatic gifts. Paul had his role confirmed when he and Barnabas were commissioned by the Holy Spirit, who spoke to the prophets and teachers in Antioch, who as a result acknowledged this calling by laying hands on Paul and Barnabas (13:1–3).

The Seven, as we have seen, were chosen by the congregation (13:3), although the method is not specified, while the elders in the newly founded Pisidean churches were 'appointed' (14:23). Again the method of their appointment is unspecified. If anything, as the recent discussion (mentioned above) suggests, elders were not holders of an office but those older men in the community who marked themselves out for recognition because of their wisdom and experience. Others, like Philip, seem to have taken their own initiative in pioneering evangelism, so their appointment may have been obvious (8:5), even though he had apparently been asked to undertake a different role in Jerusalem. They did not wait for authorization but gained the imprimatur for their work after the event.

What of the laying on of hands? It may have occurred more frequently than reported, but it is not evident that it was an indispensable element in the process of appointment. It is neither mentioned in reference to Matthias (1:12–26), nor in respect of the Pisidean elders (14:23). This does not, of course, mean it did not happen. We must remember that Acts was not written as a manual of church discipline, so it may simply have been unimportant for Luke to record. It is mentioned in reference to the Seven (6:6), to Paul individually (9:17–19) and to Paul and Barnabas together (13:3). Laying on hands was also practised when healing took place (19:7; 28:8) and when authentication of true discipleship was necessary (8:17; 19:6), as well as when leaders were recognized.

Most find precedence for the laying on of hands on the Seven in Moses' commissioning of Joshua (Num. 27:18) and therefore interpret the act as one of transferring authority. But, as Giles argues, there is no evidence that the Seven were subordinate to the Twelve and their gifts had already been acknowledged. So 'laying on of hands was a recognition of charismatic authority and not a bestowal of it'.[43] Similarly, Paul and Barnabas were already among the prophets and teachers when hands were laid on them. In their case, the apostles are not involved, and there is no support for any doctrine of apostolic (or even episcopal) succession here. They have hands laid on them by equals, not superiors, as an act of commissioning, and not as a bestowal of gifts.

The laying on of hands seems to have been a symbolic act capable of wide interpretation. In the sacrificial rituals of Israel, it was most often an act of identification with the animal to be sacrificed (Lev. 1:4; 3:2; etc.), although, as on the Day of Atonement, it could indicate a transference of sins (Lev. 16:21). The touch of Jesus was effective in bringing healing and blessing to people, while elsewhere in the New Testament it signifies the imparting of a spiritual gift (1 Tim. 4:14; 2 Tim. 1:6). So although it is evident that laying on hands was practised, it is difficult to make a watertight case for the practice as amounting to anything like contemporary ordination or to argue that it is indispensable before certain gifts of leadership are exercised.

The function of leaders

Four major tasks seem to stand out in Acts as the responsibility of leaders, of whatever sort. They are to *engage in teaching truth*, *pioneering mission*, *resolving conflict* and *protecting integrity*. A concomitant mark of leadership in Acts is enduring suffering.

Teaching truth

The apostles are first and foremost witnesses to Jesus, whose primary responsibility is to ensure the church is founded on truth. Hence the church devotes itself 'to the apostles' teaching' (2:42) and are called in to validate missionary expansion (8:14–17; 10:1 – 11:18). They may be confined initially to the mother church in Jerusalem (8:1), but even so are passionate about the spreading of the word of God (4:29; 6:5, 7; 10:36) and are a necessary link in the chain of gospel proclamation. Without them the authentic gospel would not be passed

---

43. Giles, 'Is Luke?', p. 17.

on to others. No summary of 'the apostles' teaching' is given, but it can be reconstructed from the preaching of Peter, who seems representative of the other apostles. They were essentially transmitting the teaching of Jesus (1:1) and proclaiming him as both the Lord and the Messiah (2:36) through whom God had brought about salvation and made the forgiveness of sins available.

The same emphasis on teaching is found in Paul, who was the chief, but not sole, instrument in extending the mission beyond Jerusalem. He is regularly shown to be instructing people in the faith (e.g. 11:26; 18:11; 19:9–10; 28:31) and strengthening the disciples (14:21–22). Teaching incorporated not only proclamation and instruction but argument and apologetic. Paul's visit to Athens may be the outstanding example of this (17:16–34; see also the visit to Lystra, 14:8–20), but he was as urgent in trying to persuade synagogue worshippers and Jewish leaders that Jesus was the fulfilment of their hopes as he was of arguing for the truth among pagan audiences (17:1–4; 18:4; 25:23 – 26:32).[44]

Pioneering mission

Another key task of leaders seems to be that of church planting, as is seen in Philip and, most of all, in Paul. It is misleading to think they were chiefly concerned with the conversion of individuals. Their primary thrust was the formation of new Christian communities, composed, of course, of converted individuals, who would be ongoing models of the gospel and transmitters of its message.[45] Although public and synagogue proclamation took place, most witnessing was based on particular households and channelled through the workshop where Paul plied his trade of tent-making.[46] Once a nucleus existed, various strategies were quite naturally adopted to form them into a community. The administration of baptism, the celebration of the Lord's Supper and the use of language, which distinguished insiders from outsiders, were all part of this and contributed to their being bound together in love. It was not that Paul and others were manipulating people by the conscious adoption of

---

44. This is not the place to discuss their missionary methods in detail, for which see Michael Green, *Evangelism in the Early Church* (Eastbourne: Eagle, 1995); and Eckhard J. Schnabel, *Early Christian Mission*. Vol. 2: *Paul and the Early Church* (Downers Grove: IVP; Leicester: Apollos, 2004), pp. 1294–1309.

45. Abraham J. Malherbe, *Paul and the Thessalonians: The Philosophic Tradition of Pastoral Care* (Philadelphia: Fortress, 1987), p. 87.

46. Ronald F. Hock, *The Social Context of Paul's Ministry: Tentmaking and Apostleship* (Philadelphia: Fortress, 1980).

sinister strategies; they instinctively, or taught by the Spirit, did that which would build strong communities.[47]

Resolving conflict

With advance came inevitable conflict as the church faced new, even unanticipated, questions. Chief among them was whether the Gentiles could be admitted to the church, and if so on what terms. The issue came to a head in what has grandly been called 'The Jerusalem Council', which makes it sound more institutional than it probably was. But, as Conzelmann has commented, 'it is not by chance that the Apostolic Council occupies the middle of the book. It is the great turning point.'[48] The conference throws up many questions.[49] Luke is not even precise about the list of attendees, but one gets the impression that all interested parties were present. What interests me is the way in which they reached their decision. It was exactly as one might expect of a family community of relative equals led by the Spirit. There is no official decree composed beforehand to which all have to submit, but rather open discussion in which many take part. After the initial problem was stated (15:1–5), Peter spoke first of the unmistakable lessons he learned in his experience at Joppa (15:6–11), and therefore the apostles, as foundational teachers, do take precedence. Barnabas and Paul then tell of their experiences of God at work (15:12–3). Then James sums up, reflecting on the words of Amos and providing guidance for the assembly (15:13–21). All this was under the guidance of the Holy Spirit (15:28) and undertaken with a remarkable ability to listen to one another, which is rare in my experience of church meetings. We have, then, a way of reaching collective agreement that involves open debate and discussion, testimony, Bible study, good theology and the Holy Spirit. No single strand stands alone, but one provides checks and balances for the others and in turn is tested by the others. Peter clearly gives a lead. He does not abdicate his apostolic authority. But neither does he pronounce *ex cathedra*.

---

47. There is a growing literature exploring these issues. In addition to Malherbe, see Wayne Meeks, *The First Urban Christians: The Social World of the Apostle Paul* (New Haven: Yale University Press, 1983), pp. 75–109, 140–164; and Derek Tidball, 'Social Setting of Mission Churches', *DPL*, pp. 883–892. See further chapter 6 in this book.

48. Hans Conzelmann, *Acts of the Apostles: A Commentary*, Hermenia (Philadelphia: Fortress, 1987), p. 115.

49. Luke T. Johnson, *Decision Making in the Church* (Philadelphia: Fortress, 1983), pp. 46–58.

Barnabas and Paul are respected when they speak and James steers them to a wise conclusion. Here is collective leadership as well as collective decision-making at work in an ideal way.[50]

Protecting integrity

Two incidents witness to the importance of maintaining the integrity of the church. The way in which discipline is exercised in both cases seems fierce, and is probably more characteristic of the way in which situations needed to be handled initially rather than establishing an ongoing pattern. Ananias and Sapphira (5:1–11) lied to the apostles about the money they were donating to the Christians in Jerusalem. They had perfect freedom to dispose of their income as they wished, but had no freedom to pretend to be giving it all when they were not. So, in a scene somewhat reminiscent of the judgment on Abihu and Nadab in Leviticus 10:1–5, both husband and wife fall down dead and their bodies are carried out. We read that 'great fear seized the whole church and all who heard about these events'. From the outset, reverence for the God of truth was firmly established.

The second incident took place in Samaria when Simon, the sorcerer turned believer, sought the power of the Holy Spirit to use for his own ends (8:9–25), and was even prepared to buy it if necessary. But he lacked understanding of the nature of the power of the Holy Spirit. When confronted with Simon's request, Peter bluntly states, 'To hell with you and your money.'[51] Unlike Ananias, Simon is given the opportunity to repent, which he apparently does with alacrity. Whether the judgment falls (as in the case of Ananias and Sapphira) or not (as in the case of Simon), these early days established the need for integrity and ensured that none would attempt to play games with God.

Endure suffering

We are used to thinking that the signs of an apostle consist of powerful preaching, miraculous powers of healing, the exercise of authoritative disci-pline and unstoppable advance in mission. But it is also true that the mark of a genuine apostle, and of other Christian leaders, is *suffering*. Peter, Stephen, James, Paul, Barnabas, Silas, Jason, Gaius and Aristarchus all suffered for their commitment to Christ. Although Paul expands on the theology of his suffering in his letters, even in Acts he is reported as teaching, 'We must go

---

50. For a full discussion, see ibid., pp. 77–87.

51. This is J. B. Phillips's translation, which Howard Marshall says 'may sound like a profanity, but is precisely what the Greek says' (*Acts*, p. 159).

through many hardships to enter the kingdom of God' (14:22). Prisons and plots, riots and being roughed up seem to have been the order of the day and brought them into closer unity with the Lord of the cross whose glory they served and whose experience they shared.

Paul's address to the elders at Ephesus (20:17–38)

Paul's address to the 'elders' (*presbyteroi*) (or 'overseers' [*episkopoi*], 20:17 and 20:28 – the words seem interchangeable) at Ephesus gives us a good insight into the nature and purpose of ministry, as he understood it. In it, he reveals something of his own strategy for ministry before committing the responsibility for it into their hands.

Woven throughout the address is an emphasis on the lifestyle Paul adopted. He served 'with great humility and with tears' (20:19), passionately committed to serving the Lord and his people but not himself. The same mark of self-disinterest is evident in his refusing to hold back any teaching that would be of benefit to them, however unpopular it might have proved (20:20). His mention of the Spirit speaks of the Spirit guiding him to go to Jerusalem, but throughout his ministry he had displayed this same sensitivity to the Spirit's direction (20:22). His future was to be one of suffering but, as we have seen, his earlier and more active ministry was never free from hardship and opposition (20:23). True to the character Luke has introduced us to in his narrative of missionary progress, Paul next speaks of his determination 'to finish the race' (20:24). Ministry is full of obstacles and is not for those who will give up easily. Another familiar characteristic of Paul's service was his commitment to financial integrity, mentioned in verses 33–35. Verse 35, in fact, makes a suitable ending for Paul's reflections on ministry because it speaks, once more, of the self-giving without which ministry cannot be truly Christlike. All these features are to be found in those writings that come from Paul's own hands where he reflects on his approach to ministry, especially 1 Thessalonians[52] and 2 Corinthians. Luke's portrait is anything but fictional and encapsulates Paul's true priorities.

---

52. For a detailed comparison of this speech with 1 Thessalonians, see Steve Walton, *Leadership and Lifestyle: The Portrait of Paul in the Miletus Speech and I Thessalonians*, SNTSMS 108 (Cambridge: Cambridge University Press, 2000). Walton also points out the close identification between this speech and the teaching of Jesus (pp. 99–136).

The address shows Paul to be a model not only in respect of a leader's lifestyle but also in terms of fulfilling the responsibilities he has undertaken, which he now passes over to the elders of Ephesus to continue. They include

- teaching in public and in private (20:20)
- calling people to a decision about repentance and faith (20:21)
- testifying to God's grace in his own life (20:24)
- proclaiming the whole will of God (20:27)
- watching over his own spiritual life as well as those of the flock (20:27)
- being a good shepherd (20:28)
- preparing them to cope with the future (20:29–31)

The substance of ministry is also to be found here. It concerns the will of God and his salvation plan (20:27), the Spirit of God and his missionary dynamic (20:22, 28), the Son of God and his redemptive cross (20:28)[53] and the church of God and its future hope (20:28–33).

After comparing this speech with the teaching of Jesus in Luke's Gospel, Steve Walton has adjudged that

> This represents far more than a collection of vague platitudes; it offers a dynamic, sharply focused model of Christian leadership rooted in Luke's understanding of Jesus, in contrast with other approaches to leadership available in the ancient world (Luke 22:25).[54]

For all the apparent variety of what Acts says about ministry, these characteristics, these responsibilities and this message lie at the core of any ministry, whoever undertakes it, however and wherever it is exercised.

Conclusion

Acts does not provide us with any blueprint about the way ministry is to be structured in the church, but it does provide us with a blueprint for handling

---

53. Dunn points out that this is a unique theological reflection on the cross in Acts but one that is characteristic of Paul's teaching in his letters about the cross (Dunn, *Acts*, pp. 270, 272–273; Bruce, *Acts*, p. 434; and Walton, *Leadership and Lifestyle*, pp. 94–98).

54. Walton, *Leadership and Lifestyle*, p. 136.

a situation where church planting is the norm and growth is the order of the day. It sets before us a 'kaleidoscopic variety' appropriate to a church being born that is inevitably a 'messy, painful and risky business'.[55] It sets before us the call to be creative and inventive in the way in which we respond as new communities are formed, adapting where necessary in a church that is, or should be, always emerging. It gives us permission to take up and adapt leadership forms found outside the church, as long as they are transformed to become consistent with, and do not undermine, the nature of the church as Acts portrays it. The neatly structured forms of ministry, constrained by history and tradition, that put everyone in their place in a bureaucratic arrangement smacks of stability and complacency rather than advance and progress. Indeed, such an arrangement may actually hinder growth.

Finke and Stark, in their careful study of the progress of the gospel in America, have concluded that the remarkable growth of the church on the frontier was due to Methodist and Baptist itinerant evangelists who looked for little by way of support and authorization. At the same time, the churches of the north-eastern states went into decline in spite of, or probably because of, their well-educated, titled and scholarly ministries, which took place in proper buildings and at great financial cost.[56] Both Scripture and history point to the need for flexible and responsive patterns of leadership if the church is to grow.

Scholars are apt to dismiss this phase of the church's life as a 'pre-ecclesial' rather than 'a fully developed ecclesial situation',[57] as if there is little to gain about 'proper' ministry from Acts. It must be conceded that arrangements are bound to change as the church became established. Yet this phase has much to teach us about the true nature of 'church', and consequently its ministry, before the period of consolidation with the onset of institutionalization, especially if we see mission rather than mere preservation as a priority in the church. Acts invites us to envisage a ministry less encumbered with status and professionalism and more able to improvise in order to respond to the opportunities we face.

Bartlett has said it well in the conclusion to his study of *Ministry in the New Testament*:

> The New Testament's most structured view of ministry, foreshadowed in Acts 20 and delineated in the Pastorals, was still more charismatic than the ministerial leadership

---

55. Tetley, 'Ordained Married Couples', p. 154.

56. R. Finke and R. Stark, *The Churching of America: Winners and Losers in our Religious Economy* (New Brunswick: Rutgers University Press, 1992).

57. Gehring, *House Church*, p. 216.

of most contemporary Assembly of God churches. There were fewer hoops to jump through, fewer authorities to please, fewer professional standards.

We are who we are, a specialized people living in a specialized world, but the occasional morbidity of the church results in part from a twofold confusion. The first is the minister who thinks that he or she is not only set apart but set above, who thinks that being paid to be Christian makes it especially virtuous to do so. The second is the congregation who sees the minister as a hired hand, not fellow Christian, fellow pilgrim, but management: easy come, easy go.[58]

---

58. Bartlett, *Ministry*, p. 188.

6. PAUL: MINISTRY IN AN INFANT CHURCH

The ministry of a founding father

Approaching Paul

It is amazing that the apostle Paul never describes himself as a 'pastor,[1] and that he uses the word 'pastor' (*poimēn*) only once in his writings (Eph. 4:11), since, apart from Jesus Christ, we have more knowledge of this sensitive and skilled pastor than anyone. Admittedly, Paul is difficult to categorize. He was a gifted pioneer evangelist and an astute theologian as well as being an accomplished pastor. Much more attention has been paid to his missionary methods and his formative role as a theologian than to his pastoral work, at least until recently.[2] That partly reflects the mission interests of an activist evangelical

---

1. Ernest Best says in his opening Sprunt Lecture, 'I had intended to call these lectures "Paul the Pastor" until I discovered he never so described himself' (*Paul and his Converts* [Edinburgh: T. & T. Clark, 1988], p. 22). See also James W. Thompson, *Pastoral Ministry according to Paul: A Biblical Vision* (Grand Rapids: Baker Academic, 2006), p. 22.

2. Literature on Paul as a pastor is beginning to grow, but until recently there was little available apart from W. E. Chadwick, *The Pastoral Teaching of St Paul: His Ministerial Ideals* (Edinburgh: T. & T. Clark, 1907), which, as its title suggests, concentrates on Paul's teaching rather than on Paul himself.

church, on the one hand, and the intellectual interests of the academic world, on the other. Nonetheless, Paul serves as an exemplary pastoral model, if not a perfect one. His theology arises out of the questions thrown up by pastoral and everyday situations in the churches.[3] And his writings constantly reveal his pastoral heart, his pastoral ambitions, his pastoral techniques, his pastoral advice, and his pastoral frustrations.

Since much that is relevant occurs in more than one of Paul's letters, it would be repetitive to go through them all book by book. However, in order to do some justice to the complexity of Paul's work as a pastor, I have chosen to consider him in three chapters, representing three phases of his ministry. First, we consider his pastoral role among the churches he founded as seen in his earlier letters. Secondly, we consider him writing as an apostolic teacher to other churches, some of whom, like Rome and Colosse, he had never visited. Thirdly, we reflect on him as the elder statesman passing the baton to the next generation. It is here, particularly, that we consider his teaching regarding the nature and 'structure' of leadership in the church as the original apostles fade from the scene.

Any such analysis is bound to be artificial and there is a good deal of overlap between the phases, although I believe it holds good and suits our purposes without distorting our understanding of Paul. However, since it is artificial I shall be free, occasionally, to draw in evidence from outside the phase I am dealing with, if relevant. Adopting this scheme does not mean that I believe Paul matured through his ministry to the extent that his understanding of and teaching on the church and ministry changed as time went on, as is commonly taught.[4] In particular, the idea that he originally saw the church as a charismatic community that had become an organized institution by the end of his life, with the implications this had for ministry, is highly questionable. It will be examined in chapter 8. Moreover, adopting this scheme means we are considering the whole body of literature as 'Pauline' rather than accepting only seven of the letters as genuinely written by him. With Andrew Clarke, I agree that any study of Pauline leadership that did not include all the canonical letters of Paul is 'regrettable and regarded as deficient'.[5]

---

3. Mark Strom, *Reframing Paul, Conversations in Grace and Community* (Downers Grove: IVP, 2000), pp. 72, 159.

4. For a developed discussion of this trajectory, see Margaret Y. MacDonald, *The Pauline Churches: A Socio-Historical Study of Institutionalization in the Pauline and Deutero-Pauline Writings*, SNTSMS 60 (Cambridge: Cambridge University Press, 1988).

5. Andrew D. Clarke, *A Pauline Theology of Church Leadership*, LNTS 362 (London: T. & T. Clark, 2007), p. 4.

Paul as church planter and pastor: common themes

The correspondence Paul had with the churches he brought to birth provides us with rich material for understanding his approach to ministry. Much of what is written to these churches is characteristic of Paul's approach to any church, but there are also some distinctives that arise from the unique relationship he had with them as their founder. First, we look at themes that run through his writings to churches, whether he planted these churches or not.

Pastoral vision

Paul has a concern for individuals. The many personal references in his letters (e.g. 1 Cor. 16:1–18; Phil. 2:19–29; 4:2; 2 Tim. 1:16; 4:9–13), and the various greetings with which his letters conclude (notably, Rom. 16; Col. 4:7–18), together with the complete, if brief, letter to Philemon, shows us he was deeply concerned about the spiritual welfare of individuals and that he knew them and their needs well. Although he struggled with some who were out to do him harm (2 Cor. 10:1 – 12:21; 1 Tim. 1:18–20; 2 Tim. 1:15; 4:14–15), overwhelmingly his references to people convey a sense of love and personal commitment, which seeks the best for them. They also reveal him to be a sensitive person, touched by joy and sorrow in relationships. He never loses sight of the individual. Paul Beasley-Murray draws attention to the emphasis on individuals, even in some of the statements that set out a corporate vision. So as a father he 'dealt with each of you' (1 Thess. 2:11) and sought, according to Colossians 1:28, to warn and teach 'everyone'.[6]

However, his greater ambition is for the church as a whole and his concern is primarily for the people of God collectively. His vision is essentially to see the body of Christ transformed. In this respect, Paul mounts a profound challenge to the individualism that characterizes our Western church and culture today. James Thompson suggests this is perhaps one reason why Paul's pastoral theology is not given the attention it deserves today.[7]

When Paul writes to the Galatians, he uses the analogy of childbirth, one of several maternal images he uses,[8] to speak of his ambition to have Christ 'formed in you' (Gal. 4:19). It is a rich analogy. As the process of giving birth

---

6. Paul Beasley-Murray, 'Pastor, Paul as', *DPL*, p. 657.

7. J. W. Thompson, *Pastoral Ministry*, pp. 59–60.

8. On Paul's use of maternal imagery, see Beverley Roberts Gaventa, *Our Mother St. Paul* (Louisville: Westminster John Knox, 2007). Other maternal imagery is found in Rom. 8:22; 1 Cor. 3:1–3; 1 Thess. 2:7.

is painful, so pastoral work involves anguished labour at times. As the ambition of any mother is to see the foetus develop in the womb until full term, so Paul's ambition for the Galatian Christians is that Christ might be fully developed in them. This means that morally, ethically and spiritually they will become like Christ, a process that involves them sharing in his crucifixion (Gal. 2:20; 6:14). The 'you' in whom Paul longs to see this happen is plural, not singular. So 'formation does not belong to individual believers as a personal or private possession only. Instead, formation refers to the community of those who are called to faith . . .'[9] Another important hint about Paul's pastoral vision is hidden in this verse. He commits himself to strive with the Galatians 'until'. As with all his pastoral work, he has an eye on a future day when not only Christians will be fully restored in Christ but the creation itself will be rescued. Gaventa points to the way in which in saying this Paul puts their progress into the context of 'a new creation' (6:15) when the whole of the cosmos is renewed.

Paul uses many different analogies and expressions in his letters to state his pastoral goal, but it is always the same goal, however he puts it. He raids the building site, the nursery, the bridal suite, the gymnasium, the farm and even the marketplace to find language to express his ambition for the churches he has planted. He wants them to be based on sure foundations and then built up, using good-quality materials that will endure in the construction (1 Cor. 3:10–15; 2 Cor. 12:19;[10] 13:10; Col. 2:7). He wants them to grow up to become mature adults, no longer infants and children (1 Cor. 3:1–4; 14:20; Eph. 4:14–15). He wants the bride to be a virgin, 'betrothed to one husband', with eyes for no one else (2 Cor. 11:2). Using imagery from the gymnasium and the athletics track, he wants them to develop strength, build stamina and not be feeble in faith (1 Cor. 9:24–27; Eph. 4:16; 1 Thess. 3:2, 13; 2 Thess. 2:17; 3:3). Using agricultural imagery, he wants to see roots go down deep and fruit develop (1 Cor. 3:5–9; 2 Cor. 9:10; Gal. 5:22; Phil. 1:11; Col. 1:10; 2:7). Using educational imagery, he wants them to 'learn Christ' (Eph. 4:20 NRSV). And even from the marketplace, though the analogy is disguised in our English translations, he wants our transaction with God to be sure, one on which we shall not go back. The word 'strengthened' in Colossians 2:7 means exactly that in the commercial world.[11]

---

9. Gaventa, *Our Mother*, p. 37.

10. The word 'strengthening' in 2 Cor. 12:19 in TNIV is the word *oikodomeō*, usually translated 'build up'.

11. The word *bebaioumenoi*, translated 'strengthened' in Col. 2:6, was used legally of a guarantee. when a seller 'confirmed a purchase to the buyer in the face of claims

Whatever metaphor Paul is using, the sense of making progress towards a goal, or of travelling towards a destination, is very apparent. It is clear that none of his converts has yet arrived and, indeed, they will not do so until God completes his work in them on the day Christ returns (Phil. 1:6). Paul, then, gives no comfort to those who feel that making a 'decision' for Christ is all that matters. Nor does he admit any room for complacency or stagnation in the Christian life. Having begun the Christian life, there is strenuous work to be done so that everyone may be presented 'fully mature in Christ' (Col. 1:28–29) and the pastor has a vital role to play in achieving that goal.

Eschatological horizon

Paul is always looking forward. His approach to ministry is strongly shaped by his belief in the future. Using the metaphors of first fruits, pregnancy or of a deposit, Paul makes it clear that what is experienced now is only the initial instalment of what is to come. Consequently, he never takes his eye off the distant horizon of the end time. So much so that James Thompson can rightly claim, 'The eschatological horizon is *a central feature* of Paul's pastoral ambition.'[12]

This driving force of his pastoral ambition worked itself out in at least two respects. First, it was a constant reminder to Paul himself that he was responsible to God. While Romans 14:12 states that 'we will *all* give an account of ourselves to God', and 2 Corinthians 5: 10 reminds us that 'we must *all* appear before the judgment seat of Christ', there is an impression left that the sense of accountability was felt more urgently by Paul than by most. He was not a free agent, peddling a message he had invented, but a man with a commission who would be called upon to account for the way he had discharged it. While this freed him from kowtowing to the whims and worldly ambitions of those in the churches (1 Cor. 4:4; 2 Cor. 1:12; 4:2; 5:11–15), in other respects it constrained and compelled him (2 Cor. 1 – 4) to make decisions and undertake actions required by the gospel he believed and preached (1 Cor. 9:23). He was driven (and Paul almost certainly was a driven, type-A personality) by the fear that having preached to others he might himself be 'disqualified for the prize' (1 Cor. 9:27). In order to ensure that this did not happen, Paul disciplined himself and used every ounce of his energy to work for Christ and serve the interests of those in the church (Col. 1:29).

---

of a third party' (H. Schlier, '*bebaios*', *TDNT*, vol. 1, p. 602). For God's side of the guarantee, see 2 Cor. 1:21–22.

12. J. W. Thompson, *Pastoral Ministry*, p. 22; italics mine.

Secondly, and more positively, it gave Paul a tremendous sense of joy as he looked forward to seeing the outcome of his labours on that day. The wrestling with people, the praying for their development, the striving with their dullness of spirit and the handling of complex, even disappointing, situations would be passed and he would be able to take a rightful pride in the things he had accomplished in the name of Christ. Unlike many of us, Paul is not embarrassed to speak of the boasting he will enjoy when he sees those he has won to Christ and those he has seen mature in Christ enter into their full salvation. He will be able, on that day, to 'show off'[13] converted Gentiles (Rom. 15:16–17), troublesome Corinthians (2 Cor. 1:12–14) and eager Thessalonians (1 Thess. 2:19–20). The Philippians, whom Paul describes as 'my joy and crown' (Phil. 4:1) and the Galatian Christians will be there to prove he has not 'run in vain' (Gal. 2:2; 4:11; cf. Phil. 2:16; 1 Cor. 9:24–27). At last he will be able to enter into his reward and be presented with his crown (1 Cor. 9:25; 2 Tim. 4:8). Such an incentive keeps him going through the exceptional demands and discouragements he faces in ministry. It is the eye on the winning tape in the far horizon that often enables pastors to persevere when they are tempted to give up.

We also need to place Paul's motivation here on a wider canvas. The 'eschatological horizon' is corporate and cosmic, not simply personal. Paul is engaged in God's work of re-creation, and especially of the re-creation of humanity – a work that might be said to have begun with the calling of Abraham and, through him, Israel as the chosen people of God. Paul is a harbinger of the new age that has begun even though it is yet to be fully brought into being. The work he is doing is part of the unveiling of God's great plan for creation. It is a plan that has a vital role within it for the church (Rom. 8:18–21). So we might say, as James Thompson does, that 'in his statements about his own ministry, he [Paul] indicates that his pastoral ambition is to work with God toward the completion of God's work'.[14]

Neither the corporate dimension nor the eschatological horizon that determines Paul's pastoral approach can be said to be uppermost in the thinking of

---

13. I. Howard Marshall explains, 'it may be taken for granted that Paul is not looking forward here to any sort of proud display of his apostolic achievements before the Lord Jesus, but is rather thinking of the joyful exultation which he will be able to feel when the work which God has done through him (1 Cor. 5:10) is recognised' (*1 and 2 Thessalonians*, NCB [Grand Rapids: Eerdmans; London: Marshall, Morgan & Scott, 1983], p. 87).

14. J. W. Thompson, *Pastoral Ministry*, p. 59.

too many pastors today. The driving ambition of some and the besetting temptation of many is to keep individuals happy and maintain their ongoing commitment to the church's programme rather than directing the church corporately towards the goal of maturity and readiness for the day of Christ. Returning to Paul's priorities would mean not only rediscovering God's priorities for those in leadership in the church, but would also free us from the tyranny of having constantly to please members in an attempt to win their loyalty.

Paul as church planter and founding father: distinctive themes

Several issues are considered here, all of which relate to each other and impact each other. The primary framework that provides us with an understanding of Paul's role and the application of his pastoral leadership is that of a family, in which he serves as the father. This is consistent with the teaching and practice of Jesus, as seen in the Gospels, and argued by Elliot.[15]

'I became your father through the gospel' (1 Cor. 4:15)
Jesus instructed his disciples not to call anyone on earth 'father', 'for you have one Father, and he is in heaven' (Matt. 23:9). Paul frequently refers to God as Father in his writings, but on two occasions he refers to himself as being the father of churches he has planted. He is unique among the New Testament writers in referring to himself in this way. In 1 Corinthians 4:14, he makes a direct claim to a special relationship with the church because he is their founding father in contrast to his position with others, to whom they were listening, who were merely their 'guardians'. In the second case, 1 Thessalonians 2:11, he uses it as a simile, saying that he dealt with them 'as a father deals with his own children'.

In the light of Jesus' express command not to do so, how can Paul use such language? First, he can legitimately do so because the context is different. Paul is writing to churches in Gentile territory and using a natural reference to the role of fathers in the Roman world in the act of procreation and the subsequent care of their offspring. It fits with the social structure of the day where

---

15. John H. Elliott, 'Jesus Was Not an Egalitarian: A Critique of an Anachronistic and Idealist Theory', *BTB* 32 (2002), pp. 75–91, and 'The Jesus Movement Was Not Egalitarian but Family-Oriented', *BibInt* 11 (2003). Pp. 187–193, relate specifically to Paul.

the household was the basic unit of society and where the father had a key role to play.[16] The point is underlined by the fact that Paul refers to himself not only as a father but also speaks of being their *mother*, which we shall return to later. Paul uses parental language in the normal rather than in an especially religious way.

This is very different from the way in which Jesus was using the word in the Jewish religious context of Matthew. Paul is in no way putting himself in the place of *Abba* Father and is not even essentially using it as a status term. It is used to capture his part in the generative process that has led to their formation and to the implications that would have been understood to have followed.

Secondly, we should note that Paul carefully qualifies the statement. He became their father 'through the gospel' (1 Cor. 4:15). His commitment is always to the gospel and not to himself. 1 Thessalonians 2 equally sets the simile in the context of Paul's service to the gospel (esp. vv. 3–7) and removes it from the context of self-seeking.

If Paul is their father, then they are his children and he treats them as such. They are not his slaves but members of his family, and his role is to provide for, protect and guide them. It is true that the *paterfamilias*, the father of the family, was in a powerful position in the family and exercised authority even over grown-up children. Recent research into the role of the father has, however, revised the earlier authoritarian image of the role and presented a much softer image.[17] The father's full authority, which gave him the right to impose severe punishments, was rarely exercised and most would never have experienced it. Although the father might exercise his preference in decision-making, most would have operated on the basis of consensus. There was a real bond of affection and genuine love between fathers and sons, even if law protected the honour of the father. The picture of the relationship between them has sometimes been clouded by the picture of the relationship between the *paterfamilias* and his slaves. Again, the quality of the relationship could be very good but in this relationship the slave owner was in a real position of power, reinforced by the exercise of punishment when deemed necessary. Paul draws out this very difference strongly in Galatians 3:26 – 4:7, where he urges the Galatians to have full confidence in their being sons of God and no longer slaves.

---

16. See Best, *Paul and his Converts*, p. 29; and Wayne Meeks, *The First Urban Christians: The Social World of the Apostle Paul* (New Haven: Yale University Press, 1983), p. 76.

17. Andrew D. Clarke, *Serve the Community of the Church: Christians as Leaders and Ministers* (Grand Rapids: Eerdmans, 2000), pp. 86–95.

The outworking of this is seen in the way Paul actually relates to the churches he has planted: his fatherly instincts for them is all too transparent. There is clearly a strong emotional bond between them (2 Cor. 12:14–15; Phil. 1:3–8; 1 Thess. 2:17–20) and one that, when disturbed, caused deep hurt (2 Cor. 7:2–16). Paul is willing to spend himself for his infant churches and give himself freely for their well-being in Christ (1 Cor. 4:12; 9:1–18; 1 Thess. 2:9). He mostly does not accept their financial support and is prepared to work day and night to give his services to them for free.[18] He did this through using his skills as a leather worker, which not only provided him with financial support but an excellent platform from which to share the gospel.[19] He makes clear that his refusal to accept financial support is not a precedent for others who, indeed, should be rewarded for their work (1 Cor. 9:7–10). Like any good father, he provides for them, not them for him (2 Cor. 12:14–15).

Paul seeks to relate to his 'children' as a good parent relates to their grown-up, as distinct from infant, children. In other words, he treats them as adults, or expresses the wish that they be adults and behave as such.[20] So although there are occasions when he can issue sharp commands and places where he uses sarcasm to make his point, for the most part he seeks to reason with them. He often reminds them of things they already know (1 Cor. 3:16; 5:6; 6:2, 3, 15, 16, 19; 9:13; 12:2; 15:58; 16:15; 1 Thess. 1:5; 2:1, 2, 5, 11; 3:3; and esp. 4:2; 5:2)[21] and, affirming their knowledge rather than repudiating it, his strategy is to build on it and guide them further so that they reach a better conclusion than the one with which they started. 1 Corinthians 11:2–3 provides a very explicit example of this ('I praise you for remembering me in

---

18. This became one of the sources of conflict between Paul and the Corinthians (2 Cor. 11:7–11), who wanted to become Paul's patron so they could exercise 'ownership' over him. His more trusting relationship with Philippi enabled him to receive a gift from them (Phil. 4:10–19). See Victor Furnish, *II Corinthians*, AB (New York: Doubleday, 1984), pp. 507–508; and Murray J. Harris, *The Second Epistle of the Corinthians*, NIGTC (Grand Rapids: Eerdmans; Milton Keynes: Paternoster, 2005), pp. 756–757.

19. R. F. Hock, *The Social Context of Paul's Ministry: Tentmaking and Apostleship* (Philadelphia: Fortress, 1980), pp. 37–42.

20. MacDonald, *Pauline Churches*, p. 53.

21. There are other occasions where he challenges their knowledge (e.g. 1 Cor. 7:16), and plenty more where, by using the expression 'we know', he alludes to shared knowledge (e.g. 1 Cor. 8:4).

everything . . . But I want you to realise . . .'). But 1 Corinthians as a whole provides many examples of this approach, covering topics like marriage and singleness, food sacrificed to idols, behaviour at the Lord's Supper, the covering of the head in prayer, spiritual gifts or the resurrection. He gives them space to come to their own decisions and does not exempt them from taking the responsibility in doing so, as his handling of the case of incest (1 Cor. 5:1–5), his encouragement to them to think for themselves (1 Cor. 10:5) or his refusal to assert his authority beyond the revelation he has received (1 Cor. 7:12) shows. The gospel is about freedom, and pastor Paul is not going to rob them of it (Gal. 5:1).

As mentioned above, Paul balances the fatherly image by reference to maternal imagery. Twice Paul alludes to his role in the spiritual nursery. He tells the Corinthians he has fed them 'with milk, not solid food' (1 Cor. 3:2), and to the Thessalonians he writes not only about acting as their father but also about caring for them gently, as a nurse (1 Thess. 2:7). The word 'nurse', *trophos*, almost certainly means 'nursing mother' as opposed to the professional nurse found in a modern maternity unit. Hence Paul is saying that he is not only a father but also a mother. In Malherbe's view,[22] the phrase 'gentle as a nurse' relates to a wider discussion in the ancient world about the style adopted by wandering philosophers in propagating their views, some of whom advocated harshness, boldness and outspokenness and ridiculed gentleness as weakness. Paul seems to be picking up on that debate, given the language he uses in the surrounding verses, and saying that as a Christian pastor he comes down on the side of the mothers!

'The authority the Lord gave us' (2 Cor. 10:8)

Recent years have seen a debate about Paul's use of authority rage. Paul clearly understood himself as having apostolic and fatherly authority in the church (2 Cor. 10:9; 13:10), but he very rarely calls attention to it as a finger-wagging exercise.[23] 1 Corinthians 4:14–21 and 2 Corinthians 13:1–4 are exceptions. Rather,

---

22. Abraham J. Malherbe, '"Gentle as a Nurse": The Cynic Background to 1 Thess ii', *NovT* 12 (1970), pp. 205–210; and Derek Tidball, *Builders and Fools: Leadership the Bible Way* (Leicester: IVP, 1999), pp. 87–96. For a critique, see Gaventa, *Our Mother*, pp. 29–39.

23. Copan concludes, 'the authoritative dimension of the father role is . . . downplayed and the nurturing, caring aspects are accentuated' (V. A. Copan, *St Paul as Spiritual Director: An Analysis of Imitation of Paul and its Implications and Applications to the Practice of Spiritual Direction* [Milton Keynes: Paternoster, 2007], p. 222).

seeing himself as a father, it is an authority directed to building the church up, not keeping its members in their place.[24] The exercise of authority by a good father is always aimed at helping children reach, at the appropriate time, their full potential as adults and not at reinforcing his own position of power. Some, me included, accepting the integrity of Paul's writing and the genuineness of his strategy as set out in the paragraph above, see Paul's use of authority as restrained, consistent with this goal, and only called strongly into play when necessary for the preservation of essential gospel truths.[25]

Others, however, read Paul's letters more suspiciously and detect within them techniques of manipulation which lead them to conclude that whatever Paul says, he is actually controlling, a unilateral authoritarian and even abusive. His emphasis on his unimportance and weakness (1 Cor. 3:5 – 4:13) is not to be taken seriously, and his apparent empowering of the church to take decisions is really just pretence. The criticisms have particularly, but not exclusively, emanated from feminist theologians and been greatly influenced by some philosophic writings on power that tend to view all power as negative.[26]

All leadership does involve the exercise of power, but, as Andrew Clarke has recently discussed, power is a complex set of transactions and too often Paul's critics have approached the question in simplistic and black-and-white terms. If put in the context of the family, then, Clarke concedes that 'well-meaning parents do, on occasion, entirely misjudge a situation and apply disproportionate control that is immediately or later regretted'. And there may be 'evidence of momentary regret on the part of Paul' that is consistent with that.[27] But Clarke's careful review both of the text and the literature does not support those who regard Paul as an authoritarian. He concludes that 'for Paul, while leadership entails the exercising of power, the task of leadership is not about power'.[28]

'Therefore I urge you to imitate me' (1 Cor. 4:16)

Many contemporary leaders, as well as scholars, feel themselves very ill at ease with the invitation Paul issues more than once for his converts to imitate him.

---

24. Ernest Best, 'Paul's Apostolic Authority', *JSNT* 27 (1986), pp. 3–25.

25. See my *Skilful Shepherds: Explorations in Pastoral Theology*, 2nd ed. (Leicester: Apollos, 1997), pp. 114–118.

26. For a recent introduction to the literature, too full to detail here, and an excellent discussion of the topic, see Clarke, *Pauline Theology*, pp. 104–130.

27. Ibid., p. 116.

28. Ibid., p. 130.

The discomfort arises for some because of a feeling that Paul is setting himself up in an unwarranted way as a model and betraying some lack of humility in doing so. Others, like E. A. Castelli,[29] argue this is clear evidence of an abuse of Paul's power and he is seeking to impose an illegitimate conformity on his churches and being repressive. It is, they think, a power play.

The Corinthians are invited twice to imitate Paul (1 Cor. 4:16; 11:1) and the Philippians once (Phil. 3:17), while the Thessalonians are both commended for imitating him (1 Thess. 1:6) and encouraged to keep doing so (2 Thess. 3:7). Paul is not only interested in encouraging people to imitate him but uses the language of imitation and modelling quite widely in respect of others. In proportion to the length of their writings, other New Testament authors refer to the idea more frequently than Paul, but he is the only one to invite people to imitate him.[30] The frequency of this language should alert us to question further the meaning of Paul's invitation, since it is obviously more than a personal power play.

We note that Paul invites only believers in churches he founded to imitate him. He does not invite those in other churches to do so. This is not only because the former have had the opportunity of observing him,[31] but also because he has a special relationship with them as their founding father. In the social context of the day, it is unlikely Paul would be thought to be imposing himself in any unacceptable fashion on those churches, but rather behaving as any father should. Imitation of respected people (not only fathers but also teachers, rulers and good men) was the way in which character developed and maturity was reached. Their example was viewed in principle as positive and worthy of copying.[32] It was a matter of honour that fathers should act as models to their children and that their children should take pride in imitating them. To fail as a model would have been to fail in his fatherly relationship with these churches.

---

29. The argument is forcefully, but not exclusively, expressed in E. A. Castelli, *Imitating Paul: A Discourse of Power* (Louisville: Westminster John Knox, 1991). See critique in Copan, *St Paul*, pp. 181–218; and Clarke, *Pauline Theology*, pp. 104–106, 122–123, 174.

30. Clarke, *Pauline Theology*, p. 173.

31. Best, *Paul and his Converts*, p. 68.

32. The best recent discussion of the question of imitation is Copan, *St Paul*. On its place in the classical world, see pp. 40–71, 219–220. See also Best, *Paul and his Converts*, pp. 68, 70, who, like Copan, produces primary evidence from the ancient world about imitation (pp. 60–63).

We should also note more precisely what Paul is inviting his converts to imitate. As W. P. de Boer points out in his study of this motif in Paul, 'he is not seeking a copy of himself which will reproduce him in finest detail'.[33] He never asks his converts to imitate his personality or eccentricities. He is cautious, even in such matters as singleness and manual labour, to advocate his own position as preferable but leaves them as a matter of freedom. There is no insistence on imitation in these areas. Rather, the call to imitation always lies in the context of humility, not insisting on one's right and of self-giving. In 1 Corinthians 4, the invitation comes immediately after Paul has described himself, almost recklessly, as unimportant, and like the 'scum of the earth' (1 Cor. 4:13), while 11:1 concludes a discussion of freedom and individual rights in which believers are urged to take the lower place and consider the interests of others as more important than their own.

The same emphasis occurs in Philippians 3:17, where the lifestyle he wants them to imitate is one where he knows 'the power of his [Christ's] resurrection and participation in his sufferings, becoming like him in death' (Phil. 3:10). His call to imitation is none other than a call to be conformed to Christ's cross.[34]

The example of his hard work, advocated in 2 Thessalonians 3:17, is at heart a question of serving others freely and humbly rather than expecting to be served by them. Although he only once explicitly says so, each of these calls to imitation is limited in reality by the qualifying phrase 'Follow my example, *as I follow the example of Christ*' (1 Cor. 11:1; my italics).

For Paul, imitating Christ is what drives his ministry. The events that lie at the heart of the gospel he proclaims are not events he merely reports but events he embodies as they become the pattern for his own ministry.[35] His proclamation of the gospel is not completed once he has spoken the words, but takes place through his life and actions. As Christ emptied himself, became a servant and submitted to the cross before experiencing resurrection, so does Paul, for the sake of others. His self-giving, weakness, suffering, discomfort, brushes with death and sheer weariness result in life, both for himself but, even more importantly, for others. The theme runs like a thread throughout his writings (e.g. 1 Cor. 3:5–9; 2 Cor. 12:1–10; 13:4; Gal. 2:20; 6:14; Phil. 3:10;

---

33. W. P. de Boer, *The Imitation of Paul: An Exegetical Study* (Kampen: Kok, 1962), p. 207.

34. Copan, *St Paul*, p. 222.

35. Morna Hooker, 'A Partner in the Gospel: Paul's Understanding of his Ministry', in E. H. Lovering, Jr., and J. L. Sumney (eds.), *Theology and Ethics in Paul and His Interpreters* (Nashville: Abingdon, 1996), pp. 83–100, esp. p. 92.

Col. 1:24–28; 1 Thess. 2:1–12; 2 Tim. 1:11–12), but is most explicitly encapsulated by Paul in his discussion of ministry in 2 Corinthians 4:10–12:

> We always carry around in our body the death of Jesus, so that the life of Jesus may also be revealed in our body. For we who are alive are always being given over to death for Jesus' sake, so that his life may also be revealed in our mortal body. So then, death is at work in us, but life is at work in you.

Here, Paul is not claiming something unique to him as a servant of the gospel; it is applicable to all men and women who believe and grasp the gospel.[36] Nonetheless, it is particularly relevant to one who is called to proclaim the gospel and form new Christian communities.

The social context of our day is very different and imitation is not prized as much as individuality. Yet children still do naturally imitate their parents, consciously or not, whether they admit it or not, as all parents know when they hear their pet phrases thrown back at them and see their attitudes and actions reproduced by their offspring! Other non-beneficial models abound, particularly in a celebrity-driven culture. In such a culture, pastors can and should still serve as models and strive, if not always successfully, to 'set an example for believers in speech, in conduct, in love, in faith and in purity' (1 Tim. 4:12). They have special responsibilities to serve as a model for those they bring to Christ and churches they plant. Their modelling, however, is restricted. It gives no liberty to pastors to insist that they are models in everything, or in respect of secondary and personality issues where Christians rightly differ from one another, but only in so far as they model self-giving and carrying the cross of Christ.

'And what is Paul? Only a servant' (1 Cor. 3:5)

One final aspect of Paul's role as a founding father is to look at the question of the status he enjoyed. Equivalent leaders in the wider community or other voluntary associations would have enjoyed prestige in their positions. And there is undoubtedly, as we have seen, an understanding of elementary hierarchy in Paul's modelling of leadership. Not only is he the father of the family, and so has some status, but in using the image of the body for the church he explains that while everyone in the church is significant and their worth is not to be judged by their prominence or appearance, nonetheless God has given '*first* of all apostles, *second* prophets, *third* teachers, *then* miracles, *then* gifts of

---

36. Hooker, 'A Partner', p. 100.

healing, of helping, of guidance, and of different kinds of tongues' (1 Cor. 12:27; my italics). Galatians 2:6–10 shows respect for the 'pillars' of the church at Jerusalem. Given this, it is inappropriate to call the early church an egalitarian community in any simplistic way, and therefore the question of the kind of status leaders could expect becomes relevant.

Paul's teaching on the status of leaders runs counter to that found in the wider world, which 'had an exceptionally developed pattern of social hierarchy where high status was clearly recognised and publicly honoured'.[37] Paul protests, even if some of it is ironic, that he is of no importance (1 Cor. 3:2–15), a fool for Christ (1 Cor. 4:9–10; 2 Cor. 10 – 12) and 'the garbage of the world' (1 Cor. 4:13). He regards himself as a servant, even a slave, rather than a leader who has servants. The use of the servant imagery is more complex than is often imagined. Some servants had honourable positions and exercised great influence. And Paul is clearly not only a servant: he adopts different roles when the occasion demands. Even so, this might be said to be the constant subtext of his understanding of Christian leadership. For him, being a servant leader is not a convenient technique for getting his way but is required by the gospel itself. After all, he represents one who became nothing, and 'took on the nature of a servant' (Phil. 2:1–11), and therefore must model that same humility in the style he adopts as a leader.

Clarke points out Paul shuns words that begin with *arch* (from *archon*, 'leader') and 'distances himself from any who would call themselves his followers or disciples'.[38] In preferring the language of servant, he is being totally counter-cultural.[39] He also rejoices in the prefix *syn* (together, with) and frequently mentions people as fellow workers, fellow servants and fellow soldiers. Again, this needs to be nuanced, as it does not imply equality (Paul sends his colleagues on errands!) so much as cooperation in a joint enterprise and goal.[40]

The picture, then, is somewhat more complicated than often presented.[41] As a founding father Paul does have a position, authority and status. To

---

37. Clarke, *Serve the Community*, p. 249.

38. Ibid., pp. 249–250. See 1 Cor. 1:10–17.

39. On the nuancing required in using 'servant leadership', see Clarke, *Pauline Theology*, pp. 95–102.

40. Ibid., pp. 94–95.

41. Strom is, I think, a little incautious in saying, 'Paul avoided the vocabulary of leadership . . .', even though he is right to add, 'preferring to use metaphors of service and care from work and the household' (*Reframing Paul*, p. 180). Paul uses a range of leadership concepts, but these are all transformed by the gospel.

describe his approach to leadership solely in terms of being a servant is inadequate. Nonetheless, it is abundantly clear that Paul never has any desire to shelter behind his status, boost it or abuse it. His leadership style goes against the grain of his world, and ours, in working cooperatively with others, in a Christian family where they serve each other mutually. Paul summarized this at a difficult time in his relationship with the Corinthians in these words: 'Not that we lord it over your faith, but we work with you for your joy . . .' (2 Cor. 1:24; cf. Matt. 20:25; Mark 10:42; Luke 22:25; 1 Pet. 5:3).

Community formation

Recent sociological studies have examined how the early Christian communities were formed.[42] The churches came into being by the work of the Spirit, through the preaching of the apostle, and seem to have been reasonably spontaneous formations. They were, however, not fluid conglomerations of people who touched each other's lives briefly and then went their own ways, as if participating in a fast-flowing eddy of water. They formed communities that met and functioned together, standing for something and living in a particular way. So, without detracting from the movement of the Holy Spirit, it is also true that the churches Paul founded were human communities that necessarily ran along certain sociological lines. Communities do not just happen; they are formed. Communities are not just groups of people who know each other well and have close face-to-face relationships;[43] they are more than that. And Paul, consciously or otherwise, demonstrates the way in which this formation takes place in the early church in such a way as to enable them to grow, survive in a world of competing options and become stable.

---

42. The two most fertile studies relating to Paul are MacDonald, *Pauline Churches*, and Meeks, *First Urban Christians*. A related seminal study on Luke's Theology is found in Philip F. Esler, *Community and Gospel in Luke-Acts: The Social and Political Motivations of Lucan Theology*, SNTSMS 57 (Cambridge: Cambridge University Press, 1987). See also Eckhard J. Schnabel, *Early Christian Mission. Vol. 2: Paul and the Early Church* (Downers Grove: IVP; Leicester: Apollos, 2004), pp. 1370–1373.

43. Some pastors and churches have recently sought to overcome the institutionalization of the church and to restore the personal face-to-face relationships of the church by rejecting rituals, anniversaries, rules and boundaries. But this leads to sociological formlessness rather than community.

Several elements, all of which are to be found in Paul's leadership of the infant churches, can be detected in the formation of communities.[44] Clear definition of their identity is essential and this usually entails them being plainly set apart from other groups, especially those that are similar but not identical. Positive identity is gained from an outlining of the group's beliefs and of its lifestyle. These are reinforced by the adoption of customs and certain rituals. Boundaries are drawn that, while permeable so that others may join, are firm. Initiation or entry rituals, like baptism, play a significant role in marking people crossing the boundaries, while meetings for worship, teaching and communion (from a sociological perspective) reinforce group belonging and identity. Without such rituals the community dissolves into a collection of mere individuals or nothingness. Some governance structures, at least of an elementary kind, also have to be in place. The evidence is that people will join and remain committed where there is some cost to pay for doing so, rather that when a group is so open that it lacks definition and permits anyone to drift in.

A group's identity is also formed negatively as 'outsiders' who do not belong are identified, heresy is defined, problems and puzzles explained, and by the exercise of discipline and even the expulsion of the disruptive or wayward. Negative experiences such as conflict and opposition may also help to form and maintain a group, since it helps to define a group clearly over against others.

It takes little imagination to see the apostle Paul addressing all these issues in his letters, especially his early correspondence to Corinth, Thessalonica and Galatia. Sometimes he does this explicitly, such as when he is teaching on matters of correct belief (e.g. 1 Cor. 15; Gal. 1 – 3; or 1 Thess. 4:13–18) or correct behaviour (1 Cor. 6; Gal. 6; 1 Thess. 4:1–12). He explicitly addresses questions of their identity as a community under the cross (1 Cor. 1:26 – 2:16). He calls for the exercise of discipline where behaviour is incompatible with the community's expected practice (1 Cor. 5). He speaks of the rituals of baptism and communion (1 Cor. 1:14–16; 11:17–34). On other occasions, he is implicitly building the community by the use of family language or the mention of 'outsiders' (1 Thess. 4:12; Col. 4:5), and of opposition (Gal. 3:1;

---

44. As well as the literature mentioned in n. 42, most standard literature in the sociology of religion contains details about these matters. Christian Smith's *American Evangelicalism: Embattled and Thriving* (Chicago: University of Chicago Press, 1988) provides a particularly insightful applied discussion of some of it to the contemporary American church.

6:12–13; 1 Thess. 3:1–5). In doing so, he is putting in place the foundations that will enable the churches he has founded to become strong.

Other leaders: a briefer comment

It would be wrong to give the impression that Paul was a solitary figure as a leader in the churches he founded. Reference has already been made to other members of his team whom he acknowledges in his writings: 'our brother Sosthenes' (1 Cor. 1:1); Barnabas (1 Cor. 9:6; Gal. 2:1, 9, 13); Aquila and Priscilla (1 Cor. 16:19); 'Timothy our brother' (2 Cor. 1:1; Phil. 1:1); Titus (Gal. 2:1–3); Epaphroditus, 'my brother, co-worker and fellow-soldier' (Phil. 2:25); and Silas (1 Thess. 1:1; 2 Thess. 1:1). These exercised some form of leadership within the churches, but usually of a secondary or delegated kind. There is no indication that they acted alone.

There are, however, local leaders into whose hands Paul commits the leadership of the churches once his mission has taken him away. Acts 14:23, as previously mentioned, reports Paul and Barnabas appointing elders in the churches on their first missionary journey. We know nothing of the method of their appointment, nor is any description of their responsibilities given. Similarly, in Philippians 1:1 a greeting is sent to 'overseers and deacons' as well as to the whole church, which, apart from marking them out as a distinguishable group within the church, tells us nothing. More revealing is the comment about Stephanas in 1 Corinthians 16:15–18. The implication is that he was the relatively wealthy *paterfamilias* of a household where a Christian group met. It would be natural because of his social standing for him to act as patron of the group. It was the way things were done. Being patron would not only mean providing a setting for them to meet, and hospitality for travelling preachers, but it would probably have involved a teaching function as well.[45] So it is unsurprising that Paul encourages the believers to 'submit to such as these' (1 Cor. 16:16).[46] In passing, we should note that Paul's exhortation does not apply to

---

45. For a full discussion, see R. W. Gehring, *House Church and Mission: The Importance of Household Structures in Early Christianity* (Peabody: Hendrickson, 2004), pp. 196–210, 266.

46. Note a similar comment about the undefined leaders in Thessalonica (1 Thess. 5:12). See Gehring, *House Church*, p. 200, who lists ten different functions one commentator identified, which those who cared for the church undertook. But these are assumptions.

Stephanas alone. He is but one example of good leadership that deserved respect. We know nothing of Fortunatus and Aristarchus, but they could be among the 'such as these' of which Paul writes.[47]

What is more important, however, and what we are likely to miss, is the amazing transformation that has taken place in the role Stephanas plays as a patron.[48] Patrons were usually served by clients: it was the responsibility of others to serve them. But here Stephanas and his household are commended for having 'devoted themselves to the service of the Lord's people' (1 Cor. 16:15). They have undergone a role reversal. Here, and elsewhere, Paul rejects the normal understanding of patronage, the understanding many in Corinth still hold (1 Cor. 1:10–17). So Paul works with the normal social structures and does not overthrow them (Stephanas cannot deny his wealth or status) but transforms them. Hence the role becomes not about privilege but about service, not about receiving but about giving, not about leadership so much as about ministry.

Truth to tell, it is impossible to say much with any certainty about local leadership in these early Pauline churches because so little is said in Paul's letters. What is said, however, suggests that there was not much interest in developing hierarchies of leadership, that leaders were not accorded any exalted status, least of all as a separate class of Christians, even though submission to them was encouraged, and it is clear that 'formal positions within the communities are nowhere in mind'.[49]

Conclusion

In discussing Paul's ministry among the churches he founded, one model of pastoral leadership has come to the fore: that of the *founding father*. Paul's special relationship with these churches means his relationship with them is

---

47. For a discussion on the names of people Paul mentions in his correspondence, see Meeks, *First Urban Christians*, pp. 55–63. Fortunatus and Aristarchus are sometimes considered to be freedmen or slaves, but Winter thinks they, as well as Stephanas, 'possessed social status', even if they were not householders (Bruce W. Winter, *After Paul Left Corinth: The Influence of Secular Ethics and Social Change* [Grand Rapids: Eerdmans, 2001], p. 197).

48. See Winter, *After Paul*, pp. 184–205, where he discusses not only Stephanas but Phoebe as well (Rom. 16:1).

49. Robert Banks, *Paul's Idea of Community* (Exeter: Paternoster, 1980), p. 150.

different in some respects than it is with other churches. He acts very much as the father of their family and so exercises some authority over them and serves as an example to be imitated by them, as well as fulfilling his responsibilities to provide for them and educate, direct and guide them. This fatherly role explains some of the aspects of pastoral leadership that appear to us to be in tension with each other. The relationship is mutual but not equal. The relationship is warm but firm. The relationship is affectionate but occasionally tense. The relationship is marked by humility and yet demands respect, even obedience. The relationship concerns the present but equally has an eye on preparing for the future. From their viewpoint, as any parent knows, the parental role is that of a servant: cooking meals, cleaning rooms, driving the taxi and opening up the wallet! From the child's viewpoint it looks very different. Where it goes wrong is when the chores are done and the service is rendered without love. But no one could ever doubt the bond of affection Paul felt for his converts, a bond that arose because they had all experienced the love of Christ and were partners in grace (Phil. 1:7).

7. PAUL: MINISTRY IN A MATURING CHURCH

The ministry of an apostolic teacher

Although the apostle Paul never calls himself a 'pastor', he is not shy of refer-ring to himself as a 'teacher'. He views himself in this light in every phase of his ministry (e.g. 1 Cor. 4:6; Col. 1:28; 1 Tim. 6:1). Shortly after his conversion to Christ we read of Paul, in company with Barnabas, teaching 'great numbers of people' in Antioch (Acts 11:26), and he continued to teach throughout his life (Acts 20:20). He claims the title of teacher for himself most boldly in the pastoral letters, for understandable reasons, since it is there he instructs the next generation of leaders about handling false teaching.[1] In 1 Timothy 2:7, linking his appointment as the teacher with that of the herald and apostle, he claims to be 'a true and faithful teacher of the Gentiles'. In 2 Timothy 1:11, he makes the same threefold claim to be a herald, an apostle and a teacher but adds no further description to the titles. Add to these self-references Paul's acknowledgment of the gift of the teacher (Rom. 12:7; 1 Cor. 12:28–29; Eph. 4:11) and his injunctions to others to teach (1 Tim. 4:11, 13; 6:2; 2 Tim. 2:2; 4:2; Titus 1:11; 2:1, 2, 3, 7, 9, 15) and we must agree with Andrew Clarke that 'for Paul, teaching is of supreme importance and a key function of the leaders in

---

1. A. D. Clarke, *A Pauline Theology of Church Leadership*, LNTS 362 (London: T. & T. Clark, 2007), p. 152, n. 105, lists 1 Cor. 4:17; 14:6; Col. 1:28; 2 Thess. 2:15; 1 Tim. 2:7; 2 Tim. 1:11; 2:2.

the church'.[2] Or, to use the words of a popular preacher of an earlier generation, 'The Christian pastoral ministry in the Apostle's view is distinctly educational in its design.'[3]

Paul's appointment as apostle and teacher

It might be expected that Paul would exercise a teaching role in the churches he founded or among the younger men he mentored, but significantly he equally exercised a teaching role among churches he had not yet visited, namely Colosse and Rome. Moreover, if we assume, as most do,[4] that Ephesians is really a circular letter rather than addressed solely to the church he had founded in that city, we gain a picture of the widespread ministry he exercised as a teacher in the Gentile churches. The reason why Paul felt no hesitation in instructing churches he had not visited in these places was because he was called to be an apostle to the Gentiles (Rom. 11:13), and his teaching role was inextricably bound up with his role as an apostle. It was not only his pleasure and right to address them but his duty to do so.

Most of his letters begin with a reference to his being an apostle, which of course puts down a gentle marker about his authority and is intended to give his readers a reason why his teaching should be heeded.[5] His earlier letters to the Thessalonians, his happy, mainly pastoral, letter to the Philippians, and the personal note to Philemon are exceptions to this, for in those letters he does not refer to himself as an apostle. He stresses that he has become an apostle through the commissioning of Jesus Christ (Gal. 1:1). It was 'through him we received grace and apostleship to call all the Gentiles to faith and obedience for his name's sake' (Rom. 1:5). In situations where his apostleship is challenged, he reminds them in the body of the letter of his credentials (as in 1 Cor. 4:9; 9:1, 2; 15:9; 2 Cor. 10:1 – 12:28; Gal. 2:8).

---

2. Ibid., p. 152.

3. Alexander Maclaren, cited by W. E. Chadwick, *The Pastoral Teaching of St Paul: His Ministerial Ideals* (Edinburgh: T. & T. Clark, 1907), p. 321.

4. The chief reasons for this relate to the absence in some manuscripts of Ephesus as a destination and its less personal tone. The reference in Col. 4:16 may also have a bearing on the matter. See Peter T. O'Brien, *The Letter to the Ephesians*, PNTC (Grand Rapids: Eerdmans; Leicester: Apollos, 1999), pp. 84–86.

5. He mentions in 1 Thess. 2:6 he was an apostle, not to stress his rights or authority but rather the reverse.

The origin of the concept of apostle, in its more restricted sense,[6] has been much disputed. Some have tried to link it to the Jewish idea of šalîaḥ, where a representative was sent by someone, carrying that person's full authority, to fulfil a commission. Whether the link explains the origins or not,[7] it is evident that Paul saw himself as an ambassador of Christ (2 Cor. 5:20; Eph. 6:20) and having his authority to announce and explain the gospel, thus exercising both an evangelistic ministry in the world and a teaching ministry in the church. It was a commission he had received on the Damascus road (e.g. 1 Cor. 9:1; 15:8–10).[8]

Despite all that Paul has said sincerely about his insignificance (1 Cor. 3 – 4),[9] he also sees the apostles as people of importance. In Ephesians 2:20, he asserts that the apostles, with the prophets, are the foundation of the church. This is a step forward in Paul's thinking. In 1 Corinthians 3:11, he lays the original foundation: Christ himself. But in Ephesians, he, along with the other apostles and the prophets, are also described as the church's foundation.[10] It is not that they have displaced Christ, who is now spoken of as the cornerstone or capstone of the church, rather than its foundation. It is just that the image serves more than one purpose in Paul's writing. They are foundational because they are the essential link to the original events at the heart of their faith, witnesses to the life, teaching, death and resurrection of Jesus, and entrusted by him to be the guardians of the normative tradition. They are not, therefore, dispensable but are crucial to the upbuilding and stability of the church.

We have seen that Paul in 1 Timothy 2:7 and 2 Timothy 1:11 connects being an apostle to being a teacher. In explaining the connection, Philip Towner has written that 'the term "teacher" fills out the job description of the "apostle"'.[11] Acts 2:42 makes a similar link in referring to 'the apostles' teaching'. The original Twelve had spent much time with Jesus, more than, and much more intimately than, that of the crowds who followed him, listening to his teaching, making sense of his ministry and receiving his instructions. Paul was not party

---

6. Paul uses the term to describe the Twelve and himself, but also in a more general sense of those engaged in mission (e.g. Rom. 16:7).

7. See the summary discussion in P. W. Barnett, 'Apostle', *DPL*, pp. 45–46.

8. See Antony Bash, *Ambassadors for Christ: An Explanation of Ambassadorial Language in the New Testament* (Leiden: Mohr, 1997).

9. See discussion in chapter 6.

10. Andrew Lincoln, *Ephesians*, WBC 42 (Dallas: Word, 1990), pp. 152–154.

11. Philip H. Towner, *The Letters to Timothy and Titus*, NICNT (Grand Rapids: Eerdmans, 2006), p. 188.

to that original teaching but probably underwent his own personal training in the Arabian desert (Gal. 1:17), thus qualifying him to be an authoritative teacher in the early church.

In this way, it was the apostles, including Paul, who were called and qualified to determine what was legitimate to believe and to distinguish that from the false ideas that would inevitably swirl around a newborn church. Equally, they were concerned to spell out what the correct lifestyle was for disciples of Christ and to correct unacceptable patterns of behaviour. Like it or not, this would necessitate the drawing of boundaries and the question of how to discipline those who did not conform to the acceptable standards of belief and practice.

Paul as teacher in Romans, Ephesians and Colossians

Since these letters are free from the intense personal emotions and sometimes tempestuous relationships that characterize the letters to the churches he founded, Paul can write about his apostleship in a more 'dispassionate way'. In these letters he has no need to defend it. We find, therefore, perhaps 'a more normal and more "balanced" expression of his apostolic consciousness', as Colin Kruse has put it.[12] It is not the intention here to outline Paul's teaching in these letters, so much as look at that consciousness and see what Paul sees himself as doing in the role of the teacher.

Some have questioned the extent to which we can take Paul's letters as representative of his teaching, since they are a different medium of communication. But Paul's letters have the characteristic of being oral communications, written down probably by an amanuensis. They are, in Nai Ming Tsang's words, 'part of an ongoing conversation with his audience' and therefore 'the best available records that allow us to catch good glimpses of his oral teaching with his audience'.[13] They are a good basis for studying Paul as a teacher.

Paul had no lesser ambition for these churches than for the churches he had founded. His motives were the same. They are summed up in Colossians 1:28:

---

12. Colin G. Kruse, *New Testament Foundations of Ministry* (London: Marshall, Morgan & Scott, 1983), p. 126. Clarke, *Pauline Theology*, pp. 167–168, comments that the 'language of persuasion' is less common in letters to the churches he has not visited.

13. Nai Ming Tsang, 'Paul as Teacher in 1 Thessalonians 1:2–2:12 – from Exegesis and Pedagogy to Dialogue' (PhD diss., Brunel University, 2006), p. 62.

'We proclaim him, admonishing and *teaching* everyone with all wisdom, so that we may present everyone fully mature in Christ' (my italics). His aim was to strengthen believers, provide them with further knowledge about their identity and salvation, give them a great appreciation of and confidence in Christ and his work, encourage their unity as a reflection of the gospel of reconciliation and instruct them in ethical living.[14]

The teacher recalls tradition

For those who think Paul 'invented' the gospel for the Gentiles, it comes as something of a surprise to realize how much Paul speaks of 'tradition'.[15] He speaks of it explicitly and on several occasions in his first letter to the Corinthians. He congratulates them on 'holding to the traditions just as I passed them on to you' (1 Cor. 11:2), and then reminds them of the tradition about the Lord's Supper (1 Cor. 11:23) and the tradition about the matters of 'first importance' that concern Christ's 'death, burial and resurrection' (1 Cor. 15:3). He also encourages the Thessalonians to 'stand firm and hold fast to the traditions [TNIV 'teachings'] we passed on to you' (2 Thess. 2:15; see also Rom. 6:17; 16:17). These traditions include ethical teaching as much as doctrinal beliefs, as we see from 2 Thessalonians 3:6 and, as set out more fully, for example, in Romans 12:1–21; Galatians 5:1 – 6:10; Ephesians 5:21 – 6:9; Colossians 3:1 – 4:6. They also include allusions to the sayings of Jesus, such as those found in Romans 12:14; 13:8–10; 14:14.[16]

Often the language of tradition is somewhat disguised in our English translations. So, for example, when Paul writes to the Colossians about their having 'received Christ Jesus as Lord' (2:6), he is not referring to the individual and existential conversion experience of modern evangelicalism but of their having agreed with and owned the apostolic message that Jesus Christ is Lord. To 'receive' means to accept the tradition and live by it. When in Colossians 1:19, 20 Paul speaks of 'the gospel', he clearly has in mind that 'the gospel embodies a core of fixed tradition committed to the apostles'.[17] This is the

---

14. Adapted from Lincoln, *Ephesians*, p. lxxxi.

15. The word group involved includes *paradosis* (noun, 'tradition'); *paradidōmi* (verb, 'I pass on') and *paralambanō* (verb, 'I receive' [the tradition]).

16. On Paul's use of various traditions, see M. B. Thompson, 'Tradition', *DPL*, p. 944; and on Paul's connecting with the Jesus tradition in 1 Corinthians, see E. Earle Ellis, 'Traditions in 1 Corinthians', *NTS* 32 (1986), pp. 481–502.

17. George Eldon Ladd, 'Revelation and Tradition in Paul', in W. Ward Gasque and Ralph P. Martin (eds.), *Apostolic History and the Gospel* (Exeter: Paternoster, 1970), p. 228.

gospel he passionately champions, even against a fellow apostle when that apostle is going back on it (Gal. 2:11–21).

These traditions are not viewed as restrictive, as matters of dispute, or targets to tilt against. Rather, they are foundational. These traditions soon stood for what was authoritative in Christian teaching as it was transmitted to others.[18] Tradition went hand in hand with revelation and was not in conflict with it. Though Paul claims to have received his gospel through a revelation from God (Gal. 1:11–12, 15–17; 2:2), the gospel he has received in this manner is the same one the earlier apostles believed and taught.[19] Tradition also went hand in hand with the dynamic work of the Holy Spirit. The message of the gospel is tied to the historic events of Christ's life, death and resurrection (the tradition element) but it is also a living word communicated through preaching and made alive and real to people and cultures through human preachers to whom the gospel has been committed (the Spirit dimension). George Eldon Ladd points out that, on the one hand, the tradition is fixed and unalterable, while, on the other hand, 'the Spirit can add to [but not change] tradition by granting through the apostles and prophets an unfolding and outworking of the redemptive work of Christ'.[20] In saying this, Ladd has in mind the unfolding of the 'mystery' of the gospel, to which we shall turn in the next section. The tradition, then, is a living tradition, where the teachings and the Spirit work together in perfect harmony. It is not a mere parroting of facts but a lively communication of those facts and their implications for the hearers. There is, in Ladd's words, a 'kerygmatic-pneumatic character to the tradition'.[21]

Originally, the handing down of the tradition would have been through oral communication, and the responsibility of teachers in this phase was to expound the sayings passed around. But increasingly, the traditions were written down, and Paul's letters are a crucial factor in this. The responsibility of teachers today is to be expositors of the apostolic teaching as recorded in the New Testament, faithfully applying it to the contemporary world and making it live for people, transforming them through the anointing of the Holy Spirit.

---

18. Antony C. Thiselton, *The First Epistle to the Corinthians*, NIGTC (Grand Rapids: Eerdmans; Carlisle: Paternoster, 2000), p. 810. Thiselton cites Polycarp, Irenaeus, Clement and Origen in support.

19. M. B. Thompson, 'Tradition', p. 944.

20. Ladd, 'Revelation and Tradition', p. 228.

21. Ibid., p. 229.

The teacher unravels mystery

The task of any teacher is to instruct the ignorant, to make clear what is opaque and to enable students to understand plainly what has mystified them to this point. In line with this, the apostolic teacher, Paul, had the responsibility of making known 'the mystery of God' (1 Cor. 2:1 NRSV).[22] The normal religious, intellectual and political leaders of the world were left in the dark. They had no understanding of the way God worked, nor especially of what God had done through Christ crucified. But what they failed to understand had been revealed to the apostles and prophets (Eph. 3:5) and, through them, was made known to the believers 'by his Spirit' (1 Cor. 2:6–16). The mystery, then, was no longer hidden but 'an open secret'.

Ephesians and Colossians are particularly concerned with 'the mystery'. Paul believes himself to have been commissioned both to understand the mystery (Eph. 3:3–4) and to make it known plainly to others (Eph. 3:9; 6:19; Col. 1:25–26; 4:3). His goal in teaching is that his 'students' may know the meaning of the mystery in all its richness (Col. 2:2).

What was the mystery? It was nothing other than the plan God had for the salvation of the world, including the Gentiles, through the action of Christ. No wonder the mystery remained a closed secret and an impenetrable conundrum to many. How could God possibly effect the rescue of the world through a crucified carpenter's son from Nazareth, when all the wise intellects of the world, all the wise politicians, all the military powers and all the other rich resources of the world had failed to do so? No wonder the mystery needed explaining! Jesus was not just a Galilean peasant but also the Christ who embodied all wisdom and knowledge (Col. 2:3). His death on the cross (Col. 1:20) was God's way of reconciling Jew and Gentile (Eph. 2:11–22; Col. 1:21–22). It was his plan that through the Gentiles the salvation of Israel (Rom. 11:25–26) would be brought about and, indeed, that the whole of his fallen creation (Col. 1:20) would be redeemed, renewed and restored. This mystery had already begun to unfold, for, not only were Gentiles being converted, to the consternation of many Jews, but Christ himself had already made himself at home in the lives of those who grasped and believed 'the open secret'. 'Christ in you [was the promise of] the hope of glory' later (Col. 1:27) when the mystery would be finally unveiled to all at the return of Christ (1 Cor. 15:51–52).[23]

---

22. Twenty-one of the twenty-seven NT references to mystery are found in Paul (Peter T. O'Brien, 'Mystery', *DPL*, p. 622).

23. Paul's teaching on mystery is much fuller than represented here. For a good overview, see ibid., pp. 621–623.

The gospel of Christ remains a mystery to a large segment of the world, and it is still the responsibility of teachers to make it known and explain it so that people may grasp its meaning and believe it. Paul kept the mystery of the gospel central to his teaching and so should we. Sadly, some people are known as brilliant expounders of mysteries in the Bible, but fail to teach that which is essential. Tantalizing trivia are set out before a congregation, while the gospel itself is sidelined. This is what Spurgeon called 'holy trifling', which he said reminded him of 'a lion engaged in mouse-hunting'.[24] If, by following Paul's example, we keep 'the boundless riches of Christ' (Eph. 3:8) as the focus of our teaching, we are unlikely ever to be short of a relevant message.

The teacher enhances understanding

Paul's teaching aims to help people understand the gospel and its implications more clearly and deeply than they obviously do. The questions they have raised or the reports he has received suggest they have not quite understood it as they should. So he engages in a sustained exposition of the gospel, relating it to their circumstances and needs. Paul never really does anything more than unfold the gospel itself. It is not that there is a basic gospel and then deeper teaching that is something different. Indeed, Acts 13:12 speaks of Paul's evangelistic witness to the proconsul of Cyprus as 'teaching'. It is not a question of there being a stage 1 and a stage 2 to his teaching – everything goes back to the basic gospel that needs to be expounded and understood more thoroughly. 'The gospel . . . speaks as much to believers as to unbelievers; they continually need to be reminded of it as Kate Hankey's hymn "Tell me the old old story . . ." drives home.'[25] As I have written elsewhere, 'Pastoral work is simply bringing to full flower the bud of the gospel.'[26]

The letters to the Romans, Ephesians and Colossians are classic examples of this. There is no agreement on what motivated Paul to write to the Romans

---

24. C. H. Spurgeon, *Lectures to My Students*, First Series (London: Passmore & Alabaster, 1900), p. 79.

25. Ernest Best, *Essays on Ephesians* (Edinburgh: T. & T. Clark, 1997), p. 165. Similarly, James W. Thompson, *Pastoral Ministry according to Paul: A Biblical Vision* (Grand Rapids: Baker Academic, 2006), in his discussion of Romans as pastoral theology states that we 'learn from Paul, transformation occurs where the community is constantly reminded of the story that called it into existence' (p. 117).

26. D. Tidball, *Skilful Shepherds: Explorations in Pastoral Theology*, 2nd ed. (Leicester: Apollos, 1997), p. 100.

as he did, other than to share with them his travel plans (15:23–33).[27] It is likely that Paul had several reasons for writing what is a masterly exposition of the heart of the gospel. He clearly had some knowledge of the situation in Rome, perhaps through his friendship with Priscilla and Aquila (16:3), even if the letter is less personal than many. Reading between the lines, as well as reading what is on the lines, makes it probable that his letter was intended to address divisions in the Roman church between Jewish and Gentile believers. Much of the theological argument, with its emphasis on faith in Jesus Christ as the means of being justified, and the only requirement for satisfying and receiving the righteousness of God, can readily be seen to relate to that issue. Similarly, the more applied section in 14:1 – 15:13 deals with the issue of division in the church. But, as many have observed, the tensions in Rome were by no means unique to them. Douglas Moo resists the temptation to think that 'the specific problem in Rome gave Paul a good excuse to write about this widespread tension', but that is perhaps not far off the mark.[28] Paul's approach here is classic. He does not focus too much on the church's needs and certainly draws back from dealing with the tensions at a pragmatic level. Rather, he takes them back to the gospel, gets them to look more thoroughly at its basis and shows them how it is inconsistent for them to do anything other than 'accept one another, then, just as Christ accepted' them (15:7).

The Christians at Colosse were in danger of falling into syncretism. They saw Christ as one of the answers to their problems, but sought to gain salvation and spiritual assurance through a portfolio of religious options.[29] They still clung to the practices of the Jewish synagogue but, most likely, also adopted the ceremonies found in the mystery religions and picked up elements of folk religion as well. This resulted in the Jesus in whom they believed being a very different person from the one proclaimed in the Christian gospel. So Paul takes them back to look afresh at Jesus and what Christians believe about his pre-eminent place in creation and the new creation coming to birth (1:15–20). All else flows from Paul's assertion of the supremacy of Christ. They need have no fear of 'powers and authorites', for he has 'disarmed' them and held them up to ridicule on his cross (2:15; see also 1:16; 2:10). There is no point in adopting ascetic religious rituals or seeking ecstatic spiritual experiences (2:16–23), since Christ is the only reality on whom to depend (2:17).

---

27. See D. J. Moo, *The Epistle to the Romans*, NICNT (Grand Rapids: Eerdmans, 1996), pp. 16–22.

28. Ibid., p. 20.

29. Clinton E. Arnold, *The Colossian Syncretism* (Tübingen: Mohr, 1995).

They have failed to grasp that this Christ is one with whom they have been united. They have died with him, risen with him and now have the victory over opposing forces, since Christ is seated at the right hand of God (3:2). This has direct implications for their personal character (3:5–10), social relationships (3:11 – 4:1) and Christian witness in the world (4:2–6). Everything they need to face the challenges of living in their little town of Colosse is to be found in the gospel.

As for Ephesians, 'Having addressed a specific problem in Colossians,' Peter O'Brien writes, 'Paul has remodelled his letter for a more general Christian readership.'[30] It does not seem that Ephesians is written to address any specific false teaching. Like the Colossians, however, the letter's readers seem to live in fear of cosmic power and evil spirits. In the past, their magical practices were bent on appeasing these powers (Acts 19:17–20).[31] Now Paul writes to further their understanding of Christ as a cosmic and exalted Saviour through whom God is 'to bring unity (*anakephalaiōsasthai*) to all things in heaven and on earth under Christ' (1:10 my tr.). The word *anakephalaiōmai* is usually used to mean 'to sum things up', and the idea here is that Christ will bring everything together and, hence, restore harmony in the universe. This means that the forces that resist his plan, that make for disintegration, disharmony and destruction, need to be overcome. Those forces include 'the rebellion of the powers' and 'the alienation of Jews from Gentiles' and the separation of both from God.[32] The particular slant Paul gives to the gospel in Ephesians addresses these issues, with the focus in 1:15 – 2:1 being on the powers, and the focus shifting seamlessly in 2:3 – 4:13 to the alienation of people from each other and from God. Once that groundwork is laid, Paul explores from 4:1 onwards the implications of this gospel for their behaviour. It is appropriate that he should address the issue of spiritual warfare as the climax of his letter (6:10–18). Given their fear of malevolent powers, this is a related topic and teaching that enables them to appropriate the victory of Christ for themselves.

Each of these letters demonstrates Paul in his role as an apostle teaching the churches that fall within his sphere of influence as Gentile churches, even though, as we can be certain in the case of Romans and Colossians, he is not personally known to them. His method is to start with Christ and his gospel

---

30. O'Brien, *Ephesians*, p. 57.
31. Clinton E. Arnold, *Ephesians: Power and Magic, the Concept of Power in Ephesians in the Light of its Historical Setting*, SNTSMS 63 (Cambridge: Cambridge University Press, 1989).
32. O'Brien, *Ephesians*, p. 113.

and unfold their meaning in a way applicable to each church's situation. He never strays from the gospel. He has no need to introduce new or different teaching, for the inexhaustible riches of this multifaceted gospel are always sufficient to meet the church's needs.

Although the analogy he uses needs to be used with care, Mark Strom summarizes this well:

> Paul was first of all preoccupied with a person, Jesus Christ. The story of Jesus formed Paul's message or 'gospel' of good news. Paul's preoccupation with Christ and his story gave coherence to all his letters and enabled him to translate his message for each new audience and circumstance. In many ways, . . . Paul was like a jazz musician improvising on a theme. The theme was Christ and his story; the improvisations were the various ways in which he brought his knowledge of Christ to bear upon the changing circumstances of his own life and the lives of those in the fledgling *ekklēsiai*.[33]

The teacher applies truth

Paul's letters are rich in theology, but they are always *pastoral* theology. The most obvious example of this is the way in which he applies his theological teaching practically in the second half of his letters. This used to be presented almost as if there were two letters largely unrelated to each other but stitched together uneasily in the middle – the first, theology, and the second, practice. But the theology was practical and the practice was theological. The truth is that they were more seamless than this suggests. So the discussion of disunity in the church in Romans 14:1 – 15:13 grows directly out of the teaching in the earlier chapters about the level-playing field of grace on which we all stand. The use of 'therefore' in Colossians 3:5 and Ephesians 4:1[34] shows that in Paul's mind he is not changing the subject but drawing out the implications of what he has just written. In Colossians, we can live a holy life, letting the peace of God rule, because we have died with Christ and live in the light of his victory and exaltation. In Ephesians, we live in unity in the church and purity in the world, fighting the spiritual battle, because Christ died to make us one, rose to shed his light in the dark world and is exalted, victorious over his enemies.

In this respect, Paul is a master teacher. He never fails to make the connections between belief, values and behaviour. He does not assume that Christians

---

33. Mark Strom, *Reframing Paul, Conversations in Grace and Community* (Downers Grove: IVP, 2000), p. 72.

34. The Greek text uses the same word, *oun*, in both cases, even though TNIV translates one as 'therefore' and the other as 'then'.

will be able to work things out for themselves. It is his task to point things out. Nor does he make the mistake of laying moral burdens on people by issuing pragmatic edicts devoid of adequate reasoning. The basis for his moral exhortations and ethical teaching is found in his gospel. The balanced relationship between theological depth and practical application is one for which all those who teach the apostle's doctrine should strive.

The teacher offers worship

The apostolic teacher does not see the teaching task as one of detached professionalism but as an act of worship. There is only one occasion when the New Testament speaks of ministry in priestly terms, and it is a guarded reference. In Romans 15:15–16, Paul writes of 'the grace God gave me to be a minister of Christ Jesus to the Gentiles', which he then explains by writing, 'He gave me the priestly duty of proclaiming the gospel of God, so that the Gentiles might become an offering acceptable to God, sanctified by the Holy Spirit'. Nowhere else does the New Testament remotely speak of Christian leaders or ministers as 'priests'. There is only one priest: Christ himself.[35]

There is some dispute over what Paul means in describing himself as 'a minister'. The word *leitourgos* is used to refer to priests but, following Barth, some believe the service Paul offers to God is more likely akin to that of the Levites (those who assisted the priests) than of the priests themselves.[36] But even if Paul does mean 'priest', he clearly uses the word metaphorically, for, as Hodge comments, he clearly does not mean that he is literally sacrificing the Gentiles to God.[37] He immediately goes on to explain the meaning of this priesthood. It is in serving Christ by his preaching and teaching, not by the literal offering of ritual sacrifices, that Paul fulfils his 'priestly duty'. This makes, as Cranfield remarks, Paul's service subordinate to Christ's priestly service.[38] In this way, and because of the work of the Holy Spirit, the Gentiles are given the opportunity to respond to the gospel and become God's people. So the sacrifice that pleases God is the ingathering of the Gentiles into the church.

---

35. See further the discussion on the priesthood of all believers in chapter 11, pp. 190–192.

36. C. E. B. Cranfield, *The Epistle to the Romans*, ICC 2 (Edinburgh: T. & T. Clark, 1979), p. 755, adopts this view. For the contrary position, see James D. G. Dunn, *Romans 9–16*, WBC 38b (Dallas: Word, 1988), pp. 259–260; and Moo, *Romans*, p. 889, n. 30.

37. Cited by Moo, *Romans*, p. 890, n. 38.

38. Cranfield, *Romans*, vol. 2, p. 756.

Any notion of priesthood Paul entertains, therefore, relates very closely to his preaching of the gospel and his role as apostle and teacher. It is neither as liturgist nor as mediator that Paul uses the term. But his service is just as real an act of worship, just as set on pleasing God, just as concerned about offering an acceptable sacrifice as the most elaborate rite that any religion could perform. In the daily routine of exercising ministry, Christian leaders are conducting worship and this should inspire all their service for Christ. It is unnecessary to oppose the offering of worship with professionalism, for the quality of worship should always reach a high standard, worthy of God. Even so, the greater need today is to conceive of ministry through the lens of spiritual worship rather than through the lens of cool professionalism so common in our modern world.

Paul's educational method

Several problems face us if we begin to discuss Paul's educational methods and attempt any adequate discussion of the subject. First, there is the complexity of education in Paul's world and the uncertainty as to how much he bought into Jewish educational methods or used the contemporary rhetorical approaches of the philosophers of his day, and if so, which ones. Then there is the complexity of contemporary education and the competing theories and frameworks by which we understand it today. It is a recent field of research and one where much work has to be done.[39] In the light of that, I venture only a few comments.

True education is about more than the impartation of knowledge. It is recognized today that several dimensions compose a rounded education, including a *cognitive* dimension, which is to do with what we know; an *affective* dimension, which is to do with attitudes, will and values; and a *behaviour* dimension, which is to do with our actions. Each of these dimensions is evident in Paul's teaching.[40] Much of his writing, as we have seen, is devoted to explaining the content of the gospel, that his readers might grasp more fully the significance of the events and nature of the truths that lie at the heart of their faith. But he equally addresses the affective dimension when he encourages certain attitudes and values. Galatians 3:28, 'there is neither Jew nor Gentile, neither slave nor free, neither male nor female, for you are all one in Christ

---

39. See discussion in Tsang, 'Paul as Teacher', pp. 5–24.

40. Ibid., pp. 19, 92. Tsang is drawing on Kent Johnson, *Paul the Teacher* (Minneapolis: Augsburg, 1986).

Jesus', states one of the most important values to arise from the gospel. He seeks constantly to impart the deeper values of honour, freedom, purity and integrity. And throughout his letters Paul is seen to be encouraging the early Christians to love one another, forgive one another, be patient with one another agree with one another, put the other's interest first and so on.

The affective dimension is seen in another way in Paul's letters, in terms of emotions. His teaching regularly drives him to express praise. It is never about cold abstractions. His educational method is doxological. Illustrations of this are found in Romans 11:33–36; 15:13; 16:25–27; Ephesians 3:20–21; and Colossians 1:15–20. Then he addresses specific behaviour patterns, most notably, but not exclusively, in the household codes of Ephesians 5:21 – 6:9 and Colossians 3:18 – 4:1.

The context in which Paul teaches is an encouraging one and he is always concerned, with one exception, to ensure a warm and positive relationship between himself and those he is teaching. The exception, of course, is in his letter to the Galatians, where the situation is so catastrophic and their stance so destructive to the cause of the gospel that shock tactics are called for. So although he wishes them his conventional greetings of 'Grace and peace' (1:3), he does so only after being fairly heavy-handed about his apostleship (1:1), and then immediately launches into them with 'I am astonished . . .' (1:6). However, this is entirely atypical.

Paul's affection for the churches he founds is very evident, but the same is true of the churches to whom he writes where he is unknown, even if the intensity of feeling is not as marked. He always shows great sensitivity to their situation. To the Romans, in some respects the most measured of his letters, he writes, 'I long to see you that I may impart to you some spiritual gift to make you strong' (Rom. 1:11). His conclusion to the letter in chapters 15 and 16 is similarly personally warm. His prayer for the Ephesians (1:15–22) and the Colossians (1:9–14) is equally full of love and his longing that they may know the fullness of God's grace and power. All this suggests that Paul knew the best framework for teaching was a positive and relational,[41] not a formal or institutional, one.

Paul's style of teaching is to engage in dialogue. He strives constantly to engage his students rather that to talk at them. His letters are full of dialogue of different kinds.[42] There is the dialogue when Paul asks them to recall what

---

41. Tsang, 'Paul as Teacher', p. 135.

42. In searching for a model to characterize Paul's theology, James D. G. Dunn concludes that the model of dialogue is the best fit (*The Theology of Paul the Apostle* [Grand Rapids: Eerdmans; Edinburgh: T. & T. Clark, 1998], pp. 713–716).

they already know, as in 1 Corinthians 2:3, 3, 9, 15, 16, 19 and 9:24, or 1 Thessalonians 2:9. Then he includes dialogue with imaginary debates that raise the questions his readers may well have in their minds, as in Romans 9:19 or 11:19. Then he constantly appears to be thinking aloud, as if engaged in an ongoing conversation with his students, 'What shall we say . . . ?', which occurs in one form or another seven times in Romans.[43] Throughout, his desire is not to rob his readers of their freedom but rather to try to get them to think for themselves (Rom. 2:3; 1 Cor. 1:26; 10:12; Phil. 4:8). According to Tsang,[44] Paul's dialogical approach is best considered to be of an instructional kind as opposed to a dialogue where he is merely making an inquiry, conducting an open conversation or engaging in debate. In this form of dialogue, the teacher does have a particular end in view but probes the students, supplying them with sufficient information for them to reach the right conclusion for themselves. Paul may not always use this method – he is capable of giving firm instructions that are not to be questioned. But much of the time he enables his readers to work things through for themselves, which usually produces a deeper understanding and a firmer ownership of the answer than might otherwise be the case.

Paul was unavoidably a child of his day and to some extent his teaching benefited from the training in rhetoric commonly available.[45] The shape of his letters and the nature of his arguments demonstrate this. Yet in 1 Corinthians 1:18 – 2:16 he takes a strong stand against such rhetoric.[46] Why? The reason is that the philosophic rhetoric of his day was based on entirely the wrong premise – that human wisdom and strength would save the world. Greek philosophical schools encouraged teachers to make a public display of oratory

---

43. Throughout Romans, Paul uses inclusive language: 'What shall *we say* . . . ?' In 1 Cor. 11:22, where he admonishes the Corinthians, he writes, 'What shall I say to you?'

44. Tsang, 'Paul as Teacher', pp. 221–226.

45. Duane Litfin, *St Paul's Theology of Proclamation: 1 Corinthians 1–4 and Greco-Roman Rhetoric*, SNTSMS 79 (Cambridge: Cambridge University Press, 1994). See also the discussion in Clarke, *Pauline Theology*, pp. 159–172.

46. Eckhard J. Schnabel, *Early Christian Mission*. Vol. 2: *Paul and the Early Church* (Downers Grove: IVP; Leicester: Apollos, 2004), p. 1359, writes in a somewhat understated way, 'Paul dissociates himself from certain methods of public speech. It is obvious and unsurprising that he, a Hellenistic Jew, is knowledgeable of rhetorical methods. A passage such as 2 Cor 11:4 demonstrates that Paul certainly was aware of the problematic nature and appropriateness of rhetorical methods for the proclamation of the gospel.'

and draw attention to themselves. The messengers and their oral communication skills were considered a crucial factor in the success or otherwise of their persuasion. It is this aspect of the teaching methods of his day that Paul is so fundamentally against, for it draws attention away from Christ and God's counter-cultural way of working through the folly and weakness of the cross. Paul seeks not to manipulate people into belief with clever oratorical tricks but to set 'forth the truth plainly' (2 Cor. 4:2) and wait for God to open people's eye to that truth (2 Cor. 4:3–5). Here is a teacher aware not only of the responsibility that lies on his shoulders, but also that he does not shoulder it alone.

Other teachers

As an apostle, Paul had a special teaching function. But the gift of the teacher did not die out with the apostles, nor was it ever exclusively confined to them. We are aware of teams of people who assisted Paul in his missionary endeavours[47] and, although no one else is specifically called a teacher, it is obvious that others exercised the gift of teaching (Acts 11:16; 13:1). Romans 12:7, 1 Corinthians 12:28–29 and 14:26 mention them and Galatians 6:6 acknowledges them as a distinct group worthy of financial support.

In writing to the Ephesians, however, Paul states that among the key gifts the ascended Christ has given for the ongoing life, growth and health of the church is that of the teacher (4:11). The words 'pastor' and 'teacher' here are linked by a single definite article and therefore some have concluded they are one. That may be claiming a little too much and it may be that 'two groups are envisaged', but that there is no 'rigid separation between them', as Ernest Best concludes.[48] They do seem closely linked and have functions that relate to each other. O'Brien resolves the question by saying that, in practice, all pastors are teachers, 'since teaching is an essential part of pastoral ministry but not all teachers are also pastors'.[49] This may be so, but I know of pastors who seem to lack a teaching gift and I get anxious about teachers who are not closely related to people's lives. It is best to hold on to the view that Paul evidently does think that these gifts are closely related without attempting to be too precise or strict in our interpretation of that relationship.

Andrew Lincoln sums up the task of the teacher as 'preserving, transmitting,

---

47. An exhaustive list is given in ibid., pp. 1426–1427.
48. Best, *Essays*, p. 168; *Ephesians*, ICC (Edinburgh: T. & T. Clark, 1998), pp. 392–393.
49. O'Brien, *Ephesians*, p. 300.

expounding, interpreting, and applying the apostolic gospel and tradition along with the Jewish Scripture'.[50] But whether these teachers held office or not is probably the wrong question to be asking of Scripture. They are clearly distinguished from other believers by virtue of the gifts they exercise, but there is no sense here that they hold an office or are set apart as 'clergy' distinct from the 'laity'.[51] Neither the pastor nor the teacher is described as a 'leader'; they are not given 'authority over' the church, nor are we told that they are to preside over its services.[52] In line with Paul's teaching about the body in 1 Corinthians 12 – 14, they simply contribute their gift, as do others, for the benefit of the church as a whole, but by the nature of their gift, they exercise a more significant influence over the churches' beliefs and behaviour than other members of the body.[53]

Two passages in Paul's letters appear to rule out women from being teachers in the church. They are 1 Corinthians 14:34–35 and 1 Timothy 2:11–15. Unfortunately, both passages are problematic. The first, which is wider than the question of teaching, instructs women to keep silent in the church and to ask questions of their husbands at home. The difficulty with the passage is that 1 Corinthians 11 clearly envisages women participating vocally in worship and the chapters on spiritual gifts do not ban women from exercising gifts like prophecy and tongues in the congregation. 1 Timothy 2:11–15 is explicit about

---

50. Lincoln, *Ephesians*, p. 251.

51. Best, *Essays*, p. 172, thinks 'Ephesians may be said to have hastened the division between clergy and laity, begun the sacralization of the ministry and at the same time to have supported the idea that ministry of a non-spontaneous nature was necessary for the good estate of the church.' See also, p. 176.

52. Best, *Ephesians*, p. 391.

53. Strom's statements about leadership, in *Reframing Paul*, pp. 178–181, are basically in the right direction but somewhat clumsily stated. While I agree that Paul does not allow any room for 'individual superiority' and 'there were no cultic acts to be performed by any consecrated or appointed person. There was no ordination. There was no room for personal power or office,' it is untrue that there is no notion of leadership. To claim this neglects the role of the apostles, and of people like Timothy and Titus. Paul does speak about leadership in a variety of ways and leadership is seen to function. The question is not whether there was leadership but what kind of leadership, and there Paul fights to maintain the character of Christian leadership as profoundly counter-cultural. See Andrew D. Clarke, *Serve the Community of the Church: Christians as Leaders and Ministers* (Grand Rapids: Eerdmans, 2000), part 2.

a woman not being permitted 'to teach or assume authority over a man' but rather to learn in quiet. The injunction is backed up by a reference to Adam and Eve and by what must surely qualify as one of the most obscure statements in Paul's writings, that 'women will be saved through child-bearing'. The unusual vocabulary Paul uses in these verses also raises questions about how widespread a command this is.

The interpretations of these passages are endless and it is impossible to resolve the problems in a few sentences here, even if I were capable of doing so.[54] Suffice it to say, several factors encourage me to think that these verses do not represent a fixed, transcultural position in which the church is forbidden for all time to recognize appropriately qualified women teachers. There is clearly a trajectory in the New Testament that provides more and more liberty and opportunity for women in the church.[55] We know that in practice women did take leadership roles in the early church that would have involved a teaching element. Some would argue that the logical outworking of Galatians 3:28 is that women should be able to function as teachers.[56] Paul's main concern seems to have been to address particular situations where problems were arising (especially the false teaching circulating in Ephesus) and also to have an eye, as the surrounding contexts suggest, to what public decorum would have found acceptable as far as women's participation was concerned. In addition to all this, the verses may well be legitimately interpreted in such a way that they do not imply a blanket ban on women as teachers. Therefore, in our own very different day, I believe Scripture would not only permit but even encourage us to appoint qualified and gifted women to teaching positions within the church.

Today, many good teachers hold offices because they are recognized by denominations, but others emerge and are recognized more informally, yet exercise an equally valuable gift of instructing others. The important thing is that whenever the gift of teaching is sidelined, whenever the apostolic tradition is considered unessential, and wherever the mystery of the gospel and its

---

54. On the various interpretations, see the standard commentaries, esp. Thiselton, *Corinthians*, pp. 1146–1161; I. Howard Marshall, *The Pastoral Epistles*, ICC (Edinburgh: T. & T. Clark, 1999), pp. 452–471; and Towner, *Timothy and Titus*, pp. 212–224.

55. William J. Webb, *Slaves, Women and Homosexuals: Exploring the Hermeneutics of Cultural Analysis* (Downers Grove: IVP, 2001).

56. E.g. F. F. Bruce, *Commentary on Galatians*, NIGTC (Exeter: Paternoster, 1982), pp. 189–190.

implications are considered secondary to a contemporary agenda, the church is in danger and its health threatened.

Conclusion

Paul's calling as 'an apostle to the Gentiles' means not only that he teaches the gospel to audiences who have never heard it, and plants churches in virgin territory, but that he has an ongoing responsibility to teach the gospel. His responsibility extends beyond the churches with whom he is personally involved and embraces other churches in the Gentile regions. His teaching consists of instructing believers in apostolic doctrine consistent with that taught by the Twelve and, indeed, with the teaching and traditions about Jesus. In his letters, he is seen to 'reframe'[57] the gospel of Jesus to fit the everyday experience of those he addresses. The gospel itself is more than adequate to serve as his syllabus. He has no need to look elsewhere for additional teaching to supplement it. Even if he incorporates some of the general moral teaching of his age, as in the household codes, it is all transformed by the gospel. This gospel speaks about the core of their faith; the meaning of their salvation; their identity in Christ; the values, virtues and attitudes they should cultivate; and provides them instructions regarding the ethical decisions they must reach. The cognitive, affective and behavioural dimensions are all to be found within it.

Paul is not the only teacher. Others exist and one of the gifts of ministry the ascended Lord bestows on his church is the gift of teaching, closely partnered by that of pastoring. The wise teaching of apostolic doctrine remains a vital need in the church today. Its absence spells decline and death, while its presence signals health and growth. It may not be the only secret to churches maintaining their health in the inhospitable environment of a pluralist world. But it is an indispensable one.

---

57. Strom, *Reframing Paul.*

8. PAUL: MINISTRY IN AN AGING CHURCH

The ministry of the elder statesman

Desmond Tutu chairs an international group called 'The Elders'. Composed of ex-presidents, their wives and prime ministers (like Nelson Mandela, Graça Machel, Jimmy Carter and Kofi Annan), they devote themselves to using their experience to resolve world conflicts. Since they are not running for office, they have no vested interests and can speak freely to a hurting world. The world can trust them. Thank God for those who bring the wisdom of the elders to bear on current problems. And thank God for Paul, who played just that role in his final letters to Timothy and Titus.[1]

The pastoral letters are crucial for any study of ministry because they 'reflect an interest in church organization that is unparalleled in the rest of the NT'.[2] But there is much more to them than the questions of church order. In fact, these questions occupy only a sixth of the letters and there is much discussion of doctrine and the ethical practice that grows out of it besides

---

1. The view that Paul did not write these letters is widely accepted in contemporary scholarship. But they form part of the Pauline corpus and make immense sense as his autobiographical final letters.
2. Philip H. Towner, *The Goal of our Instruction: The Structure of Theology and Ethics in the Pastoral Epistles*, JSNTSup 34 (Sheffield: Sheffield Academic Press, 1989), p. 223.

questions of internal organization.[3] Apart from anything else, from a ministry viewpoint, much is to be gained by looking at the relationship between Paul and those to whom he writes.

The role of Paul

Paul himself

A sense of retrospective broods over these letters. In Titus, Paul continues to anticipate an effective ministry ahead but, rather than pressing forward, as he might previously have done, he has decided to winter in Nicopolis (3:12). Even though when he writes 1 Timothy, Paul still hopes to visit Timothy in Ephesus (3:14; 4:13), it is clear he writes as if such a visit will not actually take place. He gives advice therefore about 'how people ought to conduct themselves in God's household' (3:15) and is clearly preparing Timothy for the leadership of the church (6:20). In 2 Timothy we have a portrait of a confined man, who is probably frail (4:13) and knows that 'the time of [his] departure is near' (4:6). Consequently, he writes in the past tense: 'I have fought the good fight, I have finished the race, I have kept the faith' (4:7).

Paul's experience equips him to give some perspective on the needs of the church during this time of transition. There is still a sense of tremendous confidence in the gospel to which he has devoted his life. There is also a tremendous sense that God, who through Christ destroyed death (2 Tim. 1:10), will be the judge of the living and the dead (2 Tim. 4:1) and will reward his servants at 'his appearing' (2 Tim. 4:8; see also 1 Tim. 6:14). After all, he is 'the blessed and only Ruler, the King of kings and Lord of lords' (1 Tim. 6:15). Paul's vision of 'the blessed hope – the appearing of the glory of our great God and Saviour, Jesus Christ' (Titus 3:12) remains undiminished. On the other hand, there is no sense of any triumphalism or superficial claims about the triumph of the church in the world. Rather, Paul writes with tremendous realism about the setbacks that have taken place and the threats the church faces. Some believers have shipwrecked their faith (1 Tim. 1:19–20); others have proved unreliable, leaving Paul with a sense of isolation (2 Tim. 1:15; 4:10, 16); while Alexander is said to have done him 'a great deal of harm' (2 Tim. 4:14). Paul knows people are abandoning the faith (1 Tim. 4:1; 2 Tim. 3:1–9), and that others are being sucked into facile arguments (1 Tim. 4:7; 6:4–5;

---

3. I. Howard Marshall, *The Pastoral Epistles*, ICC (Edinburgh: T. & T. Clark, 1999), pp. 52, 100.

2 Tim. 2:14–16) and seduced by false teachers (1 Tim. 4:2–5; 6:3–5; 2 Tim. 2:14–19; 4:3–6) and by money (1 Tim. 6:6–10).

It is this blend of unfailing confidence in God and the gospel and of perceptive realism about people and the church that makes Paul the perfect pastor who can assist the next generation of Christian leaders through the period of transition. His seasoned maturity is evident in the way in which he never loses sight of the ideal, but is able to live with what is real, without becoming despondent or cynical.

Paul as mentor

Great leaders do not always serve well those who follow them. They are sometimes so confident in their own abilities and so unaware that they will be on the scene only temporarily that they pay no attention to preparing others to step into their shoes. As the South Indian proverb says, 'Nothing grows under the Banyan tree.'[4] The tree is so great and spreads so widely that nothing has a chance to grow under it. So it is with some leaders, but not with Paul. He obviously delights in working with others.[5]

Among the younger leaders Paul encourages are Timothy and Titus. Paul speaks of Timothy in 1 Timothy 1:1 as 'my true son in the faith' (see also 1:18) and as 'my dear son' in 2 Timothy 1:2. This kinship language is more than formal and 2 Timothy 1:3–5 gives a glimpse of the relationship Paul has, not only with Timothy but with his mother and grandmother as well. The great bond of affection between them is evident. In Paul's eyes, although Timothy may have lacked confidence (2 Tim. 1:7) and suffered some ill-health, perhaps because of stress (1 Tim. 5:23), he has proved himself to be exceptional in the concern he has for others and the lack of interest he has shown in furthering his own 'career' (Phil. 2:19–23). Paul has mentored Timothy, as we would say today, through investing time and friendship in him, by, no doubt, correcting him on occasions and by entrusting him with increasing responsibility. Because Timothy has proved trustworthy, Paul has not only enjoyed him as a travelling companion and fellow letter writer but on more than one occasion as an envoy (1 Cor. 4:16–17; 16:10–11; 2 Cor. 1:1; Phil. 1:1; 2:19–24; Col. 1:1; 1 Thess. 1:1; 3:1–13; 2 Thess. 1:1; Phlm 1). In this way Paul has grown a younger leader for

---

4. Cited by Leighton Ford, *Transforming Leadership* (Downers Grove: IVP, 1991), p. 24.

5. F. F. Bruce writes, 'Dr Samuel Johnson described one of his acquaintances as an "unclubbable man". That is the last adjective that anyone who knew Paul would use of him. He was eminently "clubbable", sociable, gregarious' (*Paul: Apostle of the Free Spirit* [Exeter: Paternoster, 1977], p. 457).

the church and, according to the pastoral letters, Timothy was in Ephesus as 'an apostolic delegate', with the heavy responsibility of sorting out the affairs of the church on behalf of Paul.

Paul's greeting to Titus is similar to that of Timothy, but perhaps the relationship is not as close. Titus (1:4) is also 'my true son' who shares a common faith with Paul. We know less of Titus, except that he was a Gentile (Gal. 2:3) who had been a trusted travelling companion of Paul's since early days (Gal. 2:1). Like Timothy, he had been sent by Paul to serve as his envoy at Corinth (2 Cor. 2:13; 7:6–16; 8:16–24) well before the writing of this letter to him. Again, the ability of Titus to handle the tricky situations he would meet in the Cretan church must have been in no small measure due to Paul's mentoring of him in earlier years.

The pastoral letters contain much good advice to these young leaders about the task they are to perform. Yet there seems an equal, if not greater, concern about their characters and how they are to perform it. Paul not only wishes to be encouraging to Timothy, in view of his likely diffidence and youthfulness (1 Tim. 4:12; 2 Tim. 1:6–8), but is anxious for him to earn credibility because he is seen to be mature in his temperament, diligent in his performance, gentle in his disposition and godly in his character. Much space is devoted to these things (1 Tim. 4:6–16; 6:11–16; 2 Tim. 2:14–26; 3:10 – 4:5). The concern is less apparent in Titus but still present (as in 2:15; 3:9–11), possibly because the letter was shorter or because Titus was older.

Paul, then, had proved himself not only to be a faithful leader but a wise one in looking to the future and fully preparing the next generation of leaders so that they would be ready when he and the other original apostles had left the scene. His concern for them was a rounded one. He was concerned about their achieving the task, but was even more concerned about the kind of people they were. This is wonderfully consistent with what Paul had set out in Acts 20:17–38. It is the approach of a statesman.

Paul and church leaders

Timothy and Titus: Paul's delegates

In addition to looking at the personal relationship between Paul, Timothy and Titus, we must address the question of the role they played in the churches to which he sent them. How would their mission and status be viewed? From reading the letters we can conclude that their task was 'to promote the growth of the churches under [their] charge, by teaching, appointing leaders, safeguarding the gospel, and opposing false teachers'.[6] That puts them in a powerful position as well as imposing heavy burdens on them. So can we be more precise about their role?

Neither Timothy nor Titus was given a title for his role, but they serve as Paul's envoys to the churches of Ephesus and Crete in a manner similar to the way diplomatic envoys functioned in the world of Paul's time.[7] This means there would be a very close identity between them and Paul. The way the church received and responded to them would be the way they would have received Paul and responded to him. To reject them would have been tantamount to rejecting Paul himself. At the same time, they would have been considered to have significant power to speak on Paul's behalf: they represented him in every way. Through them, therefore, in addition to writing letters, Paul was able to extend his apostolic ministry, and even when prevented from going in person to visit the churches, he could still guide and instruct them through his younger co-workers.

To be an envoy of Paul, however, is not the same as being a bishop, at least as that role later developed in the time of Ignatius. There are several reasons for distinguishing them from bishops, as they were subsequently conceived. Paul never calls Timothy and Titus bishops. He uses the term in reference to some local leaders and it would surely have been confusing if he had used the same term for two very different roles within a short compass. Timothy and Titus' duties are temporary and they have no open-ended authority. The whole atmosphere of the pastoral letters, in Kelly's view, is much simpler than the hierarchical atmosphere that developed later.[8] Nothing requires them to be viewed as bishops in order to achieve their mandates.[9]

These leaders, then, are appointed personally by Paul to achieve a particular mission. They do not particularly fit with any grand scheme in which apostles, overseers, deacons, teachers or prophets all know their place, because no such integrated system exists in the New Testament. They are legitimate leaders, however, not simply because they are entrusted with their tasks by an

---

6. Towner, *Goal of our Instruction*, p. 228.

7. Margaret M. Mitchell, 'New Testament Envoys in the Context of the Greco-Roman Diplomatic Epistolary Conventions: The Example of Timothy and Titus', *JBL* 111 (1992), pp. 641–662.

8. J. N. D. Kelly, *A Commentary on the Pastoral Epistles*, BNTC (London: A. & C. Black, 1963), p. 14.

9. Fuller arguments can be found in Donald Guthrie, *The Pastoral Epistles*, TNTC (Leicester: IVP, 1990), pp. 31–33.

apostle but because they function according to the nature of Christian leadership and character, as several passages within the letters make clear. Here is another example of the form of New Testament leadership being shaped by the need of the hour.

Local leaders

What Paul has written in these letters concerning elders and deacons has generated most interest. It is here that Paul may be seen to be the elder statesman ensuring that good thought has been given to the requirements of the next generation of leaders in the church. He is concerned about the question of succession, but not of apostolic succession in the way in which that has sometimes been interpreted.

People have frequently read him as describing offices that had emerged in the early church once the excitement of a Spirit-led, more spontaneous community, way of living had passed over and more steady institutional structures had emerged. They have also read into what he has written the threefold structure of ministry, namely that of bishops, priest and deacons, which later became established in many of the churches worldwide.[10] First we shall look at what Paul says in these letters and then turn to the question of whether his writing gives signs of the church moving away from a charismatic community to a more formal institution.

Paul assumes that local leadership is in the hands of elders and deacons. According to Acts 14:23 he appointed elders in the churches he founded and the letter to the Philippians is addressed to the overseers and deacons. But neither statement is elaborated and it is not until the pastoral letters that their role is spoken of further. This in itself is remarkable. Clarke points out that 'given that the surrounding society and community contexts laid so much store by the widespread and public use of titles, it is noteworthy that Paul devotes so little space to addressing either the selection or use of titles of office'.[11]

When Paul does address the issue, his main concern is that those who serve in the various leadership capacities should be worthy of doing so. So the indisputable emphasis of 1 Timothy 3:1–13, 5:17–22 and Titus 1:5–9 is on their character and personal suitability to undertake such 'a noble task' (1 Tim. 3:1). A few hints are given about how they function, but any insight into their actual

---

10. See, *Baptism, Eucharist and Ministry*, Faith and Order Paper 111 (Geneva: World Council of Churches, 1982).

11. Andrew D. Clarke, *A Pauline Theology of Church Leadership*, LNTS 362 (London: T. & T. Clark, 2007), p. 47.

role or position is almost incidental. Paul never envisages these people as serving alone. The assumption is of a plural leadership who act collectively, even though the term 'overseer' is used twice in the singular.[12]

Whether he is writing about elders (*presbyteroi*), overseers (*episkopoi*) or deacons (*diakonoi*) (we shall discuss the meaning of these terms below), the thrust of his teaching is the same. There is no higher standard required of one office over another.[13] These are responsible roles within the church and it is important that people who undertake them do not have a character flaw that brings the church's God and gospel into disrepute. The personal requirements revolve around their being mature people, stable and self-controlled, and free from weaknesses in the area of drink, violence, argumentativeness, money and pride. The relational requirements require faithfulness in marriage and good household management, which means not only having good control of their children but also the willingness to provide hospitality to others. The church was still not at this time a large centralized body, meeting in a special building in the town, but was composed of several small house-based churches. It was natural, therefore, that the household image should influence their thinking and it lies behind much of what is said about the leaders. They must also be in good standing with those outside the church.

A few differences in what is said about the elders or overseers and the deacons are significant. Overseers should be 'able to teach' (1 Tim. 3:2). The same point is repeated in Titus 1:9, where it becomes clear that they have responsibility for passing on the apostle's doctrine and safeguarding the tradition of 'sound doctrine'. Apart from the general comment about elders 'who direct the affairs of the church' (1 Tim. 5:17),[14] this is the nearest we get to finding out about their specific duties. If part of the elders'/overseers' responsibility is to teach the faith, then it is safe to presume that they know the faith

---

12. 'Overseer' is plural in Phil. 1:1 but singular in 1 Tim. 3:2 and Titus 1:7. But it is reading too much into this that one overseer was to be appointed over the whole town and its scattered household churches.

13. Marshall, *Pastoral Epistles*, p. 472, comments that 'On the whole, the qualities required are the same for both overseers and deacons and are also such as would be required in any member of the Christian congregation . . . ; there is no "higher standard" for church leaders but it is expected that they will show the qualities that are desirable for all believers.'

14. Paul uses the word *proïstēmi* several times in terms of general leadership or management, and it does not carry the overtones some have imposed on it of 'ruling' in any authoritarian sense. See Rom. 12:8; 1 Thess. 5:12; 1 Tim. 3:4.

well and have made it their own. Little is said of the tasks deacons are to under-take, but it is generally assumed that their role is more to do with practical service and looking after the welfare of people in the congregation. They do not therefore have a teaching function and, perhaps for that reason, the church might slip into appointing caring people to the role who did not share fully in the church's beliefs. Therefore, Paul emphasizes that these people also need to 'keep hold of the deep truths of the faith with a clear conscience' (1 Tim. 3:9).

Unfortunately, the terms Paul uses in 1 Timothy 3 have given rise to a great deal of debate. He speaks of the overseer (*episkopos*) and of elders (*presbyteroi*). The term *epsikopos* occurs three times (Phil. 1:1; 1 Tim. 3:2; Titus 1:7) and the related word *episkopē*, which refers to the task of overseeing, once (1 Tim. 3:1). It also occurs in Acts 20:28 in Paul's speech to the Ephesian elders.[15] The word was widely used in the Greco-Roman world as well as in some of the Jewish literature to denote those who were 'supervisors' in a whole range of com-mercial, military and public situations.[16] From 1 Timothy 3:2 and Titus 2:9 it is evident that, in addition to general oversight, as mentioned above, the over-seers had a specific teaching function.

'The elders' was an equally common term and would have entered the lan-guage of the church quite naturally via its Jewish roots.[17] They equally appear to have a general leadership role within the congregation of caring for its affairs and directing its common life. The word *presbyteroi* is always in the plural in the pastoral letters. This could be because the leader of each separate house-hold would meet with his colleagues from other house churches, forming a college of elders. However, it is much more likely to mean that each house church would have several elders. It would appear from 1 Timothy 5:17 that some, but not all, elders might serve the church in such a way, possibly in a full-time capacity, as to deserve financial support.[18] It also appears, from the same verse, that some of them exercise a teaching ministry. So, evidently, teaching is not just the preserve of those called *episkopoi*.

Until recently, in spite of there being virtually no information about their method of appointment or other relevant issues, elders have been thought to

---

15. 1 Pet. 5:2 also uses 'overseers' (plural).

16. Clarke, *Pauline Theology*, pp. 48–49.

17. It is used frequently in Acts, often of Jewish elders, but of elders in the church in 11:30; 15:2, 4, 6, 22, 23; 16:4; 20:17, 18. Note also Jas 5:14; 1 Pet. 5:1.

18. See discussion in Philip H. Towner, *The Letters to Timothy and Titus*, NICNT (Grand Rapids: Eerdmans, 2006), pp. 363–367.

be occupants of an office.[19] The consensus is now firmly against that. R. Alastair Campbell's work has convincingly shown that it is misleading to think in terms of office when talking of the elders.[20] He points out the term was widely used by Jewish writers but without any pretence of precision. Within the synagogue the term was used of senior persons who exercised leadership, but there was no office as such. It was a term of respect and status more than anything. Though not identical, the same was largely true in the Roman world. Their power lay with wealthy families and their senior members exercised leadership in the city or community. They were people to whom others deferred instinctively. Examining the use of the title in the New Testament, Campbell concludes, '*the elders are those who bear a title of honour, not of office, a title that is imprecise, collective and representative and rooted in the ancient family or household*'.[21]

The question arises as to whether the overseers and elders are two different groups of people or are the same under a different title.[22] In favour of their being the same is the way Paul slips from using one term to another without any obvious distinction in Titus 1:5–7. (The same seamless slippage occurs between Acts 20:17–18 and 29.) Furthermore, it is hard to make any real distinction between the qualifications Paul sets out in 1 Timothy 3:1–7 regarding overseers and those he sets out in Titus 1:5–9 regarding elders. If overseers are expected to be able to teach in 1 Timothy 3:2, so are some elders in 1 Timothy 5:17.

---

19. This approach is still adopted by some on the basis of the word *episkopēs* in 1 Tim. 3:1, which may allude to 'the office of overseer'. George W. Knight III, *The Pastoral Epistles*, NIGTC (Grand Rapids: Eerdmans; Carlisle: Paternoster, 1992), pp. 153–154, 175–177, 213, for example, stresses the 'office' of the overseers and elders and speaks of a 'twofold pattern of official ministry of the church', but in view of recent scholarship I believe this is misleading.

20. Campbell's overall thesis has been well received, but not all its details. In particular, his reconstruction of two patterns of leadership coming together in the post-Pauline pastoral letters is questioned. See R. Alastair Campbell, *The Elders: Seniority within Earliest Christianity* (Edinburgh: T. & T. Clark, 1994), pp. 194–203, 242–243; and for a critique, Clarke, *Pauline Theology*, p. 55; and Marshall, *Pastoral Epistles*, pp. 179–180.

21. R. A. Campbell, *Elders*, p. 246; italics his.

22. To access the debate and vast literature on this subject, see the excellent essay in Marshall, *Pastoral Epistles*, pp. 170–181. See also Clarke: *Pauline Theology*, pp. 46–60; Knight, *Pastoral Epistles*, pp. 175–177; William D. Mounce, *Pastoral Epistles*, WBC 46 (Nashville: Nelson, 2000), pp. 186–192; Towner, *Goal of our Instruction*, pp. 223–228; *Timothy and Titus*, pp. 241–247.

The reasons some argue that they are two separate groups are principally two. First, they point out the difference between *supervisors*, spoken of in the singular, and *elders*, always spoken of in the plural. Luke Johnson says this was typical of 'intentional groups' in the first century. A single supervisor would usually coordinate a wider 'collegial leadership'.[23] Secondly, it is thought to help explain the subsequent development in which the overseers became a singular bishop over multiple clergy in a town.[24] But the former may be purely stylistic[25] or 'a generic reference belonging to a traditional code'.[26]

People have adopted various ways of trying to resolve the relationship between them. The truth is that we simply do not have enough evidence to be certain. The distinctions between them does not seem clear enough to me to claim that they were two different groups. The interchangeability of the terms persuades most scholars that they were essentially one and the same. It may be, as Marshall seems to favour, the term 'overseers' describes their work from a functional viewpoint and the term 'elder' describes it from the standpoint of their status.[27] Or it may be, as Clarke favours, that there is a great deal of overlap between the terms but that they are not synonymous. He believes that the elders functioned together in terms of general leadership but that some of them carried individual and specific leadership and teaching responsibilities and served as overseers.[28] There seems no justification for arguing that these letters envisage a hierarchical structure, where one bishop presides over a town, working with a college of elders who represent the collective leadership of the house churches, who, in turn, are served by a third tier of deacons.

The deacons are in some respects also problematic because so little is said about them. The word group to which the title *diakonos* belongs is used extensively in the New Testament, but the title itself occurs rarely.[29] Unfortunately,

---

23. L. T. Johnson, *The First and Second Letters to Timothy*, AB (New York: Doubleday, 2001), p. 218.

24. The role of Timothy and Titus is often considered significant in the development of monarchical bishops as well. For arguments against this, see W. D. Mounce, *Pastoral Epistles*, pp. 186–192.

25. It is a perfectly natural way of speaking. In this book I have alternated between e.g. 'pastors' and 'the pastor', but the difference is purely stylistic, not substantive.

26. Marshall, *Pastoral Epistles*, p. 178.

27. Ibid., p. 181.

28. Clarke, *Pauline Theology*, p. 58.

29. For an overview of both the word groups and the contemporary discussion, see ibid., pp. 60–71; and Marshall, *Pastoral Epistles*, pp. 486–488.

Paul feels no need to instruct Timothy about their role but only about the personal qualities desired in those who serve in the role.[30] There is a significant overlap between those qualities and the qualities desired in the overseers. The absence of any reference to teaching responsibilities means it is likely that they did not undertake that task, but we cannot be sure. Marshall thinks that 1 Timothy 3:9 'strongly implies some responsibility with the gospel ministry'.[31] The idea that they exercised a ministry of servanthood, caring for the practical and welfare needs of the church and its members has a long history. The idea of servanthood connects back to the Gospels, where it is spoken of widely and brought into particular focus in both Jesus' saying in Mark 10:45 and his action in John 13. But a recent study by John Collins suggests that the word 'deacon' was not confined to those who undertook menial tasks. They were also used as agents and go-betweens and were holders of a commission, even if they were usually slaves.[32] Given what is said of them and the brief place given to them, especially after the fuller discussion of the overseers, it may be that they were seen as assistants to the overseers. But once again, it is unlikely that precision reigned and that fluidity and flexibility, but not anarchy, characterized this period in the early church.

Reference should also be made of the women Paul mentions in 1 Timothy 3:11. These may be deacon's wives or, they may be female deacons. There are various arguments on both sides.[33] Mentioning them in the midst of talking about male deacons, who are required to be faithful to their wives, could be interpreted in favour of both sides. The word *gynē* might suggest a wife, but not necessarily. On the one hand, those who opt for deacons' wives as an interpretation argue that the reference here is too brief to indicate a separate group of leaders and that, in any case, if teaching were any part of the deacon's role, Paul, in 1 Timothy 2:11–15, forbids women to teach. On the other hand, by using the phrase 'In the same way' in verse 11, as he has done in verse 8, he seems to be starting a new category of leadership and Paul makes similar demands on them to those made of deacons. It is likely that Paul would not have written about 'the wives' but 'their wives'. We also know from the

---

30. The place of Acts 6 in this discussion is ambiguous. See pp. 92–93.

31. Marshall, *Pastoral Epistles*, pp. 487–488.

32. John N. Collins, *Diakonia: Re-Interpreting the Ancient Sources* (New York: Oxford University Press, 1990).

33. They are lucidly set out in Marshall, *Pastoral Epistles*, pp. 493–494. Marshall concludes that it is a reference to women deacons. For the opposite case, see Knight, *Pastoral Epistles*, pp. 170–173.

mention of Phoebe in Romans 16:1 that women deacons existed. The objection that Paul does not call them deaconesses is irrelevant since no female form of the word existed. On balance, therefore, it seems as if Paul was addressing not deacons' wives but women who were deacons in their own right.

Paul, then, gives some insight into local leadership in the churches in Ephesus and Crete. Leadership involves a number of people acting as overseers, elders and deacons, and even probably women deacons. The functions they fulfil are not clearly stated, although overseers, and at least some elders, seem to have a teaching responsibility. No clear delineation is given of any office they occupy, or of any method of appointment. The accent falls neither on their privileges, nor their position, but on their personal and spiritual fitness for leadership.

Charisma versus institution

The attention paid to these roles has led many to believe the church was moving away from being a charismatic community and becoming a more formal institution and an example of what is called early Catholicism.[34] The reason for this belief does not rest on the question of leadership alone. Other indications of institutionalization are thought to be found in the formalizing of belief and the clear delineation of boundaries; the transformation of 'faith' as a dynamic concept to 'the faith', suggesting a fixed creed; and the growing acceptance and prosperity of the church, leading to questions about civic authority and handling wealth, which indicate a growing ease with the world. But our concern here is only with the issue of leadership rather than with the general issue of institutionalization.[35]

The argument is that in Paul's early letters leadership in the church was fluid and informal. In the Spirit-led church in Corinth, for example, those who exercised the various spiritual gifts (*charismata*) led the congregation in worship. There is no reference in Corinthians to fixed offices but instead plenty of references to prophets and teachers and those who exercise a range of exciting

---

34. An early exposition of this theme is found in E. Käsemann's essay 'Ministry and Community in the New Testament', in *Essays on New Testament Themes*, tr. W. J. Montague (London: SCM, 1964), pp. 63–94.

35. On the concept of early Catholicism, see James D. G. Dunn, *Unity and Diversity in the New Testament* (Philadelphia: Westminster; London: SCM, 1977), pp. 351–359. For my wider review of the questions of institutionalization, see my *The Social Context of the New Testament*, BCL 32 (Carlisle: Paternoster, 1997), pp. 123–136.

ministries as part of the body of Christ. The early letters show a complete indifference to titles and leadership structures and portray, rather, a church that is more spontaneous and under the dynamic leadership of the Holy Spirit.[36] In the pastoral letters, however, according to Dunn, 'the concept of office has already clearly emerged: elders, overseers and deacons are all titles for well established offices . . .'[37] Dunn sees Timothy and Titus as assuming 'something of the role of *monarchical bishops*, with authority *over* the community and its members concentrated in them'.[38] Instead of forging forward in mission, their task is now one of preservation. They are to 'keep as the pattern of sound teaching' what they have learned from Paul and to 'Guard the good deposit' entrusted to them' (2 Tim. 3:13–14). True, they are to do so with 'the help of the Holy Spirit' who lives in them, but the phrase does not seem to smack of the living dynamism of earlier statements about the Holy Spirit. So, according to Dunn, 'with such evidence it would be difficult to deny that the pastorals are already some way along the trajectory of early Catholicism'.[39]

The evidence, however, is not as simple as the argument about trajectories might suggest. The case largely rests on an under-estimation of the order implicit in the concept of charisma and an over-estimation of the sense of structure and office in the pastorals.

To begin with, too much attention is paid to the Corinthian correspondence and not enough to other early Pauline letters. Ronald Fung has drawn attention to Galatians 6:6, one of Paul's earliest letters, where the existence of teachers who should be financially supported is presupposed.[40] 1 Thessalonians

---

36. Phil. 1:1 mentions them but does no more than that. Käsemann, 'Ministry and Community', p. 86, writes, 'For we may assert without hesitation that the Pauline community had had no presbytery during the Apostle's lifetime. Otherwise the silence on the subject in every Pauline epistle is quite incomprehensible.' This refers to every Pauline epistle considered by contemporary scholars to be genuine.

37. Dunn, *Unity and Diversity*, p. 352.

38. Ibid., p. 352.

39. Ibid. A fuller statement of the case from a sociological viewpoint is found in Margaret Y. MacDonald, *The Pauline Churches: A Socio-Historical Study of Institutionalization in the Pauline and Deutero-Pauline Writings*, SNTSMS 60 (Cambridge: Cambridge University Press, 1988).

40. Ronald Fung, 'Charismatic versus Organized Ministry? An Examination of an Alleged Antithesis', *EvQ* 52 (1980), pp. 195–214. The article provides an excellent critique of Käsemann's essay 'Ministry and Community', seeking to be sympathetic where possible. The argument above is based on Fung's article.

5:12 speaks of a group of people who are recognized as leading the church. Romans 16:1 and Colossians 4:17 identify others who seem to have 'some definite, recognized ministry in the church',[41] to say nothing about Philippians 1:1 and Acts 14:23.

Turning to Corinthians, where the church community is apparently indifferent to people holding offices of leadership but dominated by those who exercise certain spiritual gifts, we need to understand that the community is not thereby unstructured. The image of the body involves an implicit order and Paul explicitly states some ordering of the gifts in 1 Corinthians 12:28, 'And God has placed in the church first of all apostles, second prophets, third teachers, then miracles, then gifts of healing, of helping, of guidance, and of different kinds of tongues'. Paul knows that 'God is not a God of disorder but of peace' (1 Cor. 14:33) and provides the church with ground rules for the exercise of gifts that, if used in an unbridled way, could lead to chaos. On top of these internal considerations we also need to lay Paul's own role in these churches as their father and apostolic teacher. The other apostles, too, have an acknowledged place as transmitters of the tradition about Jesus. On the basis of the evidence, Fung concludes that Paul's 'doctrine of charisma is not incompatible with the existence of an organized ministry'.[42]

Looking at the issue from the other end, that is, from the perspective of the pastorals, Fung argues that there is no opposition between a spiritual gift and an ecclesiastical office. The words for 'serving', 'teaching', 'encouraging' and 'shepherding' are found both in the lists of spiritual gifts in Romans 12:7–8 or Ephesians 4:11 and in the pastoral letters. Fung quotes John Robinson as saying, 'The apostle would have been startled by the suggestion that bishops and deacons could execute their office aright without the divine aid of the corresponding "charisma".'[43] Käsemann talked of 'the Pauline conception of a church order based on charisma' having disappeared by the time of the pastorals to be replaced by a concept of ordained office in which the Spirit was now located and that was the guarantor of the apostolic deposit.[44] But the pastorals themselves speak of Timothy's 'gift which was given you through prophecy', adding 'when the body of elders laid their hands on you' (1 Tim. 4:14). The first half of this verse certainly sounds charismatic, even if the second half sounds more institutional, but it is not necessarily so. The work of

---

41. Fung, 'Charismatic versus Organized', p. 197.

42. Ibid., p. 203.

43. Ibid., p. 205.

44. Käsemann, 'Ministry and Community', pp. 87–88.

the Holy Spirit is much in evidence in the pastoral letters. The spiritual gifts of prophecy (1 Tim. 1:18; 4:14) and teaching (1 Tim. 3:2) are spoken of. He is active in revelation (1 Tim. 4:1) and regeneration (Titus 3:5) as well as having a vital role in empowering God's servants (2 Tim. 1:6–7, 14). The sovereign Spirit is at work in the world through the unchained word of God (2 Tim. 2:9). While some of the gifts of the Holy Spirit are not mentioned in the pastorals, it is true to say that they are not mentioned either in most of Paul's letters.

It would be foolish to deny that more attention is paid to ecclesiastical leadership in the pastoral letters than elsewhere. But there seems to be compatibility between the church as a charismatic community and the churches as an ordered community. The antithesis, as often crudely presented, between charisma and institution is a false one. The church of God needs leaders who are called, gifted and filled by the Holy Spirit. They sought and appointed them in the Acts, needed them in Corinth and spoke of them in the pastoral letters. The picture of the church, though inevitably revealing various facets of the church's life as it develops, is coherent and consistent.

Conclusion

The later letters of Paul 'reveals his character to be as *pastor pastorum*, a leader who provides continuing leadership in the churches'.[45] As an elder statesman he mentors the next generation of leaders, guiding and equipping them for their vital task at a time of transition.

The ministry of the elder statesmen is crucial for the church. Older, experienced pastors who have served God well have much to contribute to the generation of leaders who follow them when the time comes for them to draw back from being in the front line themselves. It should not be assumed that one would automatically graduate to this role, just because of age or retirement. The elder statesman, whether male or female, is required to have certain gifts, all of which are demonstrated in Paul. First, there is a relational gift. He is a mentor, able to contribute to the next generation of leaders because of the relationship of respect and love between them. Secondly, Paul shows he has learned from experience. Some people do not learn from experience; they merely repeat mistakes. The pastoral letters show how Paul's understanding of the work of the gospel has been honed by both successes and failures. He

---

45. Ralph P. Martin, *New Testament Foundations* (Grand Rapids: Eerdmans, 1978), vol. 2, p. 306.

never loses sight of the ideal but is able at the same time to live with the real and cope with the actual. Thirdly, he is in tune with the needs of the hour. Paul is perceptive about the needs of the church from which he is about to depart, and flexible in his thinking about its future. Some retired servants of God live in the past and rule themselves out from helping the next generation because they are unable to engage in the cultural and ecclesiastical changes that have occurred since they were at the height of their own ministry. But, if the biblical requirements are in place, a wonderful and strategic ministry may be exercised by the elder statesman.

9. HEBREWS: MINISTRY IN A FALTERING CHURCH

The ministry of a reflective practitioner

Most professions today encourage reflective practice as a good way of learning and developing one's understanding. It is now commonly understood that, instead of merely downloading information, learning is best achieved by doing and then thinking over what was done in relation to a wider body of knowledge. Joy Amulya believes it is the basis for purposeful learning and explains it like this:

> Reflection is an active process of witnessing one's own experience in order to take a closer look at it, sometimes to direct attention to it briefly, but often to explore it in greater depth. This can be done in the midst of an activity or as an activity itself. The key to reflection is learning how to take perspective on one's own actions and experience – in other words, to examine that experience rather than just living it. By developing the ability to explore and be curious about our own experience and actions, we suddenly open up the possibilities of purposeful learning . . .[1]

Reflection sometimes occurs in the middle of busy action, helping to guide

---

1. Joy Amulya, 'What Is Reflective Practice?', Centre for Reflective Community Practice, Massachusetts Institute of Technology, <www.crcp.mit.doc/edu/documents/whatis.pdf>, accessed 26 Apr. 2008.

decisions and shaping behaviour immediately. Sometimes it is reflection *on* action rather than *in* action and looks back at what has been done with a view to learning to handle a situation differently another time. While reflective practice may be a fashionable tool in contemporary education, the letter to the Hebrews gives us a superb example of reflective practice at work in the early church. The author, whoever he (or she) was, reflects deeply with Christians who are faltering in their commitment to Jesus Christ. He (or she) is an example of the pastor as a reflective practitioner.

Hebrews as reflective practice

What caused Hebrews to be written?

In spite of what appears to many to be some fairly obvious themes emerging in Hebrews, people have differed widely over the reason why Hebrews was written and the nature of the congregation or congregations to which it is addressed.[2] They were unlikely to be large and probably consisted of a house church, or a few house churches, perhaps in Rome.[3] It seems clearly to be addressed to Jewish Christians (although some question even this) who, for whatever reason, are being attracted back to the Jewish faith and are in danger of giving up. The evidence for this will be reviewed below.

Some, trying to be more specific, have argued that the readers were converted priests or, given what we know from the Dead Sea Scrolls, that they had been members of a Jewish sect at Qumran, attracted by its teachings about prophets, angels, Moses, Aaron and Melchizedek.[4]

Yet another very different and minority theory is advanced by Barnabas

---

2. For full discussions, see F. F. Bruce, *The Epistle to the Hebrews*, NLC (London: Marshall, Morgan & Scott, 1965), pp. xxiii–xxxv; Paul Ellingworth, *The Epistle to the Hebrews*, NIGTC (Grand Rapids: Eerdmans; Carlisle: Paternoster, 1993), pp. 21–27, 78–80; Donald Guthrie, *Hebrews*, TNTC (Leicester: IVP; Grand Rapids: Eerdmans, 1983), pp. 31–38; Donald Hagner, *Encountering the Book of Hebrews* (Grand Rapids: Baker Academic, 2002), pp. 23–26; and William L. Lane, *Hebrews 1–8*, WBC 47a (Dallas: Word, 1991), pp. li–lx.

3. Ellingworth, *Hebrews*, pp. 28–29; and Lane, *Hebrews 1–8*, pp. lviii–lx.

4. Philip E. Hughes, among others, argues for the connection with Qumran (*A Commentary on the Epistle to the Hebrews* [Grand Rapids: Eerdmans, 1977], pp. 10–15). Hughes describes this theory as 'undoubtedly the best theory yet advanced to explain the occasion and purpose of the Epistle to the Hebrews' (p. 14).

Lindars.[5] The Hebrews accepted, he argues, that the gospel spoke of complete atonement for past sin and gave them assurance of forgiveness for their past lives, and on that basis they had been baptized into the Christian fellowship. But then they ran, unexpectedly, into the problem of post-baptismal sin. 'They simply assumed they would remain in a state of grace until the parousia. But as time passed, some of them at least began to be oppressed by renewed consciousness of sin, and the gospel as they had received it appeared not to allow for it.'[6] Their former faith, Judaism, had provided rituals to deal with continuing sin. But Christianity, lacking both a temple and sacrifices, had nothing comparable to cleanse the sensitive conscience. The author, therefore, is bent on persuading them that the gospel is adequate to cover such sin and that, although there is the absence of rituals like the Day of Atonement, there is a new sacrifice and a new altar in which they can have confidence.

Still others argue it is unnecessary to look for a particular occasion to explain the setting of this letter. It is enough, they say,[7] that it provides a sustained and wonderful exposition of the work of Christ and needs no further explanation. He has written 'a word of exhortation' (13:22), which he somewhat ironically describes as brief (!), concerning the way in which God has spoken finally through Jesus who in his person and work is incomparably superior to anyone else in the religious firmament of his readers. This means that Christianity is 'absolute in character and universal in scope'[8] and a faith in which believers may have complete confidence.

If there is anything like consensus, it is to be found in the belief that the Hebrews are weary and in danger of turning their back on Jesus and being tempted to return to the more ritualistic faith of Judaism. Ellingworth has pointed out that we might look to the language used to help us reconstruct their situation and, if we do that, some of the language the author uses is passive, some active and some about external influences upon them.[9]

Passively, they are drifting (2:1), neglecting (2:3), losing hold of (4:14), and losing confidence in (10:19, 23) the faith. They have become sluggish in hearing and discipleship (5:11; 6:12), and are content to remain children in the faith (5:12–14). They are dropping out of church (10:25). They are burdened

---

5. Barnabas Lindars, *The Theology of the Letter to the Hebrews* (Cambridge: Cambridge University Press, 1991), pp. 4–15.

6. Ibid., p. 13.

7. Dr Alec Motyer expressed this position in correspondence with me.

8. Hagner, *Encountering*, p. 25.

9. Ellingworth, *Hebrews*, pp. 78–79.

(12:1), weary and discouraged (12:12–13). This means they are vulnerable and may be carried away 'by all kinds of strange teaching' (13:9). The letter, though, is not just about the pressures on them. They must take responsibility as well for what is happening. *Actively*, they manifest unbelief and a lack of faith that leads to disobedience (3:12; 4:11). They are in danger of permitting bitterness to grow (12:15) and of refusing to listen to God (12:25). Their present course, if persisted in, will hold Christ up to 'public disgrace' (6:6), and their persistent sin is akin to trampling 'the Son of God' under foot and having shown contempt for holy things and insulted 'the Spirit of grace' (10:29). *Externally*, they are subject to pressures from the state and, as their group has experienced in the past (10:32; 13:7), they are likely to face severe suffering for their confession of Christ (2:18; 12:4).

The most urgent need they face in the light of their experience, then, is to have their confidence in the gospel renewed so that they can stand firm and persevere to the end. 'You need', he tells them bluntly, 'to persevere so that when you have done the will of God, you will receive what he has promised' (10:36). They need to look to the example of the Old Testament heroes of the faith and of Christ himself to find examples of perseverance (11:27; 12:1–3). They will share in Christ, but only if 'they hold firmly to the end [their] original conviction' (3:14).

Hebrews as a sermon

Hebrews can be approached in many ways yet still not be exhausted.[10] It is clearly a letter, but is intended to be read aloud to the congregation rather than silently by an individual. Accordingly, it has all the hallmarks of a sermon in its use of language and its carefully structured sounds. It claims to be a 'word of exhortation' (13:22) and weaves exhortation throughout as well as ending with a passage of extended exhortation. Its conversational style, energy, use of present tenses, repetitions (classically, 'by faith' in ch. 11), metaphors and other verbal devices grab and sustain the attention.[11] But it is a sermon that exhibits great theological depth. No one has expressed the curious nature of this better than Thomas Long. Having argued that the key problem addressed is that of spiritual weariness, Long writes:

---

10. In *Skilful Shepherds: Exploration in Pastoral Theology*, 2nd ed. (Leicester: Apollos, 1997), I examined Hebrews as an example of the social mechanism of 'plausibility structures' at work (pp. 253–257, 262–265).

11. Fred B. Craddock, 'The Letter to Hebrews', NIB 12 (Nashville: Abingdon, 1998), p. 15; and Thomas G. Long, *Hebrews*, Interpretation (Louisville: John Knox, 1997), pp. 2–6. For a more technical discussion, see Lane, *Hebrews 1–8*, pp. lxix–lxxv.

the Preacher's response may astound us. What is most striking about Hebrews is that the Preacher, faced with the pastoral problem of spiritual weariness is bold enough, maybe even brash enough, to think that Christology and preaching are the answers. The preacher does not appeal to improved group dynamics, conflict management techniques, reorganization of the mission structures, or snappy worship services. Rather, he preaches – preaches to the congregation in complex theological terms about the nature and meaning of Jesus Christ.

The Preacher does not float around on the surface where the desires of people cluster eagerly around this or that fad; he dives to the depths, to the hidden places where profound symbols work on the religious imagination to generate surprise, wonder, gratitude, and finally obedience. As strategists go, the Preacher's approach to ministry is so out of phase, so counter-intuitive, so in violation of the notion that congregations are allergic to serious theological thinking, that it probably should be seen as refreshing, and maybe even revolutionary.[12]

It is surprising how little attention has been paid to the role of preaching in leadership in the church. As far as I am aware, only one recent book addresses the issue: *360-Degree Leadership*, by Michael Quicke.[13] He recounts the way in which several friends were nervous of the connection he was making between leadership and preaching, believing that one or other of the partnership would be adulterated and the shepherding task lost in it all.[14] But, unapologetically, Quicke explores the relationship and says that 'instead of operating independently, eyeing each other suspiciously, preaching and leadership must embrace and do gospel business together. Preaching needs leadership as much as Christian leadership needs preaching.'[15] The author of Hebrews would certainly say 'Amen' to that.

Quicke believes that if leadership and preaching are disconnected in the church, leadership will become humanistic, dispense with the Holy Spirit, will

---

12. Long, *Hebrews*, p. 7.

13. *360-Degree Leadership: Preaching to Transform Congregations* (Grand Rapids: Baker, 2006). James W. Thompson, *Pastoral Ministry according to Paul: A Biblical Vision* (Grand Rapids: Baker Academic, 2006), mentions it briefly in reference to shaping a congregation's consciousness (pp. 158–159). But for the most part, preaching is discussed as a separate topic that focuses on individual learning and transformation rather than having a significant place in leadership of the church.

14. Quicke, *360-Degree Leadership*, pp. 15–16.

15. Ibid., p. 71.

'distort theology and flatten spiritual paradoxes' and encourage pride.[16] The separation will take its toll on preaching as well, for leadership brings a realism to preaching and is ruthlessly honest about the need for change. Leadership faces rather than avoids conflict and seeks to manage it and encourage the preacher to 'intervene proactively in different situations', evaluating, exposing values, clarifying mission and fostering vision.[17]

Quicke is right. Contrary to what we see in the New Testament generally, and in Hebrews in particular, contemporary church leaders have lost confidence in preaching as an agent of change in the lives of individuals and communities. There are good theological reasons, as well as massive historical evidence, for believing in the validity of preaching as God's instrument of change and growth in people's lives. With Quicke, and the author of Hebrews, we should share the 'hope that preachers rediscover leadership *through preaching*'.[18]

The sermon is that of a reflective practitioner

But there is preaching and there is preaching. The word 'preaching' is an inclusive word and masks a whole gamut of styles and approaches, as Quicke would be the first to agree.[19] Within the range of preaching is the kind of preaching we see in Hebrews, that of the reflective practitioner.

The indications of reflective practice are evident in the overall structure of Hebrews, in the choice of style and in the detailed weft of the argument. Admitting that the scheme may be oversimplified, Fred Craddock points to the way in which Hebrews alternates exposition with exhortation. Exposition of the themes is found in 1:1–14, 2:5 – 3:6, 5:1–10 and 7:1 – 10:18, and exhortation is woven in between 2:1–4, 3:7 – 4:16, 5:11 – 6:20 and 10:19 – 13:25.[20] It is a classic dialogue between knowledge and practice.

The oral style is that of a reflective practitioner. The argument is tightly constructed and develops logically step by step. The author of Hebrews carries his audience along with him. But the reflective element is seen mostly in the

16. Ibid., pp. 62–65.

17. Ibid., pp. 65–71.

18. Ibid., p. 17; his italics.

19. Michael Quicke, *360-Degree Preaching: Hearing, Speaking and Living the Word* (Grand Rapids: Baker; Carlisle: Paternoster, 2003), pp. 25–26, 97–104; *360-Degree Leadership*, pp. 80–82. Quicke explores different types of leadership as well as different types of preaching.

20. Craddock, 'Hebrews', p. 16.

exhortation passages. He uses the word 'therefore' sixteen times in his address, with twelve of these being used to apply his teaching to his listeners.[21] He uses rhetorical questions (2:1; 3:16–18; 7:11; 10:29; 11:32; 12:5), and pushes his audience to think for themselves as he punctuates his address with phrases like 'see to it' (3:12; 12:15, 16, 25), 'let us be careful' (4:1), 'just think' (7:4) or 'consider' (10:24; 12:3; 13:7) and 'remember' (10:32; 13:3, 7). His appeal calls for a practical response. Using inclusive language, he urges his listeners to 'Let us then approach God's throne . . .' (4:16); 'let us move beyond the elementary teachings about Christ . . .' (6:1); 'let us draw near to God . . .' (10:22); 'Let us hold unswervingly to the hope we profess . . .' (10:23); 'Let us consider how we may spur one another on . . .' (10:24); and 'let us throw off everything that hinders . . .' (12:1). Time and again they are encouraged to set aside bad practice in the light of reflecting further on the positive outcome of living lives consistent with trustworthy teaching about Christ.

A systematic approach to reflective practice takes one through a number of stages. G. Gibbs, for example, has developed a cycle that identifies six phases one ideally goes through to maximize the benefit of the reflective process.[22] He has wisely developed it as a cycle because it is not a linear process that has a beginning and an end so much as a continuous process whereby one is constantly reflecting and adjusting. It begins ideally with *description* (what happened?), then addresses *feelings* (what were the participants thinking or feeling?), moves on to *evaluation* (what was good and bad about the experience?) and then *analysis* (what sense can be made of it?), before leading to a *conclusion* (what else could have been done?) and an *action plan* (how should the situation now be handled?).

All these phases can be identified in Hebrews, even if they are scattered throughout the letter. The *description* draws attention to the way in which some are falling away from following Christ (2:1; 3:12; 10:23–25) and not making the spiritual progress that may be expected of them (6:1–8). The *feeling* phase is confronted in 12:12. These Christians are weary, perhaps because of the pressures on them from their Jewish families and friends. Their arms are feeble and their knees weak. As to *evaluation*, the author gives them no saccharin assurances. Being a Christian is tough. Persecution and discomfort are part of the package, as the great heroes of the faith who carried on believing in spite of

---

21. Heb. 2:1, 3:1, 4:1, 11, 14, 6:1, 7:25, 10:19, 12:1, 12, 28 and 13:15 are the 'therefores' where application is made to believers.

22. G. Gibbs, *Learning by Doing: A Guide to Teaching and Learning Methods* (Oxford: Further Education Unit, Oxford Polytechnic, 1988).

not receiving their reward (11:1–40), as their former leaders (13:7) and, above all, as 'the pioneer and perfecter' of their faith, Jesus himself, demonstrates (12:1–3). Their experience, then, does not indicate that they are doing anything wrong but rather confirms the genuineness of their discipleship.

It is the fourth phase of *analysis* where Hebrews spends much of its time. Many are calling into question both the value and the validity of their faith in Christ. In view of what they are experiencing, have they got it wrong? Are alternative teachings, especially those found in the Jewish religion right after all? Is their acceptance of the Christian faith a fulfilment of the Old Testament hope or a betrayal of it? To answer these questions, the Preacher spends time giving a careful and sustained exposition of the superiority of Christ to angels (1:5–14), Moses (3:1–6), to the Jewish high priests (4:14 – 5:10), to Melchizedek (7:1–28), and to the tabernacle or temple and the covenant of which it spoke (8:1–13) and to the rituals practised within it, especially those exemplified by the Day of Atonement (9:1 – 10:18). Each of these elements was an active ingredient in contemporary Jewish religion and would have exercised a strong influence over faltering Christian believers. Hence Hebrews devotes itself to explaining carefully the superiority of Christ to them all (1:4; 3:3; 8:6; 9:11). The Christian faith is 'better' (*kreittōn*) in every way than the one to which some are drifting back. Donald Guthrie delightfully describes the word 'better' as 'the theme song of this epistle'.[23] It offers a better hope (7:19), a better covenant because it is effective (7:22),[24] offers better promises (8:6), is built on better sacrifices (9:23), concerns God's better plan for us (11:40) and is all based on the better word that Christ's shed blood cries out to the Father than the appeal sent out by the blood of murdered Abel (12:24). Faith in Christ, then, is no betrayal of the faith of the old covenant but rather a fulfilment of it, the destination to which it long pointed.

The detailed examination of the person and work of Christ leads to his *conclusion*. They are not misguided but need to continue with dogged commitment in the faith they have come to confess. It is not that they have done anything wrong, so much as that they have not done enough. They need to hold on firmly (3:6; 4:14), make greater efforts than they have done (4:11) and move beyond their present infantile position (5:11 – 6:3). It is not that there is anything wrong with the faith. The fault lies in their tardy discipleship, which arises from their failure to grasp the full significance of Christ and his finished work.

---

23. Guthrie, *Hebrews*, p. 263.

24. Lane, *Hebrews 1–8*, p. 188.

None of this is left in the air as a nice theological homily or even a general exhortation. The preacher is keen to see his listeners transformed and so proposes to them elements of an *action plan* that will help them through this wobbly patch in their relationship with Christ. They are to hold on (4:14; 10:23), draw near to God (4:16; 10:22), change their diet and start eating solid food (5:13–14), consider stimulating each other spiritually (10:24) and keep meeting (10:25). Overall they need to persevere (10:36), which they will be helped to do if they fix their eyes on Jesus (12:1–3). The concluding chapter sets out a number of courses of action they are to take that relate to marriage and hospitality, to contentment and worship, and to prayer and submission to leaders.

All the elements, then, of the pastor and preacher as a reflective practitioner are found in Hebrews, where the author is not reflecting *for* them on their faith and experience but *with* them, leading them to 'better things' (6:9).

Church and leadership in Hebrews

Church

In addition to modelling an effective form of pastoral leadership itself, Hebrews has a little to say about the interior life and ministry of the church. Most commentators assume that it is addressed to one or more house churches and, as we have seen, part of the author's action plan for them is to keep meeting to 'spur one another on toward love and good deeds' and to encourage 'one another – and all the more as you see the Day approaching' (10:24–25). It is envisaged that ministry is mutual, rather than dependent on a group of officers set apart from others. In the light of the second coming, they are regularly and urgently to do for each other what the author has sought to do for them in his letter, as he states it in 13:22 – exercise a ministry of exhortation.[25] Twice more in the letter, the author refers to the quality of life he hopes will be expressed in their fellowship. He longs that together they will be marked by love, peace, practical service and holiness (6:10; 12:14). Bitterness and immorality should be excluded. All should be conscious that they are dependent on the grace of God, which they both receive for themselves and their own forgiveness, and should manifest in the gentleness of their relationships with others (12:15–17).

---

25. Ellingworth, *Hebrews*, p. 529.

Leaders

Little is said about the way they are to organize their meetings. But we are made aware that however mutual the ministry of encouragement is, the church is not purely an egalitarian group, since three times in the final chapter the author refers to their 'leaders' (13:7, 17, 24). The use of the term 'leaders' (*tois hēgoumenoi*) is significant in itself, as is each of the three verses in which it is used.

The term *hēgoumenoi* is used of leadership in a wide sense in official documents and is neither a technical term nor a specifically Christian word. It may refer to military leaders, princes, pagan priests or great men in general.[26] This gives the lie to what I have often heard claimed by well-meaning Christians who are concerned to preserve a distinctly Christian ministry in the church. 'The New Testament', I have been confidently (and frequently) told, 'does not use the language of leadership.' The statement is often voiced by way of reaction to the goal-setting, task-oriented, Chief Executive Officer style of leadership seen in some megachurches, which some advocate as necessary if any local church is to grow. I understand the anxieties, but the truth is that, apart from other leadership language in the New Testament, Hebrews has no embarrassment about taking up a secular word and using it of those who lead the church.

Each of the three references to leaders gives us a different but vital insight into their place in the church. 13:7 speaks about former leaders, perhaps the founding fathers of the community, who have now passed on. Two things are said of them. First, they 'spoke the word of God to you', indicating that this was their priority in leadership. They were not essentially managers or organizers but evangelists and teachers. Secondly, the encouragement not only to remember them but also to imitate them suggests that leaders could be looked to as models and examples.

In 13:17, the members of the church are encouraged to 'have confidence' in their leaders and 'submit to their authority'. It sounds as if there was tension between the members and the leaders, possibly because of the 'strange teachings' to which some were attracted (13:9). A surface reading of the text makes it look as if the authority of the leaders is being asserted and the job of the members is presented as if they are to follow them unquestioningly. But this text does not give any encouragement to authoritarianism. Certainly, the members are called to respect their leaders but, in calling them 'to obey', Hebrews uses the word *peithesthe*, which does not mean obeying

---

26. F. Buchsel, '*hēgeomai*', *TDNT*, vol. 2, p. 908.

people mindlessly, simply because they are in positions of power. 'It is rather the obedience that is won through persuasive conversation'[27] than that of peremptory commands. The humility with which the leaders exercise their gentle authority is further underlined by the fact that, like the members of the church, they too 'must give an account' of their leadership at the Day of Judgment. Their task is described as keeping watch over the church, a term that fits with the calling of the shepherd and resonates with Paul's address in Acts 20:28 to the Ephesian elders.

The third and final reference to leaders in 13:24 simply distinguishes between leaders and 'all the Lord's people'. However mutual the ministry of the church is, and however much they all look to one High Priest, as we shall see, there is still a need and a place for leaders to direct the church humbly, faithfully and persuasively. Not every member is called or equipped to be a leader.

The high priest

What is abundantly clear is that Hebrews does not remotely envisage these leaders in the church as a new class of priests. Only one priest is to be acknowledged in the new covenant: the high priest, Jesus Christ (2:17; 3:1). Two aspects of the Old Testament teaching on priesthood are used to develop the understanding of Jesus as high priest. In 5:1–10, Psalm 110 is mentioned to speak of the way the Son is also 'a priest for ever' and 'in the order of Melchizedek' (5:6), explained more fully in 7:1–28. The point is the superiority of Melchizedek (the king of righteousness and peace, without beginning or end) to Abraham and the Levitical priesthood. The second theme is more extensive and runs through chapters 8–10 to prove that Jesus Christ is superior to the sacrificial priests of old, whose work was never done and whose service never ultimately satisfied. In contrast, 'when this priest [Jesus] had offered for all time one sacrifice for sins, he sat down at the right hand of God, and since that time he waits for his enemies to be made his footstool' (10:12–13).

The purpose throughout the exposition of Jesus as the high priest is pastoral. He need never be doubted, for he is superior to the priests known in the Jewish faith. His finished work means that believers can be assured that their sins are forgiven. Furthermore, because he has shared in our humanity and its weaknesses, though not our sin (4:15–16), we may 'approach God's throne of grace with confidence, so that we may receive mercy and find grace to help us in our time of need' (4:16).

---

27. William L. Lane, *Hebrews 9–13*, WBC 47b (Dallas: Word, 1991), p. 554.

Since we have such a supreme and unique high priest, there is no need and there is certainly no place for others to act as priests in the church, and still less if they do so in any hierarchical sense. Yet, Ellingworth explains, 'In Hebrews, the sole priesthood of Christ does not obviate the need for *pastoral leadership* in the community, but it is exercised by a group (cf. Phil. 1:1), not by a single individual.'[28] To which we might add, and is concerned with pointing to the sacrifice and mediatorial role of Christ, and not with the offering of sacrifices still, or with being a mediator between God and 'the laity'.

Understanding Jesus as the high priest by no means exhausts the rich teaching of Hebrews about Jesus. Among the many other ways in which he who is 'the radiance of God's glory' (1:3) is presented is the idea of him as the pioneer (12:2), a concept that also has leadership overtones.[29] The *archēgos* is the one who forges the path and leads the way forward for others to follow, just as Christ has done through suffering and the resurrection to complete salvation.

Conclusion

Hebrews provides some important insights into ministry in the early church. Those who exercise pastoral care do so as leaders who both teach the word of God and watch over the flock. They do so in the full knowledge that they are not autonomous managers but accountable servants. They, like all other members of the church, depend on the sole ministry of the great high priest for their salvation and strength.

Our interest, however, has focused on Hebrews as a pastoral document, modelling the ministry of the reflective practitioner. In the sermon, which we now read as a letter, the preacher, whom we now encounter as an author, aims to reflect alongside faltering members of the believing community to strengthen their faith and renew their confidence in the gospel of Christ. He analyses their experience with them, identifies their feelings, helps them to look with fresh eyes at the nature of their faith, connects them to good theology and proposes practical action to help them break out of their spiritual lethargy and make progress towards perfection. The medium he chooses to communicate his findings is not that of classroom and seminar but of pulpit and sermon. It reminds us that preaching is seldom best when delivered by

---

28. Ellingworth, *Hebrews*, p. 723; italics mine.

29. The thought is not dissimilar from the idea in 6:20 of the 'forerunner'.

someone above the congregation. It is usually much more persuasive if, like Hebrews, we preach alongside them, using the inclusive language of 'we' and 'us' rather than 'you' and 'yours'. Preaching is a vital medium of leadership, and should always aim for transformation, growth and progress in the believers, rather than just filling the air with words.

10. JAMES: MINISTRY IN A HALF-HEARTED CHURCH

The ministry of transparent wisdom

The general verdict down the centuries on the letter of James has not been altogether favourable. It has been considered doctrinally lightweight and dismissed as contributing little to our understanding of the church. It may have been valued as a practical handbook for Christian living but that has often been the most positive that could be said of it. Recent research, however, has begun to re-evaluate James and something of its richness has begun to be uncovered.

Patrick Hartin, for example, is among those who have placed it in the wisdom tradition of Israel and has argued that it has suffered from being read from too narrow a viewpoint. Read from a wisdom perspective, 'it is catechesis of the finest form instructing believers on their style of life as Christians' and 'forges a bridge between the Old and New Testaments'.[1] The whole letter is permeated with the teaching of Jesus and is far richer in doctrine and even insight into the church and its ministry than is often recognized. Douglas Moo, commenting on the practical questions that provoke James's theological answers, is surely right to protest, 'it will be a sad day for the church when such "practical divinity" is not considered

---

1. Patrick J. Hartin, *James and the Q Sayings of Jesus*, JSNTSup 47 (Sheffield: JSOT Press, 1991), pp. 22–23, 41.

"theology" '.[2] Writing to a church in danger of being half-hearted in its commitment, James proves to be a skilled pastor. The chief value for our understanding of ministry is that he sets before us an example of the understanding scribe as envisaged by Matthew. Here is the ministry of transparent wisdom at work.

James's pastoral approach

James, whom we assume to be the eldest of Jesus' four brothers and leader of the church in Jerusalem,[3] writes to 'the twelve tribes scattered among the nations' (1:1). It is a general letter intended to be circulated among the Jewish Christians of the diaspora. The opening address alerts us to the Jewish nature of what follows, and the letter is so Jewish in style and content that it has sometimes been argued that it is not essentially Christian. The argument is based on the observation that there are only two explicit references to Jesus in the letter (1:1 and 2:1), which could be later insertions, and that the rest could have been written by a Jewish sage. This argument, however, quite apart from involving the unwarranted assumption that the references to Jesus are interpolations, misses one vital fact, which is that although the letter contains no direct quotation from Jesus,[4] it is shot through with close allusions to his teaching. Various schemes estimate the number of cross-references differently.[5] J. B. Mayor believed there were fifty-seven parallels with Matthew, eleven with Luke and three with Mark.[6] Hartin, at one point, details twenty-six correspondences between James and the Synoptic Gospels, twenty-one of which relate to Matthew's Sermon on the

2. Douglas J. Moo, *The Letter of James*, PNTC (Grand Rapids: Eerdmans; Leicester: Apollos, 2000), p. 28.

3. For recent discussions of authorship, see Richard Bauckham, *James: Wisdom of James, Disciple of Jesus the Sage*, New Testament Readings (London: Routledge, 1999), pp. 16–17; and Moo, *James*, pp. 9–22.

4. Jas 5:12 is almost a direct quotation of Matt. 5:34–37.

5. The affinities between James's and Jesus' words have been widely recognized; e.g. James B. Adamson, *James: The Man and His Message* (Grand Rapids: Eerdmans, 1989), pp. 169–194; and Peter H. Davids, 'James and Jesus', in David Wenham (ed.), *Gospel Perspectives: The Jesus Tradition outside the Gospels* (Sheffield, JSOT, 1985), vol. 5, pp. 63–84.

6. Cited by Adamson, *James*, pp. 170–171.

Mount.[7] The affinities occur both with Matthew and Luke, but are particularly noticeable in connection with Matthew's Gospel, which advocates the ministry of the understanding scribe and sage.[8]

How, then, is it that James does not more obviously connect his writing with the sayings of Jesus? Why does he not quote his words and then add his own exposition, clearly distinguishing between the words of Jesus and his own? The answer lies chiefly in the way in which sages went about their calling. Disciples were not expected to quote their master (it was not after all the sort of written culture in which precise footnotes were required!) but rather to absorb their master's teaching and then re-express it in their own words, musing on them, expanding on them and creatively reapplying them as appropriate. They were not called to repeat the words so much as to be inspired by them.[9] Their own perception, creativity and artistic reformulation of the teaching were vital elements in the wisdom teacher's calling. Direct verbal correspondence and close allusions were therefore not as germane as many have thought, although any re-expression of the teaching clearly needed to be consistent with the original and not in tension or conflict with it. So, typically, James 'seems to have been so soaked in the atmosphere and specifics of Jesus' teaching that he can reflect them almost unconsciously'.[10]

In adopting this approach, we see an example of the sage and the teacher of the law whom Jesus promised in Matthew 23:34 to send out.[11] We also see a perfect example of his fulfilling the task Jesus set out for them in Matthew 13:52. Here is the one who has been instructed and immersed in the teaching of Jesus 'bringing out of the storeroom new treasures as well as old'. James provides us with a pattern of ministry that has deeply imbibed biblical teaching, but then, far from merely parroting it, transposes it into a contemporary

---

7. Hartin, *James*, pp. 141–142, 144, n. 3. For a different list, see Davids, 'James and Jesus', pp. 66–67.

8. Notwithstanding, Adamson, *James*, p. 193, finds a correspondence with uniquely Lucan material, while Hartin's attempt to identify James with the Matthean church is judged by Bauckham to be unsuccessful because it misses vital steps in the argument (Bauckham, *James*, p. 31).

9. Bauckham, *James*, p. 82. See pp. 76–83 for justification of this argument.

10. Moo, *James*, p. 7.

11. The relationship between wisdom and law was much closer in a Jewish context than we might expect. Hence James, the teacher of wisdom, pays careful attention to the law of Lev. 19 in 2:8–11. On the close relationship, see Bauckham, *James*, pp. 142–157.

idiom, picking out its themes in a way that catches the ear of the contemporary world and church. In summary, he is 'a teacher in the style of Jesus, a creative exponent of the wisdom of Jesus, a disciple who "having been fully trained" in the teacher's wisdom, has become himself a teacher of wisdom "like his teacher" (Luke 6:40)'.[12]

Typical of wisdom literature, James uses a whole toolbox full of literary instruments to achieve his end. Bauckham lists beatitudes (1:12); 'whoever' sayings (2:10; 4:4); conditional sayings (1:5, 26); synonymous couples (4:8); antithetical and paradoxical couples (1:9–10; 2:5, 18); admonitions (1:19–20; 4:8; 5:9, 12, 16); declarative statements (1:3–4; 2:26; 3:16); statements of contradiction (1:20); step sayings (1:3–4); reciprocal sayings (2:13; 3:6) and so on.[13] In addition to these pithy, even punchy, maxims, James summons into use more extended parables (1:10–11; 3:3–6; 5:7–8) and the Old Testament examples of Abraham, Rahab, the prophets, Job and Elijah (2:21–25; 5:10–11, 17–18). And within this same short letter he can engage in hypothetical dialogue (2:18–23) and strong prophetic denunciation (5:1–6). Under the surface of what appears a randomly thrown-together letter is a carefully crafted work of art, using words to their maximum effect.

James's letter is frequently seen as an example of paraenesis (a series of moral admonitions and encouragements). Scholars argue as to the precise definition of paraenesis, but many would say its place was not to persuade the unconvinced but rather to motivate and persuade people to live out what they had already accepted.[14] If so, James fits the genre superbly. He invites his readers to 'consider' (1:2), 'take note' (1:19), 'suppose' (2:2) and 'listen' (2:5; 4:13; 5:1). His predominantly short, punchy style conveys an urgency and has the marks of skilled, persuasive rhetoric about it. His use of language is equal to, though very different from, that of any poet. The whole crafting of the letter is designed not only to be striking in effect and memorable in the future, but to provide material to dwell on and provide wisdom and direction even in a different context than the immediate one addressed. By comparison, the average pastor probably spends little time considering how to communicate the truth he or she wants to convey in a sermon. The wisdom

---

12. Ibid., p. 30.

13. Ibid., pp. 35–60.

14. See discussion in ibid., pp. 30–35; John G. Gammie, 'Paraenetic Literature: Toward a Morphology of a Secondary Genre', *Semeia* 50 (1990), pp. 41–77; Lauri Thurén, *Argument and Theology in 1 Peter: The Origins of Christian Paraenesis*, JSNTSup 114 (Sheffield: Sheffield Academic Press, 1995), pp. 16–22, 226–227.

teacher needed the skill of an expert wordsmith, and James certainly displays that skill.

James's pastoral context

The list of subjects about which James displays his wisdom is wide. They are all 'focused on the practical living out of faith' and include questions of how to view social discrimination (2:1–13); how faith works out (2:14–26); how the tongue can be controlled (3:1–12); how to deal with quarrelling (4:1–12); how to plan one's future (4:13–17); how to approach wealth (5:1–6); and how to treat the sick (5:13–16).[15] Though the majority of scholars have used this list to discern the situation that lies behind the letter,[16] some emphasize the way in which traditional topics of Jewish wisdom, such as speech ethics, are to be found in the list. Then, too, it is being increasingly acknowledged that these are the sorts of issues that arise in most churches and that the letter has more of an encyclical feel about it than being addressed to one specific situation.[17] It is unwise, therefore, to seek to tie down the situation of the readers too closely.

Yet we can say that the letter is not a random collection of unrelated topics. There is at least one thread that gives it coherence. Both wisdom and poverty might be candidates for recognition in this regard, but so too might the theme of single-mindedness or single-heartedness. James addresses the question of completeness, wholeness, integrity or 'perfection' (*teleios*) in a number of ways. The opening chapter alerts us to the importance of the theme. Being complete, lacking in nothing, is seen as the objective of the Christian life (1:5), and suffering as an aid to achieving it. God is presented as the one who gives 'perfect' gifts (1:17), while his law is said to be a 'perfect' law (1:25). The word stands out for the frequency with which James uses it in comparison with other

---

15. Adapted from David deSilva, *An Introduction to the New Testament: Contexts, Methods and Ministry Formation* (Downers Grove: IVP; Leicester: Apollos, 2004), pp. 839–840. The list is not an exhaustive list of James's topics and does not do justice to the intricately structured nature of the letter he has written, where issues raised in the first chapter are revisited later in the letter.

16. A favoured, though not universally agreed, viewpoint is that it is addressed to Jewish converts in Palestine who were increasingly impoverished by the economic policies of the rich.

17. Bauckham, *James*, pp. 25–28, Moo, *James*, p. 20, and deSilva, *Introduction*, p. 839, among many others.

writings in the New Testament. Closely related language occurs on many other occasions (e.g. 1:4; 2:22; 3:2, 6).[18]

In contrast to the positive use of the language of wholeness, James betrays a horror of its opposite. He alone uses the word 'double-minded' (*dipsychos*) (1:8), admonishing those who suffer from it in the strongest terms (4:8). Instability is to be feared (1:6–8), as is restless disorder (3:8, 16). He looks for total and settled commitment in the disciples of Jesus.

The theme, however, is apparently well beyond the vocabulary used. Disciples are encouraged to be integrated persons whose inner knowledge and outward actions agree with each other. They are to demonstrate their consistency between what they learn and what they do (1:22–24), between their faith and their action (2:14–26), in their use of the tongue in different situations (3:9–13; 5:12) and in the wisdom they pursue (3:13–18). Integrity (wholeheartedness, unity) is to mark all aspects of their lives, not disjointedness, from the way they treat the poor (2:1–13) to the way they plan their futures (4:13–17). It is to have an impact on their response to suffering (1:9–12; 5:7–12) as much as their prayer life (5:13–18).

Underlying all this, James presents his readers with a stark choice. They can be either friends of God or friends of the world (4:4), but they cannot be both.[19] Set against the vigorous background of discussions of the meaning of friendship in James's time, friendship was not a light matter of affection but a relationship in which two parties shared 'the same attitudes and values and perceptions' and saw things the same way as each other.[20] To be a friend was to buy into the value-system of one's friend, and James insists that a very different, conflicting, set of values are believed and practised in the world from those revealed and modelled by God himself. There was a choice that one could make as to whose friend one wanted to be. The double-minded person wanted to live by two systems at the same time, 'and to be friends with everyone'.[21] But it was not a relationship that admitted compromises; it was a choice

---

18. For a discussion of the vocabulary, see Ralph P. Martin, *James*, WBC 48 (Waco: Word, 1988), pp. lxxix–lxxxii.

19. Luke T. Johnson, 'Friendship with the World / Friendship with God: A Study in Discipleship in James', in F. F. Segovia (ed.), *Discipleship in the New Testament* (Philadelphia: Fortress, 1985), pp. 166–183. Johnson modestly asks if he is 'over-reading' the evidence, but I think he has identified a convincing interpretative key to James.

20. Ibid., p. 173.

21. Ibid., p. 176.

that, once made, exercised a total claim on one's life. To be a friend of God, as Abraham was (3:23), required that one reject double-mindedness and shun any disjunction between faith and action, and live for and pray to God whole-heartedly. There was no place for a half-hearted church.

In an earlier book I commented that 'James' letter is best seen as pastoral first aid. He takes the immediate symptoms and problems and hands out medicine which will both bring immediate relief and prevent the patient from getting worse.'[22] I acknowledged that he was aware of deeper issues and their theological remedies, but that he did not develop them. I now believe this is to undervalue the depth to be found in James's letter both of a pastoral and theological kind. The underlying malady he addresses is that of a half-hearted faith, the attempt to live simultaneously at home in the world and at one with God. And the underlying cause is a lack of understanding of God.

James's theological depth

It is easy enough to list the theological issues James does not mention. It is true that he says little of Christ (only 1:2 and 2:1) and nothing of the Holy Spirit. Paul's view of justification by faith is left unaddressed. And even his mention of eschatology, which is pretty direct (5:7–9), is said to be 'peripheral'.[23] But this criticism falls into the category of what I have experienced to be one of the professional hazards of pastoral ministry. It is easy enough at the end of conducting a service to so dwell on those who are absent that one neglects almost altogether those who are present. We need to see what is in James's letter rather than what is not.

If friendship with God is the crucial underlying pastoral issue, then it should also be apparent that James has a very rich understanding of the God with whom that friendship should be enjoyed.[24] The God whom James serves (1:1) is a generous benefactor who promises a handsome reward to those who persevere in their love for him (1:12). He is 'the Father of the heavenly lights' who is unchanging in his nature (1:17). He regenerates his fallen creatures

---

22. D. Tidball, *Skilful Shepherds: Explorations in Pastoral Theology*, 2nd ed. (Leicester: Apollos, 1997), p. 135.

23. Andrew Chester and Ralph P. Martin, *The Theology of the Letters of James, Peter and Jude* (Cambridge: Cambridge University Press, 1994), pp. 16, 45.

24. These paragraphs owe much to Luke T. Johnson, *The Letter to James*, AB (New York: Doubleday, 1995), pp. 85–87.

through his word (1:18) and then longs for them to live a righteous life (1:20). He is a discriminating God who does not accept every form of religion as equally worthy (1:27).

The God on whom James bases his ethical teaching is on the side of the poor (2:5). He makes his will known through his 'royal law' (2:8–11). He is unique in his reality and one in his unity, as even the demons know (2:19). He is worthy of praise for he has made all men and women in his image (3:9). He longs for his creatures to express their dependence on him (4:1), but is hostile to those who oppose him (4:4–6), and is alone the ultimate lawgiver and judge (4:11–12). He disposes of our lives as he sees fit (4:15). As judge he is 'standing at the door' ready to intervene and mete out justice (5:4, 7–9). Yet he is 'full of compassion and mercy', able to heal the sick (5:15), hear prayer (5:15) and forgive sin (5:15).

The mere listing of the times James mentions God demonstrates two things. First, James's understanding of God is soaked in his knowledge of the Old Testament. The revelation of God found in Exodus 34:6–7, the revelation of God in the law, through the experiences of his people, and in the wisdom literature, especially of Proverbs, is all transparent here, as is the wisdom of Jesus.

Secondly, it demonstrates incontrovertibly that the foundation for his ethics is not pragmatic, situational, philosophical, humanistic nor secular, but theological.[25] His ethics are consequential, in the sense of stressing the consequences of one's actions, pragmatic in effect and wonderfully applied to a particular situation, while setting out major principles that apply to all situations, without being limited to that original situation. It may even be said that they enshrine the best form of humanism. But they are deeply shaped by theology. At one point (2:8–12) James interacts with Leviticus 19.[26] And although he does not refer to it, his ethics, as much as Peter's (1 Pet. 1:15–16), could be summed up by Leviticus 19:2, 'Be holy because I, the LORD your God, am holy.' By comparison with James's *theological approach* to practical Christian living, the *cost-benefit approach* or *psychological comfort approach* to ethical questions that characterize much pastoral work today seem barely to touch base with our foundation in God.

---

25. This differs in part from Chester and Martin, *Theology*, p. 35, who say, 'James' ethical teaching is controlled by his eschatological perspective.' That is only one aspect of his ethical foundation being found in God.

26. Luke T. Johnston, 'The Use of Leviticus 19 in the Letter of James', *JBL* 101 (1982), pp. 391–401.

James's ecclesiastical perspective

James is usually considered to have little of value in his letter regarding the church. Andrew Chester, for example, writes, 'James has no developed ecclesiology. The impression given by the letter is that he neither knows nor wants any formal structure, hierarchy, or organisation.'[27] But, as we have seen before, this is to gauge by the wrong measurements what is said. Rather than dismissing it as primitive, this picture of the church can be instructive and may indicate that the contemporary church is missing out because it is overstructured and organized.

Given his background and situation it is unsurprising James takes for granted that the company of Christians meeting together is the equivalent to a 'synagogue'.[28] He calls them that unselfconsciously in 2:2 – a unique use of the word 'synagogue' in the New Testament. In 5:14, however, he uses the word *ekklēsia*, the more normal word for 'church', without apparently meaning anything different by it. Synagogue and church seem to be interchangeable.[29] By James's time, synagogues 'were usually no more than large rooms' where people gathered to hear the Torah read and taught, by which they meant interpreted and applied, in the context of worship and prayer.[30] It was relatively simple in its leadership, organization and liturgies, but was a community in which learning took place.

Consistent with this picture the only 'leaders' James mentions are teachers (3:1) and 'elders' (5:16). Both have an important role to play, but neither is spoken of as exercising authority or having a position or office within the congregation. Indeed, James's concern about the teachers is a concern about their responsibility rather than their status. And, interestingly, the role of the elders to which he draws attention is a role in praying for the sick rather than a governance role.

What is more significant for James is that this community is one in which people minister to one another. So most of the letter is addressed to the whole

---

27. Chester and Martin, *Theology*, p. 41.

28. There is a discussion as to whether the word refers to the *meeting house* or the *people* who met there. See James B. Adamson, *The Epistle of James*, NICNT (Grand Rapids: Eerdmans, 1976), p. 105; and Martin, *James*, pp. 57, 61.

29. Adamson detects a slight difference, with 'synagogue' having a more local and less religious connotation than *ekklēsia*, but even so says they are 'practically synonymous' (*James*, p. 105).

30. B. Chilton, 'Synagogue', *DLNT*, pp. 1142–1143.

congregation. And even those parts of it that might be thought of as matters for the leadership, such as the seating arrangements mentioned in 2:1–13, are addressed to all the 'brothers and sisters'.

When he mentions 'teachers', he does so in a single verse before moving smoothly into the wider reference of 'we all' in the next. A similar shift occurs in 5:14–15, where, having mentioned the role of the elders in praying for the sick, he shows no interest in developing that discussion but moves swiftly to bring all the congregation into play with his injunction in 5:16 to 'confess your sins to each other'.

The essence of the image of the church as 'a community of the word' or 'a learning community' is not far off the mark.[31] But it should not be seen as this at the expense of being a community of prayer and worship, which James portrays (1:6; 5:13–16), and a community of restoration and action, as is apparent throughout his letter.

Conclusion

The letter of James is not the second-rate document it has often been dismissed as being. It is a 'letter of pastoral encouragement and, no less, of pastoral rebuke, proceeding from an unquestioned right of pastoral vocation and authority',[32] but its pastoral wisdom is built on sure theological foundations. James is a wonderful example of the 'understanding scribe' in action of which Matthew speaks. He is the model of a wisdom teacher of the new age, using every skill at his disposal, especially the skill of crafting words, to urge his readers not to flirt with discipleship and be members of a half-hearted church, but to be single-mindedly committed to friendship with God and to live by the teaching of Jesus.

Those who walk in the shoes of James today will be equally concerned with good doctrine while addressing the real-life issues, and not just the favourite church-life issues, that confront their congregation. They will bring out something old (the ancient biblical wisdom) but also something new as they apply that wisdom to the contemporary world. And like James they will seek to craft their instruction in such a clear and engaging way that there is no doubt as to its meaning. Their goal, too, will be to produce disciples who aim for perfection and live wholeheartedly for Christ.

---

31. Chester and Martin, *Theology*, p. 41, n. 37.

32. Adamson, *James*, p. 20.

The ministry of a seasoned elder

Peter's view of ministry is transparent. Twin concepts shape his understanding. First, ministry is the ministry of 'elders' and he views himself as an elder among elders (5:1); and secondly, ministry is the ministry of shepherding that human shepherds undertake in the consciousness of their accountability to the Chief Shepherd, Jesus Christ (5:4). Both aspects of Peter's understanding have been forged deeply by his own experience.[1] But equally, both aspects of ministry are appropriate for the needs of the scattered Christian communities living in exile to whom Peter is writing.

In this chapter we shall first look at Peter's statements about ministry and then see how he himself puts this ministry into practice in encouraging a despised church.

Leadership in the church (5:1–4)

Peter himself

At the start of his letter Peter introduces himself as 'an apostle of Jesus Christ'

---

1. I am assuming that the apostle Peter is the author of 1 Peter. The standard commentaries may be consulted for a discussion of the strengths and weaknesses of this position.

(1:1), but any sense of authority implicit in that title quickly recedes into the background as Peter clearly prefers to see himself as an elder, and presents himself throughout the letter essentially as an elder among elders (5:2). The term 'fellow-elder' (*sympresbyteros*) is unique in the New Testament and may have been coined by Peter for the purpose, although it is like Paul's penchant for prefixing the words 'workers', 'slaves' and 'soldiers' with the word 'fellow'. Notwithstanding any similarity with Paul, it is remarkable that one who was the chief apostle and a key foundation of the mother church in Jerusalem should speak of himself in this way. It shows an astonishing humility and a deep security in his gifts and calling. He has no need to assert himself and is free from any competitive spirit that drives him to prove himself superior to others. How different is this Peter from the raw and bumptious disciple we meet in the Gospels. He has been seasoned by experience and the Spirit of Jesus. As a result he is content to say that he is another older man called to leadership on the same terms as other older leaders in the church.[2]

Consistent with this self-perception Peter does not command his readers, as an apostle might, but 'appeals' to them, as one on the same level alongside them is more likely to do (5:1). In Selwyn's classic commentary on 1 Peter, he comments that the use of 'fellow-elder' 'expresses not only the Apostle's modesty but still more his sympathy with the presbyters addressed'.[3] In claiming to be a 'fellow-elder', Peter is intimating that the work the elders undertake within their local fellowships is the same as the work he undertakes, except that he does his work on a wider geographical scale. So Peter understands the responsibilities that are theirs.

Two clauses define further Peter's description of himself. He is also 'a witness of Christ's sufferings who also will share in the glory to be revealed'. (5:1). Peter's claim to be a witness of Christ's sufferings is not quite as straightforward as it seems. On one level it seems an obvious reference to Peter witnessing the passion and death of Christ. If so, the relevance for the present letter is obvious, for, as Cranfield writes:

> How deeply must what [Peter] had witnessed have been engraved on his memory! The indelible impression of that uncomplaining sufferer [Jesus] had broken down

---

2. The wording is based on I. Howard Marshall, *1 Peter*, IVPNTC (Downers Grove: IVP; Leicester: IVP, 1991), p. 160.

3. E. G. Selwyn, *The First Epistle of Peter*, 2nd ed. (Grand Rapids: Baker, 1982), p. 228.

his self-reliance and arrogance and transformed his character, and it was a compelling incentive to the care of the flock.[4]

But some question whether Peter was an eyewitness to the ultimate suffering of Christ on the cross (Mark 14:50; Luke 22:54),[5] and this seems intended to embrace the other elders as witnesses to Christ's suffering too. So it is more likely that the suffering referred to is the suffering that resulted from the proclamation of the gospel, rather than the events of Holy Week itself.[6]

The second clause is more straightforward. Peter has already encouraged his readers with the thought that 'inasmuch as you participate in the sufferings of Christ, so . . . you may be overjoyed when his glory is revealed' (4:13). The apostle who once saw the glory of Christ revealed on the mount of transfiguration has been transformed into the elder who knows that the glory that lies beyond suffering is a prize worth pursuing. In pointing forward to the return of Christ, Peter is not only explaining the motivating power that enabled him to persevere but also preparing the way to point his fellow-elders to the glory that will one day be theirs (5:4).

It is impossible to read 1 Peter, either in this particular passage or elsewhere, without an acute sense that the Peter who is writing is no longer the brash, self-confident disciple but a wise elder, seasoned by the experience of failure and suffering. Whether it is urging the need for godliness (2:11–25), contemplating the suffering of Christ (2:22–25), encouraging perseverance even in the face of injustice (3:8–22; 4:12–19) or his stressing the need for humility (5:6), Peter's personal experience is never far from the surface. A twin understanding of God in Christ drives him. On the one hand, he senses the need for a deep reverence for Christ as Lord (3:15). On the other hand, he equally senses the deep joy of knowing that God is 'the God of all grace' (5:10) who is greater than our failures and will bring us through suffering to eternal glory.

Elders

Peter assumes the church is led by elders.[7] He sees neither the need to explain their existence nor to speak of the method of their 'appointment'. Nothing is

---

4. C. E. B. Cranfield, *I and II Peter and Jude*, TBC (London: SCM, 1960), p. 125.

5. It may be that he was present without being referred to.

6. See further, Peter H. Davids, *The First Epistle of Peter*, NICNT (Grand Rapids: Eerdmans, 1990), pp. 176–177; and J. Ramsey Michaels, *1 Peter*, WBC 49 (Waco: Word: 1988), pp. 280–281.

7. See earlier discussion on the nature of elders, pp. 93–95, 151–155.

said about the terms and conditions of their employment. A little is said about their job description. They are to 'watch over' God's flock (5:2). In using the participle *episkopountes* of those he has previously referred to as *presbyteroi*, he adds to the impression given in the pastoral letters of Paul that there is no hard and fast distinction between elders and overseers, superintendents or bishops, in the early church.[8] Elders have the function of overseeing the church, which calls for them to be aware of their heavy responsibility and for the church to respect their authority.

While Paul is concerned about the character of elders, Peter's concern lies essentially with the style of their leadership rather than anything else. Three contrasts (5:2–3) that relate to motivation, reward and status spell out what is expected in Christian leadership as opposed to a style of leadership unworthy of those who lead in the name of Christ.

As to motivation, true Christian leadership does not serve from obligation or mere duty but with joyful consent. Leaders should not be cast in the role of the older son in the parable we (wrongly) call the 'parable of the prodigal son', but that of the younger son who, knowing how much he has been forgiven, returns home to serve his father joyfully (Luke 15:11–32).[9] Murray Harris points out something that the wider context of 1 Peter makes clear:

> most slaves served under some degree of compulsion and expected punishment for disobedience, Christ's slaves serve voluntarily, so that what motivates their service is not fear of punishment or even principally the prospect of reward, but the desire to please the Master.[10]

As to reward, true Christian leadership is not undertaken for money but for the sheer joy of service. There is a rightful strand of teaching about the rewards Christian servants will receive. Indeed, Peter mentions the leader's reward in verse 4. But the rewards are not material. The joy is in seeing the fruit of the gospel becoming ripe in the lives of those we serve (1 Thess. 2:19).

As to status, Christian leadership is not about position, and the power that goes with it, as Jesus makes abundantly clear (Matt. 20:20–28; Mark 10:35–45;

---

8. See pp. 153–155.

9. We are wrong to focus exclusively, as we often do, on the one son, since Jesus introduces it by saying 'There was a man who had two sons', and the contrast between the two is at least one important message of the parable.

10. Murray J. Harris, *Slave of Christ: A New Testament Metaphor for Total Devotion to Christ*, NSBT 8 (Leicester: Apollos, 1999), p. 97.

Luke 22:24–27), but about being an example, about leading from below rather than imposing from above. Even our most well-intentioned acts of service can become infected with the will to exercise power over others. When our service is recognized by others, we easily succumb to the temptation to enjoy the recognition and, even unconsciously, begin to replace the pure desire to serve with the corrupting desire for status. Against such temptations we need to be constantly vigilant, especially at times when we are weary in service, and adopt the attitude of the humble servant of whom Jesus spoke who, after a full day's work in the field and after preparing his master's supper, took the attitude that having done everything he was told to do, he remained an unworthy servant who had done only his duty (Luke 17:7–10).

If the above makes Christian leadership sound demanding, it is. But there is much joy in Christian service, as Peter recognizes. When Christ appears, worthy leaders 'will receive the crown of glory that will never fade away' (5:4). Using the common metaphor of a crown as a reward (1 Cor. 9:25; 1 Thess. 2:19; 2 Tim. 4:8; Jas 1:12; Rev. 2:10; 3:11; 4:4), Peter stresses that this reward is eternal, in contrast with the temporary gain sought by greedy leaders or the horticultural crowns offered to honour Greek citizens.[11] The crown of 'glory' suggests that the reward will be manifest and visible for others to see.[12] Here is the true motivation of all elders: a desire to please the coming Chief Shepherd and to seek only his reward.

Shepherds

The functional talk about eldership is cast in the metaphor of shepherding. 'The shepherd image is one of the few that is applied exclusively to leaders, and not to members of the community as a whole.'[13] So here Peter instructs the elders to 'be shepherds of God's flock' (5:2), but then immediately makes it clear that they are not autonomously in charge of the sheep but serving under 'the Chief Shepherd' (5:4), who will one day appear. The words pick up common New Testament imagery and thought. Hebrews 13:20 speaks of Jesus as 'that great Shepherd of the sheep', while the instructions to the under-shepherds recall Paul's farewell speech at Miletus (Acts 20:28). But it is really impossible to read these words without recalling the conversation between Jesus and Peter on the shore of Galilee after the resurrection (John 21:15–19).

---

11. Davids, *Peter*, p. 182.

12. Wayne Grudem, *1 Peter*, TNTC (Leicester: IVP; Grand Rapids: Eerdmans, 1988), p. 191.

13. D. Bennett, *Biblical Images for Leaders and Followers* (Oxford: Regnum, 1993), p. 129.

Peter has lamentably failed his Master but, now humbled, is restored and recommissioned to feed and take care of the flock. The elder who has fulfilled that calling since Pentecost now encourages his fellow-elders with the same words.

What does he mean by the image of a shepherd? He spends no time explaining it but rather assumes that they will understand the meaning of the image with its rich background elsewhere in Scripture. Howard Marshall helpfully summarizes it like this:

> As developed in the various biblical passages, it brings out the desperate need of sheep for a shepherd: to keep them from wandering away in their stupidity; to protect them from dangers from wild animals and thieves; to feed them; to find them, even at personal risk, when they are lost; to prevent one animal from taking advantage of others; to maintain unity within the flock; and to exercise individual care.[14]

Priesthood of all believers (2:4–10)

Throughout the New Testament there is a noticeable absence of any reference to leaders in the church being 'priests'. This is not a controversial claim but rather one that is commonly agreed.[15] 1 Peter, along with other passages, explains why. The church has assumed a priestly role and every member is now a priest, with the privilege of direct access to God through Christ the High Priest, and has the attendant responsibility to offer 'spiritual sacrifices' (see also Heb. 10:19–25). The longed-for hope of Exodus 19:6 has at last become a reality in the church. Although J. H. Elliott has argued strongly that the two references in 2:5 and 2:9 to the church as 'a holy priesthood' are collective references that refer to the identity of God's people as a community, and so do not warrant the doctrine of 'the priesthood of all believers',[16] most find his case

---

14. Marshall, *1 Peter*, p. 162.

15. One of the strongest statements in agreement with this is found in Hans Küng, *The Church*, tr. R. and R. Ockenden (London: Search, 1968), p. 364. This Roman Catholic theologian argues that many 'ecclesiologies' are in fact 'hierarchologies' and goes on to give a robust exposition of the doctrine of the priesthood of all believers (see pp. 363–387).

16. J. H. Elliott, *The Elect and the Holy: An Exegetical Examination of 1 Peter 2:4–10*, NovTSup 12 (Leiden: Brill, 1966).

overstated and unpersuasive.[17] Both collectively and individually, believers are priests called to offer not the animal sacrifices of the old covenant but the spiritual sacrifices of thankful worship (Heb. 13:15), of humble service (Phil. 4:18), of intercessory prayer (1 Tim. 2:1) and of declaring the gospel (1 Pet. 2:9; 3:15). As Hans Küng has said, 'the priesthood of all believers is far from being just a theological slogan or an empty title. Behind the phrase there lies an extremely rich and concrete reality.'[18] And reality must be practised, not just claimed.

The emphasis on all being priests severely undermines the pretence that leaders in the Christian church are somehow priests in a class of their own. It is astonishing, then, that so much of the church's energy down through the centuries has been directed to proving the opposite. *Baptism, Eucharist and Ministry*, typically, admits that although there is no New Testament precedent for using the word 'priest' in reference to an ordained minister, it is more than acceptable to do so on the basis of the later practice of the early church, where the term came to be used of the one 'presiding at the eucharist'. 'They may appropriately be called priests,' claims the World Council of Churches, 'because they fulfil a particular service by strengthening and building up the royal and prophetic priesthood of the faithful through word and sacrament.'[19]

This is, however, an evasion of biblical truth and an unhelpful confusion of terminology, as the word 'priest', when applied to leaders in the church, carries so much baggage with it. It is a faulty foundation on which an unhelpful hierarchical superstructure is built.[20] It creates dependent believers who do not

---

17. E.g. Davids, *Peter*, p. 87, n. 23; Grudem, *1 Peter*, p. 101; and Michaels, *1 Peter*, pp. 100–101.

18. Küng, *Church*, p. 382.

19. *Baptism, Eucharist and Ministry* [*BEM*], Faith and Order Paper 111 (Geneva: World Council of Churches, 1982), clause 17 and commentary, p. 23. Historical, rather than biblical, justification is appealed to throughout. See e.g. clauses 19, 22. For an excellent evangelical critique, see the response of the World Evangelical Fellowship, edited by Paul Schrotenboer, 'An Evangelical Response to BEM', *ERT* 13.4 (1989), pp. 291–313. It may be noted that even evangelicals who advocate the threefold ministry of bishops, priests and deacons do so on the basis of patristic history rather than Scripture. See e.g. Peter Toon, 'Episcopalianism', in Steven Cowan (ed.), *Who Runs the Church?* (Grand Rapids: Zondervan, 2004), pp. 23–29.

20. *BEM*, p. 25, quickly moves from the historical portrait to the position of clause 23, which states that 'Among the gifts a ministry of *episkopē* is *necessary* to express and safeguard the unity of the body' (italics mine). In the light of history, I am not sure what evidence can be produced to support such a statement.

exercise their full rights as priests but shelter behind others. And it narrows the New Testament vision of ministry and robs the church of the variety of leadership we see there, all of which is devoted to building up the faithful. Küng poses the question of how difficult it is, since 'particular names like priests and clergy have no basis in the New Testament', to find alternative names for those who lead the church.[21] Schrotenboer's conclusion that *BEM* simply justifies existing practice without submitting it to biblical critique seems entirely warranted.[22]

Peter presents a view of the church where all are priests but some are called to exercise an overseeing role as elders and shepherds, which they do both with great joy and with great care, mindful of the Chief Shepherd who will shortly appear.

The elder's pastoral strategy

How does this seasoned elder himself go about the shepherding of God's flock that was under his care? There are two aspects to the question to which we must give attention. First, we must ask what the need of the flock was that he was shepherding and, only then, how he went about accomplishing his task.

The readers as 'resident aliens'

Peter's readers are believers, dispersed around several communities in Asia Minor, whose existence is governed by the fact that they do not belong. They are in exile and live as 'resident aliens' estranged from the context in which they are situated (1:2; 2:11). John Elliott has sought to clothe the terms used (*paroikia*, *paroikoi* and *parepidēmoi*) in economic and social garments, arguing that it is inadequate to spiritualize them. They may well have been, he suggests, 'numbered among the rural population and villagers who had been relocated to city territories and assigned inferior status to the citizenry'.[23] They may also have included artisans and traders who travelled throughout the towns and cities, who, whether on the move or more settled, were never accepted as equals. These people, like so many displaced persons today, experienced a sense of dislocation and were defenceless in the face of powerful forces of politics, law and bureaucracy.

---

21. Küng, *Church*, p. 387.

22. Schrotenboer, 'Evangelical Response', p. 308.

23. John H. Elliott, *A Home for the Homeless: A Sociological Exegesis of 1 Peter, its Situation and Strategy* (London: SCM, 1981), p. 48.

Given that the central and extended section of the letter deals with the question of how to handle suffering and injustice as a Christian (2:11 – 4:19), it is clear that Peter's readers are treated with contempt by those in authority, especially for their faith in Christ. They are members of a church despised by the majority, host culture in which they live. The world around them simply does not understand their devotion to Christ as Lord nor the world view that results from that commitment.

Elliott's setting of the letter in a socio-economic context reminds us that we should not constantly jump to spiritualized or idealized readings of Scripture, as we are wont to do. Scripture addresses the real-life actualities of believers, which have a great deal to do with their position in the pecking order, their treatment at work, their financial struggles or plain sense of exploitation and oppression. Good shepherds guide their sheep through the struggles of every-day reality. Good shepherds do not retreat with their flocks from the uncongenial environment of the material world to shelter and warm each other in a cosy spiritual sheepfold. They lead the sheep through the desert, protecting, guiding and feeding them as they go.

These sad realities may have disturbing implications for faith, as they evidently did for Peter's readers. Where was hope to be found in this situation? Why did God not step in to deal with injustice? What obligations were laid on the victims? What part should the church be playing in it all? How was one to live authentically for God in such an inhospitable climate? These are real spiritual questions that, left unaddressed, can cause doubt to arise and perplexity or bitterness to undermine trust. But these are often not the questions the church addresses, as it frequently succumbs to its own internal agenda that can seem petty and remote in comparison with the challenges faced in the real world.

Although, as I have strongly argued, pastors should not rush to spiritualize a text like 1 Peter, it is true that the letter has value in addressing those who feel in spiritual exile. Many members of the Western church share in the affluence and security of the nation in which they live, but feel alienated from its moral and spiritual climate. As the church moves from having enjoyed a position of privilege to being marginalized, as long-held moral laws based on the Judeo-Christian tradition are dispensed with in favour of a non-discriminatory secularism, as increasingly the public square fails to understand the language and practice of faith, 1 Peter comes into its own. If the aliens and strangers to whom it is addressed are the socially, politically and economically marginalized, they are also the spiritually downtrodden. Our understanding of those addressed needs to be inclusive.

The elder's paraenesis

1 Peter is usually assumed to be an example of paraenesis, that is, as mentioned in the previous chapter, of moral exhortation, aimed at confirming people in their beliefs and conduct rather than producing initial evidence to persuade people of what they do not believe.[24] But Peter's is a very special form of *paraenesis*, where the basis for the encouragement lies not in popular precepts but is deeply rooted in Peter's understanding of Christ. Throughout, Jesus Christ is presented both as a Saviour to be trusted and an example to be followed (see e.g. 2:21–25).

Peter shows himself to be a skilled craftsman who, like James, constantly shapes wonderfully motivating phrases, although his rhetorical technique is different from James's. Urging his readers to some particular response or course of action, he litters his letter with 'because', 'for', 'so that', 'in order that', 'therefore' and so on. He constantly sets out the reason for and the results of the call not to conform to the world. But this motivational rhetoric is set in an overall framework concerning Jesus Christ and is rendered empty without this. The specific encouragements are nothing without the grand Christological and eschatological vision of being God's elect people who have a living hope through the risen Jesus Christ. Moral exhortation alone is too narrow a basis on which to make an appeal. The broader vision is what provides the truly motivating power to live a holy life. Theology and ethics are inseparable.[25]

This translates into shaping the document and its argument as a whole. Adapting the work of David deSilva,[26] we might see main arguments of the letter as follows.

1. *He focuses on their identity (1:3 – 2:3).* They may feel they are exiles but in reality are elect by God (1:1). They may be despised in the present world but are, in fact, a people with a living hope of an inheritance yet to be revealed (1:3–9). They are called constitutionally to live holy lives, and as a people set apart from others will inevitably not conform to conventional standards and thought forms (1:13–16). Their minds are not set on short-term gains but eternal realities (1:17–25). As a born-again people, who have begun to taste the

---

24. J. G. Gammie, 'Paraenetic Literature: Toward the Morphology of a Secondary Genre', *Semeia* 50 (1990), p. 70.

25. The paragraph is based on the thorough study by Lauri Thurén, *Argument and Theology in 1 Peter: The Origins of Christian Paraenesis*, JSNTSup 114 (Sheffield: Sheffield Academic Press, 1995).

26. David deSilva, *An Introduction to the New Testament: Contexts, Methods and Ministry Formation* (Downers Grove: IVP; Leicester: Apollos, 2004), pp. 847–858.

Lord's goodness, they are called to an ethically pure life (2:1–3). Their host culture may loathe them, but in God's sight they are 'a chosen people, a royal priesthood, a holy nation, God's special possession' (2:9), with a mission in the world to declare God's praise.

2. *He refocuses their attentions (1:14–15; 4:1–11).* The key question they should be asking is how to live in the light of the future. They are under enormous pressure to conform, but really need to keep their eye on the greater reality of having to give an account to the one who will judge 'the living and the dead' (4:5). Because 'the end of all things is near' (4:7), they need to serve each other 'as stewards of God's grace' (4:10) and to live for his praise (4:11).

3. *He reinterprets their experience (1:7; 2:18–25; 4:12–19).* Their suffering is not to be minimized and comes to them in various forms (1:6). But it has a number of purposes, which put it in a different light. Astonishingly, Peter explains the various positive benefits of the pressures they face. It is a 'proving ground' for their faith (1:7). It identifies them with Christ (2:18–25). It is a condition for sharing in Christ's glory (4:13–14). It is a sign of God's honour resting on them (4:14).

4. *He points to an example (2:21–25).* The twin motivations of the salvation yet to be fully revealed and the example of Jesus Christ are intricately bound together. Evangelicals who fear any sign of a doctrine of works and exalt, rightly, Christ as Saviour, are apt to play down Christ's role as a pattern for living. But Peter does so without any reservation or qualification. 'To this', he writes, 'you were called, because Christ suffered for you, leaving you an example, that you should follow in his steps' (2:21). They are Christ's people and so share in his way of living.

5. *He provides specific directions (2:18 – 3:12; 5:1–5).* Peter does not shelter behind grand theological principles but carefully applies his teaching to specific groups within the church in what looks like the pattern of a household code. He addresses slaves (2:18–25), wives (3:1–6), husbands (3:7), elders (5:1–4) and those 'who are younger' (5:5–6).[27] While the predominant error in much

---

27. The term *neōteroi* has caused much discussion. There is no evidence to support those who wish to see it as a junior level of leadership (maybe deacons) to the elders. The suggestion arises because of the contrast. If 'elders' are officers in the church, then perhaps 'the younger' are also officers of a kind. But if one takes elders to refer to older men, as previously discussed, rather than officers, the argument falls. It most probably means the younger generation in the church, or those younger in the faith. It is true to form that a younger generation should push the boundaries against elders and so need to be encouraged to submit. See Davids, *Peter*, pp. 182–184; and Michaels, *1 Peter*, pp. 288–289.

teaching today is probably that preachers give moral instructions without underpinning them theologically, some escape into theological abstractions and never bring their teaching, however wonderful, down to earth and within the grasp of their congregations. Application is a necessary element of any true exposition of the Scriptures.

6. *He exposes Satan's tactics (5:8–9)*. Peter is aware, as are all New Testament writers, that Christians are engaged in a spiritual warfare. Earlier, he referred to 'sinful desires' as at 'war against your soul' (2:1), but the enemy, in 5:5–9, is a prowling Satan who stalks Christians as his prey, yet who can be successfully resisted by 'standing firm in the faith'.

7. *He highlights God's grace (5:10–11)*. The grace of God is spoken of eight times in this letter, in one form or another (1 Pet. 1:2, 10, 13; 3:7; 4:10; 5:5, 10, 12). It is a fitting climax to the letter for Peter to remind them that God is the God of *all* grace (5:10), whose power and love will be sufficient to lead them through their present troubles to eternal glory.

Conclusion

Within the wider setting of the priesthood of all believers, Peter assumes only one form of ministry within the church: that of elders, acting as shepherds over the flock. He himself values the title of 'elder' and, in spite of being able to claim apostleship, prizes that title and perspective on ministry more than any other. He spends no time explaining the role, nor detailing any terms and conditions of appointment. His letter, however, demonstrates what it is to serve as an elder over a scattered group of Christian communities despised for their faith, as well perhaps as for their social position. The tone of the letter and its gentle, yet robust and inspiring, exhortations reveal the way in which a young, brash disciple of Jesus has been honed by experience and refined by the Holy Spirit into a seasoned elder. His own closeness to Jesus, his own failures, and his own experience of suffering make his call for humility and perseverance anything but hollow. Using great rhetorical skill, he never lets words outrun his theology. It is Christ, above all, who motivates him to carry on living a holy life of service. He exhibits exactly the qualities of a shepherd who not only takes care of the sheep but also serves as an example to them. In spite of the bleakness of his readers' apparent situation, he keeps his eye firmly on the glory to come, a glory he once witnessed first hand on the mount of transfiguration.

12. JOHN'S LETTERS: MINISTRY IN A COMPROMISED CHURCH

The ministry of experienced truth

The letters of John are generally considered to shed no light on the question of ministry in the early church. David Bartlett, for example, says that in these letters 'ministry is most evident by its lack'.[1] James Dunn similarly concludes that 'throughout these writings there is no real concept of ministry, let alone office', because they continue the individualism of the Fourth Gospel and are chiefly concerned about the immediate relationship between a believer and Jesus.[2] Judith Lieu grants that 'church and ministry are implicitly or explicitly' a concern of 2 and 3 John, but believes that such concerns are absent from 1 John.[3] Such verdicts, however, are unnecessarily negative and the letters of John reveal more about ministry than is usually supposed.[4]

---

1. David Bartlett, *Ministry in the New Testament*, OBT (Minneapolis: Fortress, 1993), p. 113.
2. James D. G. Dunn, *Unity and Diversity in the New Testament* (Philadelphia: Westminster; London: SCM, 1977), p. 119.
3. Judith Lieu, *The Theology of the Johannine Epistles* (Cambridge: Cambridge University Press, 1991), p. 91.
4. I am assuming a common authorship between the Fourth Gospel and the three letters. For a discussion of the validity of this position, see the standard commentaries.

The elder

1 John plunges straight into its subject without any of the customary notes of introduction. So there is no indication of who is writing, to whom, nor any note of greeting. In contrast, 2 and 3 John have full introductions. They come from 'The elder' (2 John 1; 3 John 1). The second letter is addressed to 'the lady chosen by God', a poetic and personified way of speaking about the church, while the third letter is addressed to an individual called Gaius. Both contain a greeting (2 John 3; 3 John 2).

'The elder' is obviously well enough known by his readers to require no further introduction. Whoever he is, our interest lies in what he means by the term 'the elder', which is, as Howard Marshall notes, akin to a letter being signed 'Your vicar' or 'Your pastor'.[5] Traditionally, the term was interpreted as the name for an office and, consequently, stating such a claim at the start of the letter was a sign of authority: his words were to be heeded carefully, or else![6] But, as we have seen, recent research into the meaning of elder has called this into question.[7] The term is much more likely to refer to an older, wiser person than to an official position. It still carries with it a sense of authority, but it is the authority of relationship and of experience rather than of rank. In this case, it may have a particular edge, since the elder was part of the original band of disciples and is a direct bridge between Jesus and the churches to whom he is writing.

An unusual feature of the term is that it refers to a single 'elder'. Everywhere else in the New Testament elders act collegially, as members of a group leading their local church. Here it seems the elder stands alone. This is surely chiefly because of who he is. Just as Peter described himself as a 'fellow-elder', so John, another of the original disciple band, sees himself as adopting that role.[8] In both cases, the absence of the stress on their apostolic authority is astonishing. To persuade their readers of their case, they rely on argument and tradition rather than the power of any office.

---

5. I. Howard Marshall, *The Epistles of John*, NICNT (Grand Rapids: Eerdmans, 1978), p. 59.

6. E.g. John R. W. Stott, *The Epistles of John*, TNTC (London: Tyndale, 1964), p. 200. He quotes Westcott with approval: 'It described not age simply, but official position.'

7. See discussion on pp. 151–157.

8. I recognize that this is a minority view, but see Colin G. Kruse, *The Letters of John*, PNTC (Grand Rapids: Eerdmans; Leicester: Apollos, 2000), pp. 9–14.

The use of 'elder' in the singular may also be because his ministry is evidently different from that of the elders within a local church. The elder seems not to be so much part of a local church leadership as exercising an overseeing role more widely over a number of local churches.

Care should be taken not to read any precedence into this for the emergence of some future episcopal authority. To begin with, this elder is in the not-to-be-repeated position of having been with Jesus (1:1). Secondly, so little is said about the role and relationship that making a case for the emergence of some fixed episcopal role is certainly to go beyond the evidence. Thirdly, as we shall consider more fully in the next section, the language and atmosphere of the letters exudes a sense of family, rather than of hierarchy and institution.

The church as family

A true understanding of a situation often arises from observing the informal and incidental way in which things work rather than by listening to official statements. So it is here. Although John says little explicitly about the church, much is revealed through his passing references about the way it functions. Throughout the letters there is a sense of family.[9] This is entirely to be expected if Elliott's belief, mentioned previously, that the disciples who followed Jesus and the church in the later New Testament were not an egalitarian movement but a family, is accepted.[10] John's letters fit with what we see elsewhere.

John writes to his 'dear children', using a variety of terms ranging from those that suggest 'a small child' to those that focus on the idea of 'offspring' (2:1, 12, 14, 28; 3:7, 18; 4:4; 5:2; 3 John 4). Other family terms occur (2:12, 13; 2 John 1, 4, 13). Sometimes the focus is on their being 'children of God' rather than his children (3:1, 2, 10; 5:2, 19). Relational language predominates. The tenderness with which he addresses them, even while speaking of tough issues, suggests a committed and secure relationship between them.

---

9. In spite of Bartlett's comment that John has no interest in ministry, he details the family relationship to which I refer in this and the following passages. It is obviously a particular type of ministry he finds absent (*Ministry*, pp. 109–111).

10. J. H. Elliott, 'Jesus Was Not an Egalitarian: A Critique of an Anachronistic and Idealist Theory', *BTB* 32 (2002), pp. 75–91; and 'The Jesus Movement Was Not Egalitarian but Family-Oriented', *BibInt* 11 (2003), pp. 173–210. See also pp. 113–116 in the present book.

The language of the family is evident in other ways too. A great deal of attention is paid in the first letter to how brothers (and sisters) need to relate to one another. They are to love each other and reject hatred (3:10–12, 15; 4:20–21), walk in the light with one another (2:9–11), not cause any to stumble (2:10), share their material possessions with each other (3:17) and pray for their restoration when they fall (5:16).[11] Members of another church are described as 'the children of your sister' (2 John 13), while the church to whom John writes in his second letter is personified as 'an elect lady' (my tr.).

The whole tone is one of affection and family, where people belong to each other as more or less equals. It fits with this that the leadership exercised, though real, is informal rather than anything else and one where 'the elder' is 'more like an elder brother or father than a "bishop"'.[12]

In the light of this, although there may be no sense of a developed institutional ministry or church, we have here an authentic picture of church as family being led by an older person who guides and directs them on the basis of experience and relationship rather than status and office.

Compromise and boundaries

The elder has a very real ministerial task to achieve. Folk are trying to lead the believers astray (1 John 2:26), and the church is under threat of compromising the truth, with the result that people are also compromising on the behaviour expected of followers of Christ. Belief and behaviour are inseparable. The one affects the other and vice versa. Reading John's first letter, it is hard to know whether he is more concerned about sin in the believer or error in the church. The truth is, of course, that he is equally concerned about both because they are two sides of the same coin.

In this case, the erroneous belief concerns the person of Jesus. In three passages, John refers to the mistaken belief some have propagated concerning the Master. Essentially, some deny that Jesus is the Messiah (2:22). John repeats the accusation in 5:1. At first sight this seems a puzzling position for any who claim to be Christians, since such an affirmation seems fundamental. It is only as

---

11. It is unfortunate that TNIV has lost the family language in a desire to be inclusive and translates 'brothers' as 'fellow-believers' rather than, as others do, translating it 'brothers and sisters'.

12. Bartlett, *Ministry*, p. 109.

John fills out the details later that the teaching of these people becomes clear. They deny that 'Jesus Christ has come in the flesh [and] is from God' (4:2; 2 John 7). Furthermore, they harbour doubts about the reality of his death and its value as an atoning substitution for us (1:7; 2:2; 4:10; 5:6–8). Crucially, they call into question the authenticity of the incarnation and deny that Jesus of Nazareth, who really lived in the flesh, is permanently united as the Son of God to his Father, and is the expected Messiah.[13]

The effect of this is to devalue the importance of the material. If Christ has not come in the flesh, then they need not be concerned about the flesh – it is the spirit life, and only the spirit life, that matters. Consequently, they deny any ongoing sin in the believer (1:1–10), or the need generally to obey God's law (2:1–11; 3:4–10), or the need specifically to love other members of the Christian family in any real and practical way (3:11–18; 4:7–12). Perfection, of a sort, has already been accomplished. So they can make themselves at home in this world, lusting after all its glittering attractions without any realization that it will soon pass away (2:15–17). Such people walk in darkness (1:6) and have given in to the worship of idols (5:21), among whom the reigning idol is self.

The teaching of these false teachers is attractive. It removes from Christians the burden of moral responsibility and the pressure of having to live an ethical life. The world, the sinful flesh and the devil are all powerfully channelled through this false teaching and, given the fact of ongoing sinfulness of believers, can prove mightily seductive. So John does not toy with the false teaching but writes in the strongest terms against it. Remarkably, for a man known primarily as an advocate of love, he denounces the false teachers in the most uncompromising of ways. They are liars (2:4, 22; 4:20) and have the spirit of antichrist (2:18, 22; 4:3; 2 John 7). As in the Gospel of John, his language is dualistic throughout. We live either in light or in darkness; we either love or hate; we either know the truth or believe a lie; we are either righteous or lawless; we are either children of God or children of the devil; we have either life or no life. Such dualism reinforces strong boundaries between what is right and what is false. To permit any compromise with this false teaching is unacceptable and will spell the demise of the authentic church.

---

13. Marshall, *Epistles of John*, pp. 157–158. See pp. 14–22 for a fuller discussion of the identity of the false teachers. For an alternative viewpoint, which argues the situation is sufficiently explained in terms of Jewish apostasy, see Terry Griffith, 'A Non-Polemical Reading of 1 John: Sin, Christology and the Limits of Johannine Christology', *TynBul* 49 (1998), pp. 253–276.

While the issues are mostly different in the shorter letters, the same emphasis on the importance of truth is evident. In 2 John, the elder writes of loving the church 'in the truth' (1) and of others who 'know the truth' (1). He describes believers as 'walking in the truth' (4). Similarly, in 3 John, the elder again writes of loving them 'in the truth' (1), of rejoicing in their 'faithfulness to the truth' (3) and of their 'walking in the truth' (4) and of their work cooperatively for the truth (8). While some of these phrases clearly carry the meaning of, say, loving believers 'genuinely' or 'authentically', it is inadequate merely to interpret them in this way. The only authentic or genuine way to love is within the constraints of truthful teaching and belief.

The false teachers, whom John condemns, seem to view themselves as still within the bounds of the Christian faith, although they have left John's church. Colin Kruse suggests that 'the secessionists were Christians who once belonged to the author's community, and subsequently left because they had come to accept a different Christology from that espoused by the author and others in his community'.[14] But for John, this is not a matter of theological opinion or Christological emphasis; it is a matter of truth versus lies about something fundamental, namely Christ. The boundaries of the church cannot be stretched to accommodate these false teachers. It is not that they are legitimately forming another denomination, nor is it a variation of Christianity: it is a denial of authentic Christianity. The fences of the church have to be strong and unbreachable and drawn in such a way as to exclude these heretics.

John gives the impression of being a good pastor. His letter is written in familiar language with a warm tone and an emphasis on loving one another. But if ever there was a pastoral iron fist in a velvet glove, this is it. When it comes to such important truth about Christ, there can be no compromise. The boundaries have to be drawn clearly.

David deSilva rightly cautions us to handle John's approach with care.[15] It may, he argues, give some the impression that conservatism is always to be equated with faithfulness and provide justification for others to cause splits and dissension over a variety of issues. We should be careful to ensure that should any division become necessary, the cause of the split is about an issue of such import and as essential as the doctrine of Christ. David deSilva admits honestly that most of the splits of which he is aware are not for anything like as serious a reason. And any tension that arises in the church should be handled

---

14. Kruse, *Letters of John*, p. 105.

15. David deSilva, *An Introduction to the New Testament: Contexts, Methods and Ministry Formation* (Downers Grove: Apollos; Leicester: Apollos, 2004), pp. 473–474.

with the same spirit of love and commitment to unity as is evident in these letters. Other people should always be interpreted charitably, while those who criticize zealously, and so kill love, should be avoided.[16] Nonetheless, there may be occasions where division is right because the heart of the gospel is at stake. When that is so, it should always be 'an occasion for mourning',[17] as 1 John is, because it speaks of the failure of the church.

The theology of experienced truth

There is more to be said, however, about how John accomplished his aim. His strategy is very different from that of 2 Peter or Jude, where the future of the church is equally under threat from false teaching. Both those letters and John's are polemical and John's language may be as uncompromising as theirs about the false teachers, but he clearly has no wish to elaborate on their precarious position or their downfall, as we see in those other letters. The accusations of lying and of being influenced by antichrist (2:18; 4:3; 2 John 7) are set in an altogether different context, which draws attention to his different pastoral strategy.

John has confidence in his readers and the Holy Spirit. If he stresses the importance of truth, it is a truth he and his readers have already experienced. The abrupt beginning to the first letter testifies to the truth John himself has witnessed with his own eyes and heard with his own ears (1:1–5). But the focus is not so much on what 'I know' as on what 'we know'. The truth is also known and experienced by his readers. It is not his exclusive possession as the elder.

Truth is not a set of intellectual propositions about which John needs to convince his readers but, rather, heart knowledge they already have, which he wishes them to acknowledge. He needs them to reflect on their experience and see for themselves the certainty of what he is saying. Judith Lieu is worth quoting somewhat extensively on this point:

> Although the community of 1 John need vigilance . . . and are urged to test the
> spirits (4:1), the over-riding sense is of the assurance of what they already know,

---

16. These thoughts, among many others, are explored in Richard Baxter's *The Cure of Church Divisions* (London: Nevil Symmons, 1670). The work is précised in D. Tidball, *Skilful Shepherds: Explorations in Pastoral Theology*, 2nd ed. (Leicester: Apollos, 1997), pp. 301–305.

17. DeSilva, *Introduction*, p. 473.

have achieved, possess and are. Although he exhorts and encourages (2:15), he writes because their sins *are* forgiven, they *do* have knowledge of the one from the beginning and the father, they *have* conquered, *are* strong and *do* experience God's indwelling word (2:12–14). Victory is already there, over the evil one, over those who would oppose them, and over the world (4:4; 5:4f). . . . Life, knowledge, victory, strength are 'eschatological' realities; elsewhere in the New Testament they belong in full to the final defeat of evil and realisation of God's kingdom. For 1 John they are part of the community's present experience and a key to their confidence.[18]

John constantly draws attention to what they 'know', not to cause them to question and doubt (do they *really* know?) but to encourage them to disbelieve those who are teaching something they have not experienced. He has no reservation in making an assumption about their assurance. Their knowledge is not a matter of doubt or hesitancy. There are some thirty references to what John, or his readers, 'know', or 'have known', in his three letters.[19] Uppermost is that John's readers 'know God', know that they are 'in him' and know that they are his children and are experiencing eternal life.

The revelation and teaching of the Holy Spirit is a vital element in this. They know because it has been made known to them by the Spirit who lives within them (1 John 3:24) and who gives them a vital experience of God himself in residence in their lives. This living and divine Spirit is 'the Spirit of truth' (4:6; 5:6; see also 2:20), who testifies to Jesus Christ (5:6–8). It is plain that there is thought to be no tension between right doctrine and experience, between the word and the Spirit. The two function in perfect harmony with each other, as if partners in a perfectly flowing rhythmic dance. There is not a whiff of dead orthodoxy about John's writing.

John's pastoral theology takes Christian experience seriously and has been described by R. E. O. White as an evangelical 'mysticism'. 'The New Testament', he writes,

> does not contain a richer or more varied analysis of the inner life of the Christian than is offered in 1 John. It is remarkable that the epistle which lays so great stress upon historicity and the apostolic tradition, and which at the same time presents so rigorous an ethical challenge, should also find large place in the Christian life for mystical experience. Yet John contrives to emphasise all three, and to strengthen

---

18. Lieu, *Theology*, pp. 27–28; her italics.

19. There are other references to what God has made known.

each in counterpoint to the others. So penetrating and balanced, is his representation of Christian life.[20]

The spirituality John advances is, as the above quote stresses, of a different kind than the vague spirituality commonly spoken of today. It is not any sort of spiritual experience, however introverted, vapid or misguided. It can arise only from a belief in the apostolic and historic gospel and can be observed in a particular ethical way of living. It is not purely a matter of experiential feeling. Counterfeit spiritualities abound and some are offered by the false teachers John opposes. That is why John asserts it is necessary to exercise discernment by testing the authenticity of the spirits and rejecting false paths, however attractive (4:1–3).

True spirituality is rooted in the reality of the historic and living Christ. It is established on the facts of the faith. It is also a spirituality that, in addition to satisfying the inner quests of the soul, has immediate and observable consequences. It leads to forgiveness (1:7, 9), freedom from guilt (3:19–22) and victory over evil and Satan (3:8–9; 4:4; 5:4–5). It fosters a desire to live a righteous life (2:6; 3:2, 6–10, 24). It results in fellowship with God (1:3) and an increasing and practical love for the other members of the Christian family (3:16–17; 4:7–12). It has emotional consequences, too, leading to confidence in God's presence, to fearlessness (4:18), joy and an assured hope for the future (3:1–3).[21]

The little note to Gaius, known as 3 John, provides a glimpse of some of these things in practice. It is the only one of John's letters to use the word 'church' (3 John 6, 10), but the complexion of the note is still relational rather than institutional. As mentioned above, it refers four times in its first half to the importance of truth, but in its second half illustrates what this means in reference to two contrasting persons. Diotrophes (3 John 9) pushes himself forward and is schismatic. He erects boundaries, which as we have seen is something John himself finds essential, but they are erected in the wrong place and exclude the wrong people. Demetrius (3 John 12), however, is spoken of well by everyone, apparently from the context because he 'does good'. The one shows what it is to walk in the dark, while the other demonstrates what it is to walk in the light. Whatever Diotrophes might claim about his spirituality, the fruit of it is evident in his life and proves his spirituality to be a false one;

---

20. R. E. O. White, *An Open Letter to Evangelicals: A Devotional and Homiletic Commentary on the First Epistle of John* (Exeter: Paternoster, 1964), pp. 158–159.

21. See further ibid., pp. 159–160.

whereas, the spirituality of Demetrius demonstrates itself to be well grounded in Christ and in love and service to his people.

John recognizes that there will be seasons in the spiritual life (1 John 2:12–14). Little children sense, above all, that they are forgiven and accepted. Older people, who have walked with God for a long time, are settled in their relation with God; whereas, young people feel the heat of the spiritual battle most keenly. Our spiritual experience will develop but will also, depending on our determination to 'walk in the light' daily, ebb and flow. Yet, for all the qualifications, underlying the spirituality of 1 John is the sense of remaining in Christ, of a steady, sure and firm relationship, which John 15 introduced. As R. E. O. White writes:

> We must not be content with rare moments of ecstasy or illumination or special ritual excitement. Our fellowship with God, our mutual indwelling, is to be the constant background of Christian life. Though rising at times into exceptional power and joy, it should remain at all times the true light of all our seeing, the deep spring of all our day-to-day existence. We *remain*, steadfast, unseparated, *in Him*, going forth refreshed and armed from Him to the tasks of the kingdom in the world, returning with rest and infinite peace to Him, the Source which is also our home.[22]

Conclusion

There is an urgency about John's letters. The church is in danger of compromise and he sees the need to draw clear-cut boundaries so that his readers can be left in no doubt as to what is acceptable as Christians both in regard to teaching about Christ and living for Christ. He is concerned to establish both orthodoxy (right belief) and orthopraxis (right behaviour). In doing so, he does not mince his words. There is a sharp duality in the way he writes. And yet his purpose is not essentially polemical; it is pastoral.[23]

His pastoral approach is not to wield authority and denounce from on high. He works alongside them, gently guiding them, as it were, to understand for themselves. He is the father of the family rather than the boss in an organization. Perhaps that is why he patiently goes over the ground more than once, so that they may truly grasp it. He draws out from his 'dear children' what they already know and have experienced. From the beginning he writes positively

---

22. Ibid., p. 165; his italics.

23. Griffith, 'Non-Polemical Reading', p. 255.

about what he has experienced as a basis for knowing truth. But mostly, he asks them to consider from their experience the truth of the orthodox position in comparison with the error of the false teachers. For him, as for many in post-modern cultures, truth is not to be affirmed but to be experienced. In adopting this approach, he inevitably brings belief, spirituality and behaviour into close harmony. And in doing so, presents us with one of the most balanced models of ministry found in the New Testament.

13. JUDE, 2 PETER: MINISTRY IN AN ENDANGERED CHURCH

The ministry of pastoral polemics

The short letters of Jude and 2 Peter are very rare examples of pastoral polemic. The health of the churches to which they write is in a critical condition and there is a need for urgent action. Both churches suffer from a cancer within their bodies caused by a strain of false teaching that promotes immoral living, and the cancer is so virulent that only urgent and direct action will do. So the letters engage in vigorous denunciation of the false teachers in the hope that the churches will wake up to the danger they are in and cast the parasitic cells from their midst.

Although this gives the letters somewhat of a gloomy feel (Jude more so than 2 Peter), there is much more to both of them than mere denunciation. J. N. D. Kelly's comment that Jude has an 'almost unrelievedly denunciatory tone' is an overstatement.[1] Before we examine the distinct contribution of these letters individually, let us address some common issues.

Common issues

Similarities and differences
Although there are differences between the letters, they have sufficient in

---

1. J. N. D. Kelly, *The Epistles of Peter and of Jude*, BNTC (London: A. & C. Black, 1969), p. 223.

common to be considered jointly.[2] They both take the form of literature that falls in the category of 'last testaments' and address a very similar danger in the church, though not an identical one. Their invective against false teachers (Jude 4–18; 2 Pet. 2:1 – 3:3) follows a very similar pattern and both make use of extra-biblical Jewish writings, chiefly *1 Enoch* and the *Testament of Moses*, which were popular at the time, as well as an extensive use of the Old Testament. Both believe the answer lies in the apostolic gospel entrusted to believers. Current scholarship is virtually united in believing that 2 Peter is dependent on Jude and develops the latter's thinking more fully.

There are, of course, differences between them. Whereas Jude is almost wholly polemical, 2 Peter is wider in its approach and aims. Jude's 'style is vigorous and colourful' and he uses a rich array of vocabulary to write in excellent and smooth Greek. 2 Peter, on the other hand, is much more variable, 'revealing violent alternations in mood' and its Greek is less pleasing.[3] Because of the variation in the heresy he is addressing, 2 Peter has a much greater place for the doctrine of the second coming of Christ and its implications for Christian living than Jude has.

But for our purposes, their pastoral approach is sufficiently similar to each other and sufficiently different from other parts of the New Testament to justify bracketing them together.

Early Catholicism?

Ever since Ernst Käsemann wrote his essay on the eschatology of 2 Peter in 1952, in which he claimed that the letter was 'from beginning to end a document expressing an early Catholic viewpoint',[4] 2 Peter and Jude have been treated as prime examples of that strand of early Christianity. Käsemann's argument, in brief, was that 2 Peter, whose place in the canon he questions, seeks to reassert the tradition of apostolic teaching against adversaries who were asking major questions about the coming of Christ. In doing so, he reveals he has substituted the spirit of revelation by the letter of a fixed orthodoxy, defined by his own tradition in the church. Faith has become a matter of linking with the past rather than a living vehicle of the communication of grace. Yet, paradoxically, in restating what he considers orthodoxy, the writer

---

2. The wording is owed to I. H. Marshall, *New Testament Theology* (Downers Grove: IVP; Leicester: Apollos, 2004), p. 698.

3. The comments on style are to be found more fully in Kelly, *Epistles*, pp. 228–229.

4. E. Käsemann, 'An Apologia for Primitive Christian Eschatology', *Essays on New Testament Themes*, tr. W. J. Montague (London: SCM, 1964), p. 169.

changes it and the view of the end time presented by him is not that of the earliest Christian writers. It is less Christological and less immediate while incorporating many 'secular' views regarding time and the future of heaven and earth. So the church is seen to be at a more developed stage than it was initially.[5]

Many have adopted Käsemann's basic position. James Dunn, for example, follows Käsemann in stressing that 2 Peter is written 'in repeated reaction to the failure of apocalyptic hope' and so is 'a prime example of early Catholicism'. He describes 2 Peter's writing about the second coming as 'somewhat hollow "orthodoxy"'.[6] He also believes it shows evidence of the two other key features of early Catholicism, namely increasing institutionalization in the church and the hardening of faith into fixed forms.

But not all are persuaded. A recent examination of the question by Richard Bauckman subjects the arguments to thorough scrutiny and finds them wanting.[7] In both, 'the primitive eschatological perspective remains dominant',[8] 2 Peter's exposition is much more Christological than the advocates of early Catholicism have credited and the response to the heretics is of the same kind as Paul adopts in Galatians 1 and Romans 16:17. As to developments in the church, there is no stress on church officials exercising their authority because of their status or title and, indeed, no reference to ecclesiastical office holders.[9] As to the emergence of a fixed credal orthodoxy, an examination of the phrases Käsemann interpreted as going in this direction, phrases like the 'knowledge of our Lord Jesus Christ' (2 Pet. 1:8; cf. v. 2) or 'the faith' (Jude 3) or the emphasis on 'truth', is no more than a way of speaking about the gospel, and to read them as established credal formulae is to read more into them than the evidence suggests.[10] Bauckham's arguments are convincing and free us from reading the documents through the filter of 'early Catholicism'.

There are two reasons why this is relevant to our discussion of pastoral ministry. First, for both Jude and 2 Peter, apostolic teaching is the norm. And although, in their view, it may need to be applied and interpreted to meet the challenges of a new age, it can never be replaced. At least in this one respect

---

5. Ibid., pp. 169–195.

6. James D. G. Dunn, *Unity and Diversity in the New Testament* (Philadelphia: Westminster; London: SCM, 1977), pp. 350–351.

7. Richard Bauckham, *Jude, 2 Peter*, WBC 50 (Waco: Word, 1983), pp. 8–11, 151–154.

8. Ibid., p. 9.

9. Ibid., p. 152.

10. Ibid.

Bauckham agrees with Käsemann, since Käsemann 'emphasises the importance of the conception of the apostles and the normative character of apostolic tradition . . .'[11] These pastoral polemicists are thoroughly in line with the
original apostolic message, as all pastoral polemicists must be. The second
reason why the discussion of early Catholicism is important is that, having
concluded it is unsupported by the evidence of the letters themselves, we are
now able to read what the letters do say and the line they take, free from the
distortions that arise when a particular interpretative framework is imposed on
a writing. This should lead us to a more honest, if less predictable, understanding of the nature of pastoral ministry in all its breadth.

Apocalyptic literature?

The polemical tone of these letters assumes an exaggerated quality in our
minds because of the strangeness of the illustrations and allusions found in
the central sections where the false teachers are being denounced. While in
Jude we can recognize some Old Testament stories, we are less familiar with
angels being bound in chains in everlasting darkness (6), or Michael's dispute
with the devil over Moses' body (9), or even the words Enoch spoke (14–15),
since he appears previously only briefly in Genesis 5:21–24, where he says
nothing. From where did Jude derive such material? The same question is
raised by our reading of 2 Peter 2:1–18 and 3:1–3, which, while different in
some details from Jude, roughly follow the same line and speaks in similarly
apocalyptic terms about the false prophets and their fate.

Jude and 2 Peter both draw on apocalyptic literature widely circulating in
their day, although 2 Peter does so less explicitly than Jude. Jude 14–15 draws
on *1 Enoch*, a collective work from the third century BC, and verse 9 possibly
refers to the lost ending of the *Testament of Moses*.[12] Such literature would have
had market currency, especially against their opponents, and consequently
proves an effective weapon in the hands of the apostolic writers in their opposition to heresy. As elsewhere, we find that the breadth of imagination and
source of evidential support used to accomplish their pastoral objectives is
broad. They are neither confined merely to repeating apostolic teaching,
nor merely to expounding earlier texts, but while being true to the authentic

---

11. Ibid., p. 153. Bauckham, who believes that 2 Peter is pseudonymous and comes
    from a post-apostolic period, ties this to the question of authorship. The author,
    unlike his opponents, believes the apostolic tradition to be so important that he
    adopts Peter's name to enhance the authority of his writing.
12. For a detailed discussion, see ibid., pp. 65–76, 94–96.

teaching of the apostles, they marshal all their creative skills to ensure that the original message is heard, understood and applied to the situation they now face.

Jude

Several features of Jude's letter are significant for our understanding of him as a pastoral polemicist.

His introduction (1–2)

Jude uses his connection as a brother of James,[13] and consequently a brother of Jesus, to establish his authority in the eyes of his readers, but in no way does he labour it, nor does his argument rely on it. There is no evidence that he is vaunting any office. His readers have to be persuaded by the content of his letter, not because if its author.

How he addresses his readers, and the greeting he uses, immediately establishes the bond of respect and affection he feels for them and the good will he bears towards them. Given the harsh tone evident later in the letter it is a wise and necessary start, but, as is evident from his concluding exhortations to his 'dear friends' (17, 20), it is also a genuine expression of confidence in their spiritual position and not done merely for the effect. Somewhat typically of Jude, he uses triplets to emphasize his message. They are 'called, loved and kept', while he prays for them that they will experience 'mercy, peace and love'.[14] Before polemic is engaged, relationship needs to be established and this Jude is wise enough to do.

His priority (3)

After the opening greetings, Jude speaks of the purpose of his letter and again provides us with an insight into his wisdom as a pastor. He sets aside the agenda he wanted to pursue, because he has discovered that the need of the

---

13. For discussion on the identity of Jude, see ibid., pp. 14–16; Peter H. Davids, *The Letters of 2 Peter and Jude*, PNTC (Grand Rapids: Eerdmans; Leicester: Apollos, 2006), pp. 7–12; and Kelly, *Epistles*, pp. 231–233. The consensus is in favour of the author being who he says he is, in spite of the impressive quality of the Greek used.

14. Davids, *2 Peter and Jude*, p. 25. Davids lists other repetitive patterns of three or more sayings in Jude, in vv. 5–7, 8, 11, 12–13, 15, 19, 22–23.

church lies elsewhere. His desire is to write about 'the salvation we share'. One suspects he might have written a pleasant reflection on the faith, which would have been encouraging and comforting but would entirely have missed the point. If he had kept to his plan, he would, in effect, have been dishing out tasty sweets when the desperate need was for the less pleasant-tasting medicine that brings healing.

Pastors need to establish the priorities of their work according to the needs of the congregation. This will often mean we cannot spend our time on things we enjoy most. The series of sermons on an obscure part of the Bible that will display our brilliant homiletic skills, or the downloading on the congregation of the latest secret that has been revealed to guarantee phenomenal church growth, or the secret passion we have for this doctrinal emphasis or that missionary adventure, may not match the real requirements either of the individuals or of the community we are called to lead. Too many churches have found themselves alienated from their pastors in recent years because pastors have sought to impose on them their vision, their plan, their programmes and their strategies to lead the church forward. Not only have congregations failed to own what has been proposed to them but they have also often not found it relevant to their discipleship in Christ. As with wise physicians, pastors should study the symptoms of any ailing congregation carefully before issuing the prescription for the remedy. Pastors are inevitably ready and professional speakers, and this sometimes makes it hard for us to listen. But listening before speaking is usually the better course of action.

His attack (4–16)

The identity of those whom Jude denounces so fiercely is a matter of dispute. Evidently, they have subtly infiltrated the church and advocate antinomianism by their practice and preaching. Bauckham plausibly suggests they are 'itinerant charismatics' who, while claiming to be his followers, reject Christ's authority and indeed any moral authority, whether it is that of 'celestial beings' or Moses.[15] They appear to claim 'charismatic inspiration' (8) for their immoral behaviour, but the truth is they have flagrantly rejected Judeo-Christian ethical teaching and live the licentious lifestyle found among pagans. Their practice probably arises from having an over-realized eschatology (the belief that salvation has already been fully experienced and there is nothing left to come). Consequently, they consider themselves free from the constraints of moral living on earth, exempt from coming judgment and not subject to the

---

15. Bauckham, *Jude, 2 Peter*, p. 11.

already-but-not-yet tension in which believers have to live. Tragically, the result of such theology is that they are immoral, rebellious, greedy, arrogant and divisive.

Jude will have no truck with this, since it is opposed to the true faith and a betrayal of Jesus Christ who alone is 'Sovereign and Lord' (4). Their teaching is a cloak for ungodliness. If accepted, it will undermine the church from within, which then, having lost any distinctiveness from pagan society, will soon be subsumed by that wider culture and soon lose any reason to exist. Since this will mean certain death for the church and a rejection of apostolic teaching, Jude is unrelentingly vigorous in his condemnation. There is no room for accommodation with their teaching.

Jude employs a variety of approaches to ensure his condemnation has impact. First, he calls on Old Testament history to support his argument (5–7). Three witnesses are called to give evidence: Israel in the wilderness, the fallen angels of Genesis 6:1–4 and Sodom and Gomorrah, reported in Genesis 19. These testify that God's people are not immune from his judgment if their immoral living provokes it. Jude then connects those ancient stories with the way the interlopers in the church are behaving (8–10). These 'dreamers' (8) may claim trancelike or ecstatic experiences as the basis for their behaviour, but in reality they are slandering the angels and (like the devil arguing with the archangel Michael over Moses' body, a story known from the *Testament of Moses*) thus provoke God's wrath.

Next, Jude calls three more Old Testament witnesses to the stand (11). This time the triplet is composed of Cain, Balaam and Korah. Then, with a series of graphic images (12–13), he applies their stories to that of the false teachers. They are blemishes, examples of the false shepherds of Ezekiel 34. Using four graphic images from nature, he then describes them as rainless clouds, uprooted trees, violent waves and wandering stars. It is an unflattering picture. 'Stated in prosaic terms,' writes Ralph Martin, 'they are unable to make good on the promises they offer . . . [and] they lack stability and are as unsteady as the restless sea . . . and untrustworthy as stars that fail to hold their course and so mislead the navigator . . .'[16]

Jude's third strategy is to turn to the prophecy of *1 Enoch*, where the ungodly of the last days are forewarned of judgment (14–16). Jude reinterprets the prophecy to emphasize that it is 'the Lord' Jesus Christ who will act as judge and stresses that their guilt lies not only in their immoral behaviour but in their

---

16. Andrew Chester and Ralph P. Martin, *The Theology of the Letters of James, Peter and Jude* (Cambridge: Cambridge University Press, 1994), p. 70.

'defiant words' against God and their grumbling and conceited tongues as well. Jude cites *1 Enoch* because it is valued widely and makes his point very effectively, as a preacher today might quote a contemporary writing or film.[17] Whether the appeal to history as such would have any persuasive power today is another question.[18]

His exhortation (17–23)

There is much more to Jude than his denunciation of the false teachers, and the exhortation to his 'dear friends' (17, 20) at the end of the letter shows him to possess some sensitive and tender pastoral qualities. He was clearly not in the business of denouncing the false teachers in such dark terms because he was surly by nature but because the situation demanded it.

The exhortation begins with a note of realism (17–19), encouraging the church to face the fact that 'in the last times' contemptuous and ungodly people will abound. He then encourages them to strive for four positive goals that counterbalance the negative judgments passed on the false teachers.[19] They are to (1) be built up in faith, (2) pray in the Spirit, (3) keep themselves in God's love and (4) wait for the Lord's final act of mercy in bringing them into eternal life (20–21). Each of these is significant in its context. The faith is a 'holy faith', not to be cynically set aside as the false teachers are doing. Prayer is still to be 'in the Holy Spirit'. They are not to reject the charismatic dimension of their experience just because the opponents claim a false charismatic experience as their source of authority. Having told them at the beginning they are loved by God (1), he encourages them to do nothing that will risk the security of that love. The final positive exhortation in this section encourages them to look forward to the return of Christ, not with the fear that the false teachers should rightly feel but with joy for the mercy and eternal life that will be theirs.

The same careful balance between mercy and fear, grace and holiness, characterizes his final exhortation as he turns to the question of how to handle those struggling in the church because of the influence of the false teachers. Some who doubt require gentle coaxing and even to be given space to work things through. However, others require more urgent action if they are to be rescued from what will destroy them. There is a time for patient sensitivity and a time for uncompromising emergency treatment, and the need of the pastor, filled with the Spirit, is to have the wisdom to distinguish between the two.

------

17. Davids, *2 Peter and Jude*, pp. 75–76.

18. Chester and Martin, *Theology*, p. 86.

19. Ibid., p. 66.

His doxology (24–25)

The blend of immanence and transcendence, of gentle grace and awesome majesty continues into Jude's doxology. Aware of the pressures believers face, Jude does not berate them as he does the false teachers and does not attribute blame to them. Rather, he prays that they may be kept from stumbling. The word he uses for 'falling' (*aptaistos*) is used only here in the New Testament, but elsewhere is translated 'unharmed' or 'protected'.[20] It picks up the frequent image from the Psalms of God caring for his people so that, even if they are made to trip up, they will not be down for long (Ps. 37:24) and will be rescued by God. But there is a grander purpose too. He also prays that they may be presented to God joyfully and without blemish, like the perfect sacrifices required in Leviticus. The thought is a common one in the New Testament and may indeed have been part of the ancient liturgy (Eph. 1:4; 5:27; Col. 1:22; 1 Thess. 3:13; 2 Pet. 3:14; cf. 1 John 2:28). It rules out once and for all the believer being content with spiritual mediocrity and half-heartedness. The pastor's responsibility is not only to aspire to such personal blamelessness but to inspire others to do so as well.

The majestic note on which the doxology ends exalts the saving God in his glory for all time. Ending in this way accomplishes a number of things. It further underlines that God is not to be treated with any shred of disrespect but is to be worshipped, through Jesus Christ, by how one lives as much as by what one says. It locates Jude's confidence firmly in God. He is the one who can be trusted to bring the believers through unblemished at the end, in spite of all the distractions and temptations. In these ways, the doxology brings the letter full circle, echoing the opening sentiments about his readers as a people who are 'called', 'loved' and 'kept' for 'Jesus Christ' (1).

2 Peter

2 Peter demonstrates the same concern about false teachers and engages in the same pastoral polemic as Jude. However, other elements enter the letter, which is in the form of a farewell speech (1:15),[21] giving 2 Peter a more expansive

---

20. Davids, *2 Peter and Jude*, pp. 109–110.
21. Davids, *2 Peter and Jude*, pp. 145–149, readily agrees with Bauckham that it takes the form of a farewell speech and is probably pseudonymous, but is unconvinced that it is a testament akin to other Jewish testaments of the age. See Bauckham, *Jude, 2 Peter*, pp. 131–135, 158–162.

pastoral method than Jude. He states that his aim is to ensure his readers are 'firmly established in the truth' (1:12) and that they will never forget the things he has taught them (1:15). Though contemporary commentators usually use a more complex analysis of the letter's rhetorical form,[22] I want to draw attention to four major elements in its composition.

His exhortation (1:3–11)

The beginning of 2 Peter's pastoral admonition demonstrates a fine balance between the divine and human dimensions of faith. On the one hand, his utter confidence is in God, whose 'divine power has given us everything we need for a godly life' (1:3). Nothing is lacking that will enable disciples to escape from the corruption of the present age and 'participate in the divine nature' (1:4). The meaning of the latter is somewhat uncertain, with some believing it refers to the believer's graduation to immortality and incorruption, and others arguing that the context means it should be understood as teaching that believers will adopt an ethical lifestyle that pleases God in the present.[23]

The sufficiency of the divine resource is carefully balanced with the necessity of human responsibility. Precisely because God has provided for our spiritual preservation and growth, believers are called on to 'make every effort' to add to their faith (1:5). Without the divine provision, the encouragement to confirm one's calling by growing in the qualities listed may lead to despair. But with the divine provision, development is possible. The list of virtues Peter urges on his readers is matched by similar lists elsewhere in the New Testament (e.g. Rom. 5:3–5; Gal. 5:22–23; Jas 1:3–4), except for the choice of vocabulary that, here and elsewhere in the letter, has a particularly Hellenistic complexion to it.[24] 2 Peter also presents the qualities as a step-by-step approach, again similar to wider literature. The picture is not so much that of a chain of virtues as the picture of a telescope where one section emerges from another until it is fully extended and the perfect picture may be seen.

2 Peter's encouragement to his readers to 'make every effort' is indicative of the strenuous approach the author takes towards his pastoral responsibility. Being a disciple is no light matter, nor is being a pastor. The requirement for believers to 'make every effort' (1:5; 3:14) is matched by the requirement the author imposes on himself as pastor to 'make every effort' to ensure they will

---

22. Bauckham, *Jude, 2 Peter*, p. 135; and Davids, *2 Peter and Jude*, pp. 143–145.

23. Davids, *2 Peter, Jude*, pp. 172–176.

24. Bauckham, *Jude, 2 Peter*, pp. 174–175; and Davids, *2 Peter and Jude*, p. 178.

be firmly grounded in apostolic teaching (1:15). The effort put into confirming their calling will be richly rewarded with eternal life.

His foundation (1:16–21)

If believers are to put such effort into their faith, they need to be sure it is well founded and not based on a myth. This is especially true in the light of the false teachers and sceptics who are proving very vocal in their opposition to the orthodox faith. So Peter turns his attention to explaining why there is a 'reason for the hope' (1 Pet. 3:15) they have. The foundation is found in the eyewitness evidence of the apostle, who both saw God glorifying his son and heard God's majestic voice from heaven (1:16–18). Consequently, the faith is not a fictional invention but a truth revealed, which stems from first-hand evidential experience. The second element of his apologia is to affirm the divine inspiration of the Old Testament prophets, who support his view of the second coming of Christ (1:19). Those disturbing the church have introduced the novel idea that although the Old Testament prophets may well have had visionary experiences, their interpretations of them were matters of purely individual conjecture. 2 Peter does not so much argue the case as reassert what was commonly believed, that the Holy Spirit himself had given not only the visions but the interpretations of them too.[25]

It should be noted that 2 Peter is not content merely to inspire his readers to better things; he is concerned also to instruct his readers in their faith. The inspiration might soon evaporate, especially after his death (1:15) when he is no longer around to reinvigorate their motivation by his fine-sounding rhetoric. What will keep them going is not the inspiration that has galvanized them for a short while, but the education that will mould their thinking and behaviour in the long term. Too much of, at least Western, Christianity has become heavily dependent on the exciting event, the motivational speaker and the razzmatazz of celebratory worship, with the result that too many Christians limp from one 'fix' to another without having been sufficiently grounded in the faith to survive, still less thrive, in between. As a wise pastor, the author of 2 Peter does not want to expose his readers to that danger.

His denunciation (2:1–22)

2 Peter's denunciation of the false teachers follows closely that of Jude's, although, as noted, there are some different emphases. He changes some of the wording and inserts a section of his own in 2:19–22. While the same accent

---

25. Bauckham, *Jude, 2 Peter*, p. 225.

falls on the false teachers as antinomians who live according to their base instincts and are contemptuous of authority, he also has in view that they are particularly sceptical about the apostolic doctrine of Christ's return. The failure of Christ to have appeared to that point has led the sceptics to argue that they need not live in fear of judgment, and so can live how they like. With the removal of their sense of accountability, all moral restraints have also been removed. Such is the seriousness of this teaching and its implications that 2 Peter makes it clear that this is not a matter of one opinion against another but a 'destructive heresy' that flies in the face of the sovereign Lord (3:1) and consequently cannot be tolerated in any way.

Another difference from Jude is the focus on how the false teachers have gone back on their knowledge of the 'Lord and Saviour Jesus Christ' (2:20), and so are in a worse position than before. They are not adventurous theologians who deserve applause for their interesting new twist on the gospel: they are apostates who have denied what they once knew and reneged on their commitment to Christ. Using familiar proverbs, 2 Peter denounces their sorry state.

So, although 2 Peter nuances Jude's condemnation of the false teachers, he essentially adopts the same 'vigorous use of invective'[26] with which to attack them and ensure that the church repulses their influence.

His apologia for the coming of Christ (3:1–18)

Another way 2 Peter proves himself to be a wise pastor is by his not ending the letter on the negative note of denunciation. Having made it clear that his opponents' teaching is heretical, he now sets forth a further and positive apologia for the apostolic teaching about Christ's appearing. He pays particular attention to how we are to explain the apparent delay in Christ's second coming (3:3). Since Christ has not yet returned, the sceptics wrongly believe he will never return. But in a series of deft arguments he exposes their position as foolish.

First, 2 Peter shows evidence of God's activity in history (3:4–7). The act of creation itself, followed by the act of judgment in the flood are given as examples. Secondly, he argues about God's existence in eternity (3:8). Unlike humans, he is not bound by the normal calibrations of time. Thirdly, he points to God's patience with humanity (3:9). The reason he has not stepped back into history is not because he is unable to do so but because he wishes to give more people the chance to turn to him before the judgment falls. But when that 'appearing' does take place, it will be sudden, unexpected and total in its

---

26. Chester and Martin, *Theology*, p. 163.

impact (3:10). The universal destruction that will take place, however, is not the final word but a hopeful prelude to the reconstruction of the universe (3:12–13).

The thrust of 2 Peter's writing throughout is practical. He does not muse on the coming of Christ as a matter of speculation but as a matter of stimulation and sanctification. He wants this teaching to 'stimulate' them to 'wholesome thinking' (3:1) and even more to wholesome living (3:11, 14). If Christ is coming again, if the future promises judgment, if everything is going to be exposed, if there is to be the re-creation of all things, then we should prepare ourselves by our holy living and be ready at any time to meet our Lord.

Conclusion

The spirited letters of Jude and 2 Peter provide us with fine examples of the pastor as a polemicist. There is a time when the church is so endangered that the right approach is to confront and expose error in an uncompromising way. Tolerating everyone's opinion and seeking to accommodate anyone is not always the right thing to do pastorally. It may seem kind but can prove disastrous both for the individual and the church. The pastor often needs the gift of discernment to expose where teaching may lead, especially if it appears attractive on the surface. The kindest thing to do is to unmask error before it leads to catastrophe and ruins practical Christian living.

The calling to be a pastoral polemicist is, I believe, rare and should be taken up with due caution. We easily mistake personal prejudices for doctrinal error and make issues of secondary importance our benchmark of orthodoxy where Scripture permits latitude or is even ambiguous. It is all too easy for us to believe we are vigorously defending truth when we use an issue as a cloak for an authoritarian, argumentative, angular or a crusading spirit. We set ourselves up as the judge instead of pointing to the Sovereign Lord who alone is judge. Richard Baxter warned, 'Be very suspicious of your religious passions, and carefully distinguish between a sound and sinful zeal; lest you father your sin on the Spirit of God and think you please him when you offend him most.'[27]

The calling should also be approached with care because it calls for the sort of skill we see demonstrated by Jude and 2 Peter. They did more than

---

27. Richard Baxter, *The Cure of Church Divisions* (London: Nevil Symmons, 1670), clause 20.

pronounce anathemas on their opponents. They crafted careful arguments and engaged in communication that would open minds and hearts, not close them. The arguments they used resonated with those they were addressing because they alluded to commonly accepted arguments, undisputed history, and literature in which there was widespread interest. Their strategies may not have such an immediate impact on readers today, though, and today's pastoral polemicist will need to devise arguments persuasive in contemporary culture rather than merely recycling the culture of Palestinian Judaism in the first century.[28]

Furthermore, the calling should also be approached with care because the effect of the polemic should be positive, not destructive. The denunciations voiced by Jude and 2 Peter are both encased in longer documents that begin and end positively. They both demonstrate tender pastoral sensitivity towards their readers and it is obvious that they do not want to knock them down but rather build them up in Christ. Here are polemicists who do not rejoice in conflict for the sake of it but rather oppose error with tears, in the hope of rescuing those who will be destroyed by heresy and liberating them to enjoy the fullness of God's love and coming salvation.

Different times call for different pastoral approaches and the weapon of the pastoral polemicist is necessary in any complete pastoral armoury. But it is a weapon that should be used sparingly, perhaps in proportion to the amount of space the letter of Jude and 2 Peter take up in the New Testament.

---

28. Chester and Martin, *Theology*, p. 86.

14. REVELATION: MINISTRY IN A HOSTILE WORLD

The ministry of prophetic proclamation

Eugene Peterson put it beautifully when he wrote:

> The adjective apocalyptic is not commonly found in company with the noun pastor. I can't remember ever hearing them in the same sentence. They grew up on different sides of the tracks. I'd love to play Cupid between the two words and see if I can instigate a courtship.[1]

He's right about the distance between the words, but thankfully there are signs that others want to join him and get in on the matchmaking as well.

The mysteries that surround the book of Revelation mean that it is rarely considered too deeply as a pastoral document, even though its pastoral purpose in preparing the church for persecution is readily recognized. It is not usually thought to be a source of wisdom about the nature of pastoral ministry. Interest has rather centred on its nature as an apocalyptic document, the interpretation of its visionary symbolism, its date of composition, authorship and relevance for the contemporary political situation. Yet Revelation unconsciously reveals much about the nature of ministry required when the church

---

1. Eugene H. Peterson, *The Contemplative Pastor: Returning to the Art of Spiritual Direction* (Grand Rapids: Eerdmans, 1989), p. 39.

faces hostility and even the threat of annihilation. In particular, the author has much to say about the role of the prophet as pastor.

The church in Revelation

Wildly different suggestions have been made about when the book of Revelation was written, and consequently the situation behind it, ranging from the mid to late first century.[2] Most consider it to come from the time of Domitian, even if it incorporates earlier material. Domitian, who served as Roman Emperor AD 81–96, was the first to demand worship as 'Lord and God' and instituted a cruel persecution of those who did not do so. How extensive his persecution was is unclear, but local variations made it particularly intense against the Christians in Asia Minor. Clement of Rome, writing in AD 96, begins his letter to the Corinthians by referring to 'our recent series of unexpected misfortunes and set-backs', and speaks later about being 'in the same arena and hav(ing) the same conflict of those who had previously suffered hardships and torment'.[3] Domitian's cruelty was not limited to Christians and was of such an order that a conspiracy was eventually mounted against him and he was assassinated. The extent of his persecution is arguable, but no other period of history seems to fit the evidence of Revelation as well.

In Revelation, the persecution has not yet commenced. The book is written to prepare the church for 'what must soon take place' (1:1; cf. v. 3) so that they can remain faithful to Jesus Christ, who is himself 'the faithful witness, the firstborn from the dead, and the ruler of the kings of the earth' (1:5). The forms of opposition the church will face are extremely varied, ranging from natural to supernatural, military to economic, sacred to secular, subtle resistance to full-frontal attack. But why is the church in the firing line and what is the nature of the church that will provoke such hostility for which the church is now being prepared?

Early on in Revelation the church is described as 'a kingdom and priests to serve his [Jesus'] God and Father' (1:6; cf. 5:10). Their primary calling is to be the visible representation of God's reign on earth, demonstrating the ways of his kingdom, witnessing to his rule and remaining loyal subjects under his

---

2. Robert H. Mounce, *The Book of Revelation*, NICNT (Grand Rapids: Eerdmans, 1977), pp. 31–35; and G. K. Beale, *The Book of Revelation*, NIGTC (Grand Rapids: Eerdmans; Carlisle: Paternoster, 1999), pp. 4–27.

3. Cited by Beale, *Revelation*, p. 13.

authority. It was unsurprising that Rome finds such loyalty to a higher power subversive and threatening.

As priests they are called to serve him, in worship, intercession, instructing others and in offering sacrifices. On occasions the sacrifice offered will even be their own lives (7:14; 16:6). The priests are never presented as a special class of church member or order of leadership in the church. Rather, all members of the church are seen as priests. Under the new covenant, God's desire, expressed to Israel in Exodus 19:6 that they should be 'for me a kingdom of priests and a holy nation', has come to fulfilment in the church. This understanding of the church is, of course, shared by Peter in 1 Peter 2:9. In addition, the Christians are also all called 'saints' (5:8; 8:3; 13:7; 18:20, 24). Sainthood (being set apart and devoted to God) is part of their basic description, not a category reserved for the few who have manifest special holiness or exceptional acts of service.

We know, from the letters addressed to them in chapters 2–3, that churches gathered in various locations in Asia Minor, the area (as mentioned above) where Domitian's persecution would be felt most. The seven letters are probably meant to be representative rather than exhaustive. It is in line with the teaching that all members of the church are priests that the letters are open letters to the whole congregation and make their appeal to all. They are addressed to 'the angel of the church' (2:1, 8, 12, 18; 3:1, 7, 14), whom some have taken to refer to an office holder, but most take to refer to a personification of the church rather than any bishop-like figure.[4] The reference to the 'synagogue of Satan' in Smyrna (2:9) leaves one with the impression by contrast that John, like James (Jas 2:2), views the church as a synagogue of Christ.[5] This leads to Kevin Giles's conclusion that 'The church order reflected in the book of Revelation is undeveloped with little fixed structure.'[6]

There is, however, one point of special interest in Revelation in regard to pastoral leadership: the role of the prophet.[7] The fact that prophets are referred to eight times in Revelation (10:7; 11:10, 18; 16:6; 18:20, 24; 22:6, 9) makes it unique in the New Testament and calls for further investigation. Of the eight references, one is negative and refers to two witnesses who harm the city and people of God (11:10).[8] The rest of the references are positive.

---

4. R. H. Mounce, *Revelation*, p. 85; and Beale, *Revelation*, p. 230.

5. Beale, *Revelation*, p. 241.

6. Kevin N. Giles , 'Prophecy, Prophets, False Prophets', *DLNT*, p. 974.

7. We should also note the emphasis on 'witnesses' or martyrs in 2:13; 11:3; 17:6.

8. We should also recognize that 'prophet' (singular) is used on a number of occasions in connection with the false prophet: 16:13; 19:20; 20:10.

Prophets are servants of God (10:7; 11:18) whose words and writings he has inspired (20:6, 8) and who are on a par with apostles (18:20). They may be called to suffer martyrdom, like the prophets of old, but their martyrdom will be avenged (16:6; 18:24). Picked out for special mention in this way, prophets obviously play a key role in equipping the church to face its future. So we must examine the role of prophecy further.

An overview of prophecy in Revelation

John's own description of the collection of the visions he receives is to describe them as 'prophecy' (1:3). His words, like those of the written prophets of the Old Testament, are obviously meant to be read aloud to the Christian congregations and a special blessing belongs to those who do so.[9] But in what sense is John's writing *prophecy*, since most would assume it more naturally fits within the genre of apocalyptic literature? David Hill has explored that question in depth and pointed out that although Revelation has some apocalyptic features in it, other crucial characteristics of apocalyptic are absent.[10] It is not, for example, pseudonymous and makes no pretence to secret knowledge. Here is an open communication to be read and understood by all in the church as a word of strengthening and encouragement. Positively, it has the hallmarks of prophecy about it. It deals with the events about to unfold within history. The author is inspired by the Spirit to write (1:10–11) and instructed to record his visions (1:19). His work is marked by typical prophetic traits, including formulae like 'These are the words of . . .' (2:1 etc.), first person speech on behalf of God, and by prophetic judgments on God's people and on people who do not acknowledge him (e.g. 2:5, 16, 22; 6:1–17; 8:1 – 9:19; 18:1–24; 20:11–15). Hill agrees with A. Feuillet, who wrote, 'The profound originality of the Johannine Apocalypse is the fact that, whilst making use of the style, imagery and methods of Jewish apocalyptic, it remains faithful to that which creates the greatness of ancient prophecy.'[11] Similarly, Carson, Moo and Morris

---

9. There are seven 'beatitudes' in Revelation, of which this is the first. The others are 14:13; 16:15; 19:9; 20:6; 22:7, 14.

10. David Hill, *New Testament Prophecy* (London: Marshall, Morgan & Scott, 1979), pp. 70–87. See also G. R. Beasley-Murray, *The Book of Revelation*, NCB (London: Oliphants, 1974), pp. 19–29.

11. Cited by Hill, *New Testament Prophecy*, pp. 75–76.

conclude that it is 'a prophecy cast in an apocalyptic mould and written down in letter form'.[12]

Through his writing, John himself is seen to be the prophet par excellence, though he would not wish to elevate himself above others in this way (1:2, 9; 19:10). In one sense, he shares his prophetic experience with others, yet it is plain he has a greater authority than others, even if only by virtue of the fact that his words are written in a document for others to read and study.[13] In Revelation he undeniably stands out as the one inspired by the Spirit to receive visions (1:10; 4:2; 17:3; 21:10) and is the one instructed to make it his calling to prophesy either about or against[14] 'many peoples, nations, languages and kings' (10:11).

John not only perceives his writing to be prophetic in character but also perceives the church to have the same complexion. It is not that every individual member of the church is a prophet, as might be envisaged by Acts 2:17, but that the church as a whole is corporately prophetic. It is commonly agreed that the two witnesses of 11:1–14, referred to as prophets, symbolize the entire community. The style of the language used, when put together with parallels to the language elsewhere, show that it is the whole company of the church and not two individuals that are in mind.[15] Again the whole community, not just select prophets, are called on 'to bear testimony to Jesus, so all experience the Spirit of prophecy (12:11, 17; 19:10; cf. 6:9–11; 20:4)'.[16] The point of their receiving prophetic messages does not stop with themselves. The church is not the terminus; the world is. They receive prophecy so they may be equipped and ready 'to bear their own prophetic witness to the world', inspired by the same Holy Spirit who inspired those who spoke to them.[17] As Bauckham explains,

---

12. Cited by Beale, *Revelation*, p. 39.

13. David Hill, 'Christian Prophets as Teachers and Instructors in the Church', in J. Panagopolous (ed.), *Prophetic Vocation in the New Testament and Today* (Leiden: Brill, 1977), pp. 119–120.

14. David E. Aune, *Revelation 6–16*, WBC 52b (Nashville: Nelson, 1998), pp. 573–574. Aune argues the weight of contextual evidence means that *epi* should be interpreted as 'against'.

15. Beale, *Revelation*, pp. 573–576, advances six reasons for the corporate interpretation of the two prophets.

16. James D. G. Dunn, *Unity and Diversity in the New Testament* (Philadelphia: Westminster; London: SCM, 1977), pp. 120–121.

17. Richard Bauckham, *The Theology of the Book of Revelation* (Cambridge: Cambridge University Press, 1993), pp. 118–119.

the thought in Revelation is different (from Acts 2:17). It is connected with the idea of the church's newly revealed role of confronting the idolatry of Rome, in a prophetic conflict, like that of Moses with Pharaoh and his magicians or of Elijah with Jezebel and the prophets of Baal, and in the power of the Spirit of prophecy winning the nations to the worship of the true God.[18]

We might say, though John does not do so in so many words, that the church is a school of the prophets as much as a kingdom of priests.

The relationships of the prophet

The prophet and the Spirit
In the introduction to Revelation we are made aware of 'the seven spirits before his [God's] throne' (1:4). Building on the vision of Zechariah 4:1–14 (see esp. v. 10), these 'seven spirits' represent the fullness of God's active Spirit, who is identified with the Lamb on the throne (5:6), serves as God's eyes and does his work all over the world. But, related, there is also one Spirit mentioned chiefly as the inspirer of the prophet, who serves as a recipient of and channel for his work. He is the one who provides visionary experiences (1:10; 4:2; 17:3; 21:10) and inspires prophetic utterances (2:7; 14:3). It is beautifully consistent with this that, in conveying the messages of the exalted Christ to the seven churches, the prophet concludes each letter with the words 'Whoever has ears, let them hear what the Spirit says to the churches' (2:7, 11, 17, 29; 3:6, 13, 22). True prophets have nothing to say unless the message is borne in upon them by the Spirit. With this inspiration must also come a dose of courage, for some of the messages to be delivered are messages of rebuke for the church and of judgment on the nations. Whether in the church or the world, they are called upon to expose false idols and proclaim the coming triumph of the reign of Christ. In both arenas their message is likely to provoke a negative, if not hostile, reaction, with 'the powerful' in the church and the world asking what right the prophet has to claim the spiritual high ground. The answer is that the prophet has the authority of the Spirit.

---

18. Ibid., p. 120. On the conversion of the nations and John's universalistic vision, see Richard Bauckham, *The Climax of Prophecy* (Edinburgh: T. & T. Clark, 1993), pp. 238–337.

The prophet and Jesus

Revelation is a very Christocentric book and all that is said about prophecy works with, not against, its Christ-shaped grain. The prophetic Spirit is no independent agent but an agent of the bruised, yet enthroned, Lamb. This is summed up in a key, but difficult,[19] sentence in 19:10: 'For the testimony of Jesus is the Spirit of prophecy,' which can be translated as 'the essence of Spirit-inspired prophecy is to give a clear witness to Jesus'.

As with John himself (1:12–20), prophets are to convey the words of Jesus and the revelation they have had of him to the church to begin with (2:1 – 3:21), where 'in the Spirit' they reveal the true identity of Jesus as the slain, yet triumphant, Lamb, who alone is worthy to receive worship (4:2; 5:1–14; 7:9–17). He is the one whom the growing crescendo of voices from around the world worship because it is on him that their hopes of justice and the recreation of the heavens and the earth depend. He is the one who has the authority to orchestrate the events of history (6:3). His followers are persecuted and the agents of evil and forces of destruction would annihilate him if they could (12:1 – 13:18). But as the story unfolds, he gains the victory and overthrows all who stand in opposition to God with a finality that permits no escape (18:1 – 20:10). The response to this testimony is to cry hallelujah and to rejoice that Eden will again be restored and God and the Lamb will take their rightful place among his people (21:1 – 22:21). The testimony is that dreadful events of hostility will soon take place, but the greater testimony is that Jesus will soon be returning in triumph (22:20).

Prophets as pastors and teachers

The most obvious tasks of the prophet, as understood from the prophetic tradition of the Old Testament, would seem to be to predict the future (1:1) and

---

19. The difficulty arises from knowing whether 'the testimony of Jesus' is subjective or objective. If it is subjective, it means the testimony Jesus gives serves as the origin of prophecy (so G. R. Beasley-Murray, *Revelation*, p. 276; and R. H. Mounce, *Revelation*, p. 342), or objective, in which case it means inspired prophecy results in 'the testimony Christians bear to Jesus' (so David E. Aune, *Revelation 17–22*, WBC 52c [Nashville: Nelson, 1998], p. 1038). The former is claimed to be more consistent with the immediate grammatical context, while the latter seems to make more sense of the meaning of the phrase. Either way, the close connection between Jesus and the Spirit is established.

to proclaim God's word to the nations (10:11). John is a prime example of this and amply accomplishes both tasks. But the function of the prophet is also to be a pastor to the church. In David Hill's judgment, 'The proclamation of the prophet is *pastoral preaching* which, by its very nature, offers guidance and instruction in the community.'[20] Hill later adds that as pastoral preachers they also 'give instruction on what the Christian way requires of individual believers' as well as of the community as a whole.[21]

The prophets of Revelation fit the picture of the prophet that Paul presents in 1 Corinthians 14:3–4, where he writes, 'Those who prophesy speak to people for their strengthening, encouragement and comfort . . . but those who prophesy edify the church.' In Revelation the prophet John is seen, particularly in chapters 2 and 3, offering the churches pastoral instruction on how they may more perfectly follow Christ in testing circumstances. He does so by providing encouragement where appropriate and by recalling them to the right paths, through repentance, where necessary. He also provides the church generally with the means of coping with the persecution about to break (chs. 4–17). He directs them to the ultimate triumph of the gospel (chs. 18–22). His aim throughout is not primarily to proclaim the gospel to an unbelieving world evangelistically, though he does so by the way, but to build up the faithfulness and 'patient endurance' of believers (1:9; 13:10; 14:12). And precisely these qualities, found in exemplary form in the church of Philadelphia, merit the commendation of Christ in 3:10.

Given the politically subversive nature of his proclamation that Christ is Lord, not Caesar, he chooses a strategy of communication that, at least after a little thought, will make sense to believers but may mystify others because of the symbolism involved. John writes of beasts and bowls, of angels and monsters, of trumpets and scrolls, and of the well-known symbols of 'Babylon' and 'Jerusalem'. His writing is analogous to a contemporary political cartoon where symbols of animals and other strange phenomena, rather than the naming of persons or situations, are used to convey meaning. And 'frequently the situations depicted are deliberately exaggerated, and even made grotesque, in order that the message may be made plain'.[22]

Figuring out the symbolism may take a little knowledge or study, but would not have defeated the original readers of the prophecy. One reason for the

---

20. Hill, 'Christian Prophets', p. 114; his italics.
21. Ibid., pp. 116–117.
22. The idea of the political cartoon and the quote come from G. R. Beasley-Murray, *Revelation*, p. 16.

transparency from their viewpoint is that Revelation is steeped in Old Testament quotations and allusions. The Old Testament provides John with language and thought forms that give him a way of describing the world he faces and of interpreting and handling it. The citations or allusions frequently pay little attention to the Old Testament context and are used in a variety of ways, sometimes to spark memories of a theme, sometimes analogically, sometimes by way of contrast, sometimes by way of fulfilment.[23] Each usage contributes to make the prophecy a potent mix that, the more she drinks it in, will strengthen the church to face her enemies.

Estimates vary as to exactly how many quotations or allusions from the Old Testament there are, chiefly depending on how strictly one measures them.[24] But all commentators are agreed that the most frequently quoted books are the prophecies of Isaiah, Daniel and Ezekiel, followed by the Psalms. This certainly adds to the impression that Revelation is alive with the spirit of the Old Testament prophets and falls within that tradition. So Revelation not only fits with Paul's description of the purposes of prophecy in 1 Corinthians 14:3, but also with the Old Testament role of both foretelling future judgment and salvation, and of instructing God's people to change their ways, in line with the prophetic role mentioned in 2 Kings 17:13–14 and Zechariah 1:4–6.[25]

If much of Revelation is taken up with future judgment and salvation, the letters to the church are letters of pastoral admonition and encouragement, calling on the churches to repent and amend their ways where necessary. So Revelation is a form of Christian paraklesis (exhortation and encouragement),[26] where the role of pastor and prophet unite. The pastor-prophet becomes 'the spirit-endowed counsellor of the community who tells it what to do in specific situations, who blames and praises, whose preaching contains admonition and comfort, the call for repentance and promise'.[27]

The work of the pastor and the prophet comes together in Revelation, supremely in the person of John himself. But what of the role of the

23. Beale, *Revelation*, pp. 76–99.

24. John Swete, cited by Beale, *Revelation*, p. 77, n. 21, lists forty-six from Isaiah; thirty-one from Daniel; twenty-nine from Ezekiel and twenty-seven from the Psalms. See discussion in G. K. Beale and Sean M. McDonough, 'Revelation', in G. K. Beale and D. A. Carson (eds.), *Commentary on the New Testament Use of the Old Testament* (Grand Rapids: Baker Academic; Nottingham: Apollos, 2007), p. 1082.

25. Hill, 'Christian Prophets', p. 116.

26. Ellis, cited by ibid., p. 115.

27. G. Friedrich cited by Hill, 'Christian Prophets' p. 119.

teacher? The gift of the teacher is distinct, distinguished from that of the prophet in the passages where Paul discusses the gifts of the Spirit (Rom. 12:3–8; 1 Cor. 12:27–31; Eph. 4:15). And yet much of what has been said so far about the prophets suggests that the gifts overlap or at least lie very close to each other. Hans von Campenhausen has sought to make the distinction between them clear. In discussing 1 Corinthians 12:28 and the priority Paul seems to give to prophets over teachers as ministries within the local church, he writes:

> The work of prophecy is to bring to men the untrammelled utterance of proclamation and revelation in which Christ is preached; teaching, however, is concerned with handing on and expounding the Christ-tradition, with impressing on men the precepts and propositions of the faith, and above all with the exegesis of the Old Testament as understood by the young church.[28]

The gift of prophecy, Campenhausen claims, expresses itself more fluidly than that of the teacher, because the teacher is circumscribed by a tradition or a text in the instruction he gives, whereas the prophet conveys a more immediate and direct word from God. While both are endowed by the Holy Spirit, both preach and instruct the church, and both seek to build up the church, but do so differently. The teacher might be said to expound Scripture, which in the early days, meant expounding the Old Testament, whereas the prophet is a motivator, exhorter and proclaimer.

In John there is a very close correspondence between these gifts. He expounds the Old Testament more than most in his own imaginative and graphic way. He does not always stick close to the text in context, but which New Testament writer does? He uses the prophetic tradition to instruct the church and digs deep into the recurring themes of Scripture to provide his readers with more than mere sound-bite promises. As teacher, he is concerned to enable his readers to have sure foundations on which to build their endurance. He spurns the superficial answer that provides only a flimsy foundation and leads to catastrophic collapse when the realities of spiritual warfare are felt with all their unrestrained force by the believers. Not for him the cheap platitudes 'It may never happen', 'Don't worry', 'Look on the bright side', 'Enjoy the power of positive thinking' or even thoughtless quotations of the much beloved and true claim of Romans 8:28. He enters fully into the

---

28. H. von Campenhausen, *Ecclesiastical Authority and Spiritual Power in the Church of the First Three Centuries*, tr. J. A. Baker (London: A. & C. Black, 1969), p. 61.

horror of the onslaught they will experience, sparing them nothing, but then gives them a sure reason for hope by calling up the ways of God with his people and in his world over the centuries. It is this that leads him to proclaim, to announce as a prophet, the victory of God and of the Lamb and the triumph of a restored Jerusalem, while Babylon lies in the dust and Satan and his companions, together with all his works, are banished to 'the lake of burning sulphur' (20:10).

In Revelation John primarily acts as the prophet to a church under threat, but his role as prophet merges into that of both the pastor and the teacher in a way that suggests it is unwise to seek to prise them apart. The gifts and roles of various leaders in the church were probably not as sharply defined as we might consider necessary today, even if the central core of each gift is distinguishable from the central core of the others. The prophet may proclaim, the teacher instruct and the pastor care. But the best prophet proclaims because he has an 'instructed tongue' (Isa. 50:4) and a sympathetic heart. The best teacher instructs with a prophetically applied edge and in a pastoral spirit. While the best pastor is one who can both challenge and instruct, not merely comfort or sympathize.

Conclusion

David Hill has provided us with a useful summary of the relationship between the prophet and the community, from which we can extract the headings by way of a summary.[29]

Prophets

- are those who speak with assumed authority within the congregation(s) they address
- address a community which itself has a prophetic character
- exercise their function primarily in the setting of congregational worship
- are people controlled by the Spirit
- function as an interpreter of events in history
- reinterpret the Old Testament in the light of the Christ-event
- are not directly associated with miracles and signs
- differentiate between themselves and false prophets

---

29. Hill, *New Testament Prophecy*, pp. 87–93.

To this we must add that prophets are those who bear testimony to Jesus, proclaiming his triumph over all evil, against all evidence to the contrary.

The church benefits from the work of the prophet at all times and in all circumstances, but in a situation of persecution the ministry of the prophet has special relevance and proves ideal. The prophet's confident assertions can boost the church's sagging morale and lift the spirits of otherwise dispirited Christians. The prophet keeps the church both persevering and faithful when compromise would be all too easy. Yet, ideally, the ministry of the prophet does not stand alone. If it is to achieve the desired aim of prophecy – that of building up and encouraging the church rather than adding to its burdens, the prophet will evince not a harsh but a pastoral tone, and not a superficial skating over the surface but an educational depth that will provide the church with true insight about the activity of God in things that 'must soon take place' (1:1).

Paul, not John, encouraged the church to 'eagerly desire spiritual gifts, especially the gift of prophecy' (1 Cor. 14:1). But one can hear John on Patmos in the Spirit saying a loud 'Amen' to the wise counsel of his fellow apostle.

15. UNITY AND DIVERSITY IN NEW TESTAMENT MINISTRY

Our examination of the contours of New Testament ministry has the danger of leaving us with an appreciation of its diversity and detail but little appreciation of the unity of the whole. Are there fourteen different models of ministry in the New Testament (other writers could doubtless identify several more) from which we can pick and choose? Can we justify our negligence of some aspects of what is expected of ministry on the basis that we are called to fulfil the model found in Matthew or Jude, but not that of Mark or Luke? If there are these diverse models of ministry, is it not reasonable to ask if there is not an equal diversity of gospels that lie behind them? Is the New Testament even more fragmented than recent New Testament scholarship (represented by James Dunn's categorization of early Christianity into four distinct groups of Jewish Christianity, Hellenistic Christianity, Apocalyptic Christianity and Early Catholicism) has proposed? Should there not be many more streams of early Christianity identified than these?

In this final chapter I seek to bring the diversity into some sense of harmony by examining the implications of the previous chapters from four distinct angles, before a brief concluding comment on the essential core of ministry.

What are the implications for the unity of the New Testament?

The relationship between the models of ministry I have presented needs clarifying. Several false relationships need to be ruled out. They are neither mutually exclusive nor in conflict with each other. There is no room for competition between them; none is superior and none inferior. All are relevant, even if some especially come to the fore in particular situations and according to the specific needs of the church of the time. Paul pointed out to the Corinthians how foolish they were to divide over the people God had sent to lead them and how unnecessary it was. 'So then, no more boasting about human leaders! All things are yours, whether Paul or Apollos or Cephas, or the world or life or death or the present or the future – all are yours, and you are of Christ, and Christ is of God' (1 Cor. 3:21–23). Given our insecurities we often wish to claim our style of ministry as superior, or even the only legitimate way of ministry. If we are not so foolish as to claim that, because none of us is yet perfect, we often engage in a competitive game with colleagues in ministry where we send out subtle signals that the way we undertake ministry is really better than theirs. But we would do well to heed Paul's exhortation.

The models of ministry stand in a complementary relationship with each other. Although each has a distinct emphasis, a number clearly overlap. Several, for example, emphasize the importance of teaching, even if Matthew, Paul and James each has a different perspective to contribute on teaching. While some, like the model presented by Mark or in Revelation, appear to be at the sharp end of spiritual conflict, they are all involved in spiritual warfare. If some, like Jude or John's letters, vigorously expose heresy, all are concerned about apostolic doctrine. They belong together and together make a complete picture.

What then explains the difference between them? In a critique of James Dunn's *Unity and Diversity in the New Testament*, Don Carson proposes a more satisfactory way of 'preserving the unity of the New Testament while recognizing its diversity' than the minimalist approach Dunn adopts.[1] Carson's essay is not directed to Dunn's comments on ministry, but what he writes about the New Testament documents generally applies as much to that as to anything. Of the seven reflections he offers on harmonizing the New Testament, two are of special relevance to us. They are:

---

1. D. A. Carson, 'Unity and Diversity in the New Testament: The Possibility of Systematic Theology', in D. A. Carson and J. D. Woodbridge (eds.), *Scripture and Truth* (Leicester: IVP, 1983), pp. 65–95.

The diversity in the New Testament very often reflects diverse pastoral concerns, with no implications whatsoever of a different creedal structure.

The diversity in the New Testament documents very often reflects the diverse personal interests and idiosyncratic styles of the individual writers.[2]

The former of these principles gives due recognition to the occasional nature of the New Testament documents. They were rooted in the real pastoral needs of the original churches to which they were addressed. They were not systematic theological works, written in a vacuum and in the abstract. The second principle recognizes the role of the individual authors, which is evident from the distinct style, language, interests and emphases found in the document. There is no need for them simply to repeat each other, or for them all to comment on everything. It should be remarked that this emphasis on personality is not without limits. It does not extend to them creating different gospels from each other, but rather to their personal inclinations being used of God to express the one gospel.[3] Neither of these principles detracts from the New Testament as inspired by the Holy Spirit. What they offer is a living document that demonstrates how leaders exercised pastoral ministry in the day-to-day realities of the early church.

Accepting that there is diversity and, for good reasons, what about unity? In spite of the claim that they are complementary, are the models of ministry, in reality, so fragmented that there is little in common between them? If so, should we expect a church and ministry so diverse that they verge on the point of incoherence? Dunn argues that the four streams of church he has identified found their unity in Christ and, in particular, 'on the unity between Jesus the man and Jesus the exalted one'.[4] Otherwise, he concludes, '*there was no single normative form of Christianity in the first century*'.[5] Perhaps the picture of the contours of ministry I have drawn adds to the impression of fragmentation.

Dunn's verdict is highly questionable. If the Bible does present early Christianity as a jigsaw of diverse pieces, they together provide a coherent and

---

2. Ibid., pp. 86, 89; italics his.

3. See discussion in Donald Guthrie, *New Testament Theology* (Leicester: IVP, 1981), pp. 37–40.

4. James D. G. Dunn, *Unity and Diversity in the New Testament* (Philadelphia: Westminster; London: SCM, 1977), p. 37. For fuller argument, see pp. 369–372.

5. Ibid., p. 373; italics his.

complete picture and 'all belong to the same puzzle'.[6] There is much more unity to be discovered between the New Testament writers than Dunn's verdict suggests. Donald Guthrie is surely right when he writes:

> The idea of unity relates to the conviction that there is only one gospel which the NT presents. There is simply no evidence to show that there were many gospels. In view of this our understanding of diversity must work within the limits of this gospel. Variations in the method of presentation there certainly are, but these may be classed as diversities only in the sense of variations in the expression of the same fundamental gospel. If diversity is used in the sense of contradiction, it is difficult to see how this can be maintained without calling in question the basic gospel. Undoubtedly, different writers will vary their expression according to the different purposes they have in mind. That is to be expected; but this is very different from the theory that there was no general agreement about the basic truths, no idea of orthodoxy to set over against heresy.[7]

If Guthrie is right, as I believe he is, this has implications for the diversity of ministry we have been exploring. The diversity finds its unity in the gospel itself and is always limited by that gospel. However varied their approach, New Testament ministers are always concerned to let the one gospel of Jesus Christ have its full impact in people's lives. And their method, language and tactics conform to that gospel. They do not, therefore, use the human weapons of wisdom, cunning, power or violence to make the gospel known. They minister as servants of Jesus Christ.

We should ask if these models are normative or only illustrative? In other words, should ministry today conform to one or another of these models or might there be new models of ministry we should be creating? Some recent pastoral theologians have been concerned to construct new metaphors of ministry, and in some cases the metaphors soon metamorphose into models.[8] I think, for example, particularly of the argument that contemporary ministry should fit the model of the professional or the manager. There is certainly

---

6. The metaphor is Carson's, 'Unity and Diversity', pp. 81–82.

7. Guthrie, *Theology*, p. 59.

8. See Ian Bunting, *Models of Ministry: Managing the Church Today*, Grove Pastoral Series 54 (Cambridge: Grove, 1993); Donald Messer, *Contemporary Images of Christian Ministry* (Nashville: Abingdon, 1989); W. Willimon, *Pastor: The Theology and Practice of Ordained Ministry* (Nashville: Abingdon, 2002), pp. 56–69. See brief discussion in D. Tidball, *Builders and Fools: Leadership the Bible Way* (Leicester: IVP, 1999), pp. 10–15.

value in contemporary images and to envisage new models is both legitimate and to be expected, given the improvisation theme mentioned earlier. We should therefore be concerned to think about fresh models of ministry today. Yet contemporary models should not contradict any of the key features of New Testament ministry. A model that is hierarchical, authoritarian, abusive, singular or exalts personality, or any model that exalts tasks to the exclusion of relationship, or growth to the exclusion of truth, would not be legitimate.

Contemporary models often seem to suffer from being more rooted in culture than in Christ. Unlike the models Paul used, they have not often been as radically transformed by the gospel as his were. Rooting ourselves in New Testament models avoids that error and provides a measure of safety. The New Testament, though set in its own cultural context, provides us with both a normative and a sufficient set of models of ministry. They are normative because they come from Christ and his apostles and define the essential nature and parameters of ministry. They are sufficient because they cover such a range of situations and such a variety of approaches that they cover whatever the church today might face.

There is, then, unity as well as diversity among the complementary models of ministry to be found within the New Testament. They serve as normative for ministry today and, while we should exercise our imagination to devise new metaphors and models for contemporary ministry, it is perilous if we cut loose from our New Testament moorings and, equally, ridiculous if we substitute the richness and depth of New Testament teaching for our own superficial understandings.

What are the implications for the individual minister?

Confronted by the diversity of models of ministry, what are individual pastors to do? Are they, on the one hand, to say that that was all very well but today the church demands a bit of everything and they cannot afford to specialize? Or are they, on the other hand, to argue that the New Testament provides a pattern for contemporary ministry that encourages pastors to pursue a specific aspect of ministry rather than fulfil a general calling and the church should be radical in following the New Testament pattern? The former may lead to frustration, as pastors are required to fulfil a range of responsibilities for which they do not feel particularly gifted or trained. The latter can easily lead to misunderstanding on the part of church members who wonder why their pastor is exercising ministry so narrowly?

The answer to the straightforward question 'What is an individual pastor to do?' must take a number of issues into consideration.

Recent tradition has tended to view the pastor as a general practitioner. Although pastors are ordained to be 'ministers of the word and sacrament'[9] (the wording varies according to the denomination they serve) and, although selection committees may focus on the ordinand's ability as a pastor and preacher, hence officially giving some priority to those tasks, the truth is that pastoral leaders in the church have been expected to fulfil a wide variety of roles. The pastor is expected to be not only pastor and preacher but also a priestly liturgist, children's friend, biblical interpreter, business administrator, programme organizer, moral guide, denominational servant, ecclesiastical representative, ecumenical advocate, community organizer, social activist, gospel evangelist, prophetic voice and increasingly a media personality as well. It is unsurprising that with such an open-ended and unstructured role, a significant proportion of ministers face disillusion and burnout at some stage in their ministry.

It may be argued, by the way, that an elder in the early church would quite naturally have undertaken all these responsibilities. But that is questionable. Several of the current demands are recent inventions, such as that of ecumenical advocate, denominational servant, media personality and even children's friend.[10] But even if it were true that the early church elders had to undertake a wide range of tasks, the scale on which they functioned as the leader of a household church in towns that were small compared to ours makes their task qualitatively, not just quantitatively, different. Ministering in the context of a highly organized, densely networked, bureaucratized society, drenched in the demands of instant and frequent communication, is very different from ministering in the context of small-scale communities.

---

9. E. Earle Ellis is right to draw attention to the fact that the New Testament does not speak in these terms, but 'the later church removed the administration of the sacraments, together with the ministries of the Word, from a congregational context to the exclusive control of a clerical and priestly class' (*Pauline Theology: Ministry and Society* [Grand Rapids: Eerdmans; Exeter: Paternoster, 1989], p. 121; see also p. 101).

10. By 'children's friend' I mean not only someone who enjoys a good relationship with children but one who is expected to be gifted in doing 'the children's talk', run 'family services' or organize 'holiday clubs'. It is only in recent history that children have been considered a separate class of human being who demand the concentrated attention they now receive. The early church would have included them in mainline activities rather than catering for them separately.

It may be inevitable that the pastor of a local church has to operate as something of a general practitioner, if only for the reason that most church communities are not large enough to support specialists. The pastor is often the only full-time staff member in a church and people therefore naturally turn to him or her first of all for assistance. It is unrealistic for people to enter contemporary ministry thinking they are able to minister exclusively on the lines of one of the specialized models of ministry found in the New Testament. Nonetheless, pastors may be helped if they have an understanding of their primary calling.[11] They can then, in consultation with their churches and without neglecting their overall responsibilities, begin to shape their ministry accordingly. They can organize their time appropriately, giving quality time to what is their uppermost calling. They can gather around them others who can complement them, assisting them with aspects of their work that are not their priority. It is foolish to dissipate a special gift in the pursuit of some vague and general goal. Many of us need to recover our primary sense of vocation from the layers of doing a lot of things just to keep religious consumers happy. If we do not, as Eugene Peterson has inimitably put it, 'before we realize what has happened, the mystery and love and majesty of God, to say nothing of the tender and delicate subtleties of souls, are obliterated by the noise and frenzy of the religious marketplace'.[12]

It may be helpful to look at it this way. Some make a helpful distinction between possessing a spiritual gift and having responsibility for a corresponding role. To illustrate: I may have the gift of an evangelist but all Christians are called upon to be witnesses; I may be a pastor but every Christian is called to care; I may not have the gift of giving but I have a responsibility to contribute to 'the collection' on a regular basis. Relating this to the work of a contemporary pastor, we may say that a pastor may have particular gifts and strengths within ministry that he or she should be permitted to devote their energies to. But even so, this does not exempt them from fulfilling other roles reasonably expected of a pastor. It is a question of proportion, shape, priorities and emphasis.

The truth is, pastors are often their own worst enemies and while protesting about the range of responsibilities laid on them are often very reluctant to release any part of their work to others. They feel they need to be 'superman' or 'superwoman' and do not want to be considered a failure in the eyes of

---

11. The same is true for volunteers who serve in the church.

12. Eugene H. Peterson, *Under the Unpredictable Plant: An Exploration in Vocational Holiness* (Grand Rapids: Eerdmans, 1992), p. 173.

others because they have not done everything. Others, however, are not always as reluctant to undertake that work as pastors fear. More honest conversation between pastoral leaders and congregations about their particular gifts and calling as well as the demands and pressures of the task often yields understanding and practical response.

Recent developments in the UK health service may prove a useful model for churches considering the shape of ministry. Although family doctors are still general practitioners of medicine, there is increasing recognition of the need to permit even general practitioners to specialize somewhat and to be helped in their role by a range of other staff, or external colleagues, who offer specialized support. Churches should be encouraged not to see every minister as possessing all the gifts within himself or herself but as being able to make a vital contribution in particular ways, according to the needs of the hour, supplemented by others who will take responsibility for other aspects of ministry. I know, for example, a gifted pastor who was a great people-person, a wise spiritual guide and not a bad preacher. His church, however, expected him, by virtue of his office, to chair every business meeting and be the up-front leader of all its community events even though he was not gifted in these areas. When I sat at his desk one Sunday afternoon, preparing for my evening preach, I saw how deep his frustration was as he had doodled more than once on his blotter, 'I hate this job.' Not long after, he left the ministry and the church lost a good pastor. Years later, a place was found for him on a team where he was not expected to do everything. In the current context, churches should be encouraged to think again about what they expect their ministers to achieve.

If the argument of this book has any merit, then pastors should ask themselves questions in two areas and understand two caveats. The first area is *personal*, including questions such as 'Who am I? What do I see as my particular calling in pastoral leadership? What are my burdens? How has God particularly gifted me? Which model of ministry is a best fit for me?' This will help us to understand our strengths and the distinct contribution we might make to the church. The second area is *contextual*: 'What are the needs of this church at this time? What threats and opportunities is this church facing? What is the context in which this church is called to minister at this time?' Bringing the answers to these two sets of questions together, by asking 'Do I, with my particular gifts, fit this situation?' should provide us with a clear indication of whether we are the right person to minister in this local church at this time or whether we are best to serve elsewhere.

The first caveat is that although we may operate basically in one type of ministry throughout our lives, there may be the need to adapt to the extent that we can. Paul, for example, provides us with a good illustration of his ability to adapt to the needs of the church as time went on. The ability to change varies according to personality and usually becomes more difficult with age, but we should not be too rigid in our understanding of ourselves. God gives grace according to our needs. The second caveat is that, while clear answers to these questions are helpful, we have to live with the real and not with the ideal, and so some flexibility in applying the answers may well be called for. Specialist calling, for example, will almost certainly need to be fulfilled within the context of being something of a general practitioner.

My hope is that the models of ministry I have set out will liberate people in pastoral leadership. I trust they will function as models of permission for people to be truer to themselves as they are made and called in Christ, rather than their having to conform to an ill-suited mould or a set of expectations imposed by others. Ministry is diverse. But, as always, the theoretical position needs to be applied with wisdom.

What are the implications for denominational understanding of ministry?

Denominational perspectives on ministry are mostly trapped in history and tradition. Denominations, by their nature, have a tendency to play safe. The living Lord of the church is certainly working through denominational chan-nels but is not confined to them, and is equally working outside them as new forms of church come into being and as existing local churches adapt their leadership structures to meet the needs they face. These often outpace cum-bersome institutional structures in recognizing the gifts God is giving for the ministry and mission of the church today, leaving the denominational systems unable to adapt quickly enough to what is happening at ground level.

As one who has been in denominational leadership and who is committed to the value of history, I would hope that the positive benefits denominations have to offer can be preserved. They do offer identity, quality control, resources and support and they do force people out of their localism to look more widely at the church of Christ. But if they are to maintain their service to the church, they need, as Loren Mead has argued, to give up being regulat-ing agencies, making others conform to the centre, and learn to become resourcing agencies, enabling ministry to happen at ground level.[13]

The New Testament shows a great deal of flexibility in the way ministry is

---

13. Loren Mead, *The Once and Future Church* (Herdon, Va.: St. Alban Institute, 1991).

practised and leadership exercised. It is foolish to replace this responsiveness with rigidity. Rather than encouraging creativity and imagination, denominations have too often sought to make gifted people conform to a ministerial straightjacket. Many a David has been forced to wear Saul's armour (1 Sam. 17:38–39). The painful result is that giants have not been slain and the church has failed to have the impact it could have had.

The early church functioned in stark contrast to this. Denominations need to follow the example of the apostles in Jerusalem who, when confronted with an unauthorized mission among the Greeks in Antioch, sent Barnabas to witness 'what the grace of God had done'. His stance was not one of doubt, criticism or condescension. Rather, 'he was glad and encouraged them all to remain true to the Lord with all their hearts' (Acts 11:19–24). A similar spirit of generosity needs to be shown to the varied patterns of ministry coming into being today, even while discernment is being exercised. Undoubtedly, this will be uncomfortable and costly. Working with pioneers and people on the margins of our understanding of ministry is not easy.[14] There will inevitably be failures, experiments that do not succeed and risks that do not pay off. But overall it is worth it, as Scripture and history demonstrate.[15]

Denominations also need to pay attention to what is missing from the New Testament with regard to ministry. Ministers are never presented as organizational leaders or directors of busy congregational programmes. Little is said about the method of their appointment and only the vaguest hint is given about the 'terms and conditions' of their position. What we do know is that they can expect to be paid for their services (1 Cor. 9:7–12; Gal. 6:6; 1 Tim. 5:17). There is no emphasis on ordination, even though the laying on of hands was clearly practised. The pastoral leader is not presented as a priest or president at the sacrament. There is no clergy–laity split. Leaders are distinguished from the congregation but remain firmly a part of it and their role in no way detracts from the emphasis on all believers ministering to one another.

Of course, times have moved on and the fact that churches now live in a

---

14. The Evangelisation Society once supported William Booth for his work in the East End Mission. Their minutes complained frequently of the way he acted (and spent money) and asked afterwards! But pioneers behave like that and the result was the eventual founding of the Salvation Army.

15. The history of the church in America bears out the value of the work of 'unauthorized' pioneers, as told by R. Finke and R. Stark, *The Churching of America: Winners and Losers in our Religious Economy* (New Brunswick: Rutgers University Press, 1992). Similar histories could be written of the church in the UK.

very different culture, which in the Western world is a culture of a bureaucratized and highly legislated state, means that denominations have to operate differently than the groupings of churches did in the New Testament period. Much of what denominations do assists churches and ministers to operate within the current legal framework as far as employment, buildings, finances and so on are concerned. Even so, we have moved too far from our biblical moorings in our views of ministry and need to recover something of its variety, flexibility, responsiveness and priorities of teaching the gospel.

What are the implications for an ecumenical understanding of ministry?

The ecumenical movement needs to come clean on ministry.[16] In its major statement on ministry, *Baptism, Eucharist and Ministry*, the World Council of Churches acknowledges several times that there is no single New Testament pattern of ministry. But rather than exploring this further as a paradigm for ministry today (as already mentioned earlier in this book), it argues that 'during the second and third centuries, a threefold pattern of bishop, presbyter and deacon became established as the pattern of ordained ministry throughout the Church'.[17] It further acknowledges that down the centuries this threefold pattern has undergone changes as it has adapted to contextual needs. It somewhat grudgingly comments that 'other forms of the ordained ministry have been blessed with the gifts of the Holy Spirit', but sees these as exceptions and claims that 'nevertheless' the threefold pattern 'may serve today as an expression of . . . unity'.[18]

---

16. See an important but relatively unknown essay by James Dunn, 'Ministry and the Ministry: The Charismatic Renewal's Challenge to Traditional Ecclesiology', in *The Christ and the Spirit*. Vol. 2: *Pneumatology* (Grand Rapids: Eerdmans; Edinburgh: T. & T. Clark, 1998), pp. 291–310, where he reviews a number of ecumenical documents and 'requestions' the restriction of ministry to 'the ministry' and the traditional concept of ordination in the light not only of the charismatic renewal but New Testament evidence. His more detailed argument in this paper provides much background support for my argument here as well as in earlier chapters.

17. *Baptism, Eucharist and Ministry*, Faith and Order Paper 111 (Geneva: World Council of Churches, 1982), clause 19.

18. Ibid., clause 22.

History, of course, cannot be ignored, nor should it be. But why does the ecumenical church take its stance on history and tradition, or rather a partial historical development and one stream of tradition, rather than on Scripture? Why does the document not commend to churches the opportunity of rediscovering something of the dynamism of the forms of New Testament ministry, while at the same time emphasizing the need for ministry to be conducted according to the biblical principles of being gospel-centred, always plural rather than single, contextual and requiring that those who lead the church are people of holiness? Why does it perpetuate an unbiblical view of apostolic succession through the episcopate 'as a sign, though not a guarantee, of the continuity and unity of the Church'? Why is this the pattern of ministry to be adopted for any future united church, instead of a pattern whereby diverse ministries are respected and recognized with due humility? And why does it only reluctantly acknowledge that a considerable proportion of the worldwide church does not see ministry in terms of the historic threefold order and that among such churches 'apostolic faith, worship and mission' has continued? After all, it is among these churches that growth is occurring, while most of the historic institutional churches are experiencing decline. A truly ecumenical movement should surely be more inclusive and representative of all churches around the world rather than merely those that have retained the threefold order of ministry.

The New Testament is far more radical in its approach to ministry than any ecumenical statement and that radicalism needs to be rediscovered if the Western church is to recover from the decline it has experienced now for over a century.

Conclusion

William Willimon writes:

> The great ethical danger for clergy is not that we might 'burn out' . . . not that we might lose the energy required to do ministry. Our danger is that we might 'black out,' that is lose consciousness as to why we are here and who we are called to be for Christ and his church.[19]

To be 'a minister of the gospel' is a wonderful calling. We dare not trade in our

---

19. *Calling and Character: Virtues of the Ordained Life* (Nashville: Abingdon, 2000), p. 21.

birthright because of the pressures of the moment – as Esau did, for a bowl of lentil stew (Gen. 25:29–34).

The New Testament presents us with no blueprint for ministry, but rather sets before us a number of models that reflect the particular emphasis of the writers and the needs of the churches to which they write. In all its diversity, however, there is a clear coherence and unity. Ministry is

about preaching the historic Jesus,
who is both Lord and Messiah,
in words and action,
enabling people to respond to his message,
enter his kingdom,
and grow in their appreciation of this gospel,
its depth and its implications,
and grow to maturity in Christ,
in the new community of which he is head,
whatever circumstances they face,
by people who are qualified in gift, understanding and holiness,
working together with others,
for the glory of God's name.

BIBLIOGRAPHY

ABRAHAM, W., *The Logic of Evangelism* (London: Hodder & Stoughton, 1989).

ADAMSON, J. B., *The Epistle of James*, NICNT (Grand Rapids: Eerdmans, 1976).

—, *James: The Man and His Message* (Grand Rapids: Eerdmans, 1989).

AGNEW, F. H., 'The Origin of the NT Apostle-Concept: A Review of Research', *JBL* 105 (1986), pp. 75–96.

AMULYA, J., 'What Is Reflective Practice?', Centre for Reflective Community Practice, Massachusetts Institute of Technology, <www.crcp.mit.doc/edu/documents/ whatis.pdf>, accessed 26 Apr. 2008.

ARNOLD, C. E., *The Colossian Syncretism* (Tübingen: Mohr, 1995).

—, *Ephesians: Power and Magic, the Concept of Power in Ephesians in the Light of its Historical Setting*, SNTSMS 63 (Cambridge: Cambridge University Press, 1989).

ASCOUGH, R., 'Matthew and Community Formation', in AUNE, *Gospel of Matthew*, pp. 96–126.

AUNE, D. E., *Revelation 6–16*, WBC 52b (Nashville: Nelson, 1998).

—, *Revelation 17–22*, WBC 52c (Nashville: Nelson, 1998).

— (ed.), *The Gospel of Matthew in Current Study* (Grand Rapids: Eerdmans, 2001).

BANKS, R., *Paul's Idea of Community* (Exeter: Paternoster, 1980).

Baptism, Eucharist and Ministry, Faith and Order Paper 111 (Geneva: World Council of Churches, 1982).

BARNETT, P. W., 'Apostle', *DPL*, pp. 45–51.

BARTLETT, D., *Ministry in the New Testament*, OBT (Minneapolis: Fortress, 1993).

BARTON, S., *The Spirituality of the Gospels* (London: SPCK, 1992).

BASH, A., *Ambassadors for Christ: An Explanation of Ambassadorial Language in the New Testament* (Leiden: Mohr, 1997).

BAUCKHAM, R., *The Climax of Prophecy* (Edinburgh: T. & T. Clark, 1993).

—, 'James and the Jerusalem Church', in R. Bauckham (ed.), *The Book of Acts in its Palestinian Setting* (Grand Rapids: Eerdmans, 1995), pp. 427–441.

—, *James: Wisdom of James, Disciple of Jesus the Sage*, New Testament Readings (London: Routledge, 1999).

—, *Jesus and the Eyewitnesses: The Gospel as Eyewitness Testimony* (Grand Rapids: Eerdmans, 2006).

—, *Jude, 2 Peter*, WBC 50 (Waco: Word, 1983).

—, *The Theology of the Book of Revelation* (Cambridge: Cambridge University Press, 1993).

— (ed.), *The Gospel for All Christians: Rethinking the Gospel Audiences* (Grand Rapids: Eerdmans, 1998).

BAXTER, R., *The Cure of Church Divisions* (London: Nevil Symmons, 1670).

BEALE, G. K., *The Book of Revelation*, NIGTC (Grand Rapids: Eerdmans; Carlisle: Paternoster, 1999).

BEALE, G. K., and MCDONOUGH, S. M., 'Revelation', in G. K. Beale and D. A. Carson (eds.), *Commentary on the New Testament Use of the Old Testament* (Grand Rapids: Baker Academic; Nottingham: Apollos, 2007), pp. 1081–1161.

BEASLEY-MURRAY, G. R., *The Book of Revelation*, NCB (London: Oliphants, 1974).

—, *John*, WBC 36 (Waco: Word, 1987).

—, *Preaching the Gospel from the Gospels* (Peabody: Hendrickson, 1996).

BEASLEY-MURRAY, P., 'Pastor, Paul as', *DPL*, pp. 654–658.

BENNETT, D., *Biblical Images for Leaders and Followers* (Oxford: Regnum, 1993).

BEST, E., *Ephesians*, ICC (Edinburgh: T. & T. Clark, 1998).

—, *Essays on Ephesians* (Edinburgh: T. & T. Clark, 1997).

—, *Mark: The Gospel as Story* (Edinburgh: T. & T. Clark, 1983).

—, 'Paul's Apostolic Authority', *JSNT* 27 (1986), pp. 3–25.

—, *Paul and his Converts* (Edinburgh: T. & T. Clark, 1988).

BOER, W. P. DE, *The Imitation of Paul: An Exegetical Study* (Kampen: Kok, 1962).

BOICE, J. M., *Witness and Revelation in the Gospel of John* (Exeter: Paternoster, 1970).

BOISMARD, M.-E., *Moses or Jesus: An Essay in Johannine Christology*, tr. B. T. Vivano (Minneapolis: Fortress, 1993).

BROWN, R. E., *The Gospel according to John I–XII*, AB (New York: Doubleday, 1966).

BRUCE, F. F., *The Acts of the Apostles: Greek Text with Introduction and Commentary*, 3rd ed. (Grand Rapids: Eerdmans; Leicester: Apollos, 1990).

—, *Commentary on Galatians*, NIGTC (Exeter: Paternoster, 1982).

—, *The Epistle to the Hebrews*, NLC (London: Marshall, Morgan & Scott, 1965).

—, *Paul: Apostle of the Free Spirit* (Exeter: Paternoster, 1977).

BRUEGGEMANN, W., *Biblical Perspectives on Evangelism* (Nashville: Abingdon, 1993).

BUCHSEL, F., '*hēgeomai*', *TDNT*, vol. 2, pp. 907–908.

BUNTING, I., *Models of Ministry: Managing the Church Today*, Grove Pastoral Series 54 (Cambridge: Grove, 1993).

CAMPBELL, A. V., *Rediscovering Pastoral Care* (London: Darton Longman & Todd, 1981).

CAMPBELL, R. A., *The Elders: Seniority within Earliest Christianity* (Edinburgh: T. & T. Clark, 1994).

CAMPENHAUSEN, H. VON, *Ecclesiastical Authority and Spiritual Power in the Church of the First Three Centuries*, tr. J. A. Baker (London: A. & C. Black, 1969).

CARSON, D. A., *The Gospel according to John*, PNTC (Grand Rapids: Eerdmans; Leicester: IVP, 1991).

—, 'Matthew', in F. E. Gaebelein (ed.), *The Expositor's Bible Commentary* (Grand Rapids: Zondervan, 1984), vol. 1, pp. 3–599.

—, 'Unity and Diversity in the New Testament: The Possibility of Systematic Theology', in D. A. Carson and J. D. Woodbridge (eds.), *Scripture and Truth* (Leicester: IVP, 1983), pp. 65–95.

CASTELLI, E. A., *Imitating Paul: A Discourse of Power* (Louisville: Westminster John Knox, 1991).

CHADWICK, W. E., *The Pastoral Teaching of St Paul: His Ministerial Ideals* (Edinburgh: T. & T. Clark, 1907).

CHESTER, A., and MARTIN, R. P., *The Theology of the Letters of James, Peter and Jude* (Cambridge: Cambridge University Press, 1994).

CHILTON, B., 'Synagogue', *DLNT*, pp. 1142–1143.

CHRYSOSTOM, J., *On the Priesthood*, NPNF[1], vol. 9 (Grand Rapids: Eerdmans, 1889).

CLARK, A., 'The Role of the Apostles', in I. H. Marshall and D. Peterson (eds.), *Witness to the Gospel: The Theology of Acts* (Grand Rapids: Eerdmans, 1998), pp. 169–190.

CLARKE, A. D., *A Pauline Theology of Church Leadership*, LNTS 362 (London: T. & T. Clark, 2007).

—, *Serve the Community of the Church: Christians as Leaders and Ministers* (Grand Rapids: Eerdmans, 2000).

COLLINS, J. N., *Diakonia: Re-Interpreting the Ancient Sources* (New York: Oxford University Press, 1990).

CONZELMANN, H., *Acts of the Apostles: A Commentary*, Hermenia (Philadelphia: Fortress, 1987).

COPAN, V. A., *St Paul as Spiritual Director: An Analysis of Imitation of Paul and its Implications and Applications to the Practice of Spiritual Direction* (Milton Keynes: Paternoster, 2007).

CRADDOCK, F. B., 'The Letter to Hebrews', NIB 12 (Nashville: Abingdon, 1998), pp. 3–173.

—, *Luke*, Interpretation (Louisville: John Knox, 1990).

CRANFIELD, C. E. B., *I and II Peter and Jude*, TBC (London: SCM, 1960).

CRANFIELD, C. E. B., *The Epistle to the Romans*, ICC 2 (Edinburgh: T. & T. Clark, 1979).

CULLMANN, O., *Peter: Disciple, Apostle, Martyr*, tr. F. V. Filson, 2nd ed. (London: SCM, 1962).

CULPEPPER, R. A., 'The Gospel of Luke', NIB 9 (Nashville: Abingdon, 1995), pp. 1–490.

DAVIDS, P. H., *The First Epistle of Peter*, NICNT (Grand Rapids: Eerdmans, 1990).

—, 'James and Jesus', in D. Wenham (ed.), *Gospel Perspectives: The Jesus Tradition outside the Gospels* (Sheffield, JSOT, 1985), vol. 5, pp. 63–84.

—, *The Letters of 2 Peter and Jude*, PNTC (Grand Rapids: Eerdmans; Leicester: Apollos, 2006).

DESILVA, D., *An Introduction to the New Testament: Contexts, Methods and Ministry Formation* (Downers Grove: IVP; Leicester: Apollos, 2004).

DOBSCHUTZ, E. VON, 'Matthew as Rabbi and Catechist', in STANTON, *Interpretation of Matthew*, pp. 19–29.

DUNN, J. D. G., *The Acts of the Apostles*, Epworth Commentaries (Peterborough: Epworth, 1996).

—, 'Ministry and the Ministry: The Charismatic Renewal's Challenge to Traditional Ecclesiology', in *The Christ and the Spirit*. Vol. 2: *Pneumatology* (Grand Rapids: Eerdmans; Edinburgh: T. & T. Clark, 1998), pp. 291–310.

—, *Romans 9–16*, WBC 38b (Dallas: Word, 1988).

—, *The Theology of Paul the Apostle* (Grand Rapids: Eerdmans; Edinburgh: T. & T. Clark, 1998).

—, *Unity and Diversity in the New Testament* (Philadelphia: Westminster; London: SCM, 1977).

EDWARDS, J. R., *The Gospel of Mark*, PNTC (Grand Rapids: Eerdmans; Leicester: Apollos, 2002).

ELLINGWORTH, P., *The Epistle to the Hebrews*, NIGTC (Grand Rapids: Eerdmans; Carlisle: Paternoster, 1993).

ELLIOTT, J. H., *The Elect and the Holy: An Exegetical Examination of 1 Peter 2:4–10*, NovTSup 12 (Leiden: Brill, 1966).

—, *A Home for the Homeless: A Sociological Exegesis of 1 Peter, its Situation and Strategy* (London: SCM, 1981).

—, 'The Jesus Movement Was Not Egalitarian but Family-Oriented', *BibInt* 11 (2003), pp. 173–210.

—, 'Jesus Was Not an Egalitarian: A Critique of an Anachronistic and Idealist Theory', *BTB* 32 (2002), pp. 75–91.

ELLIS, E. E., *Pauline Theology: Ministry and Society* (Grand Rapids: Eerdmans; Exeter: Paternoster, 1989).

—, 'The Role of the Christian Prophet in Acts', in GASQUE and MARTIN, *Apostolic History*, pp. 55–67.

—, 'Traditions in 1 Corinthians', *NTS* 32 (1986), pp. 481–502.

ESLER, P. F., *Community and Gospel in Luke-Acts: The Social and Political Motivations of Lucan theology*, SNTSMS 57 (Cambridge: Cambridge University Press, 1987).

FEE, G. D., and STUART, D., *How to Read the Bible for All Its Worth*, 3rd ed. (Grand Rapids: Zondervan, 2003).

FINKE, R., and STARK, R., *The Churching of America: Winners and Losers in our Religious Economy* (New Brunswick: Rutgers University Press, 1992).

FORD, L., *Transforming Leadership* (Downers Grove: IVP, 1991).

FRANCE, R. T., *The Gospel of Mark*, NIGTC (Grand Rapids: Eerdmans, 2002).

—, *Matthew: Evangelist and Teacher* (Exeter: Paternoster, 1989).

FUNG, R., 'Charismatic versus Organized Ministry? An Examination of an Alleged Antithesis', *EvQ* 52 (1980), pp. 195–214.

FURNISH, V., *II Corinthians*, AB (New York: Doubleday, 1984).

GAMMIE, J. G., 'Paraenetic Literature: Toward the Morphology of a Secondary Genre', *Semeia* 50 (1990), pp. 41–77.

GASQUE, W. W., and MARTIN, R. P. (eds.), *Apostolic History and the Gospel* (Exeter: Paternoster, 1970).

GAVENTA, B. R., *Our Mother St Paul* (Louisville: Westminster John Knox, 2007).

GEHRING, R. W., *House Church and Mission: The Importance of Household Structures in Early Christianity* (Peabody: Hendrickson, 2004).

GIBBS, G., *Learning by Doing: A Guide to Teaching and Learning Methods* (Oxford: Further Education Unit, Oxford Polytechnic, 1988).

GILES, K. N., 'Is Luke an Exponent of "Early Protestantism"? Church Order in the Lucan Writings', *EvQ* 55 (1983), pp. 3–20.

—, 'Prophecy, Prophets, False Prophets', *DLNT*, pp. 970–977.

—, *What on Earth Is the Church?* (London: SPCK, 1995).

GLASSON, T. F., *Moses in the Fourth Gospel* (London: SCM, 1963).

GOODING, D., *In the School of Christ: A Study of Christ's Teaching on Holiness, John 13–17* (Port Colbourne, Ont.: Gospel Folio, 1995).

GOULDNER, M. D., *Midrash and Lection in Matthew* (London: SPCK, 1974).

GREEN, J. B., 'Good News to Whom? Jesus and the "Poor" in the Gospel of Luke', in J. B. Green and M. Turner (eds.), *Jesus of Nazareth: Lord and Christ: Essays on the Historical Jesus and New Testament Christology* (Grand Rapids: Eerdmans, 1994), pp. 59–74.

—, *The Gospel of Luke*, NICNT (Grand Rapids: Eerdmans, 1997).

—, *The Theology of the Gospel of Luke* (Cambridge: Cambridge University Press, 1995).

GREEN, M., *Evangelism in the Early Church* (Eastbourne: Eagle, 1995).

GRENZ, S. J., and KJESBO, D. M., *Women in the Church: A Biblical Theology of Women in Ministry* (Downers Grove: IVP, 1995).

GRIFFITH, T., 'A Non-Polemical Reading of 1 John: Sin, Christology and the Limits of
    Johannine Christology', *TynBul* 49 (1998), pp. 253–276.

GRIFFITHS, M., *The Example of Jesus*, The Jesus Library (London: Hodder & Stoughton,
    1985).

GRUDEM, W., *1 Peter*, TNTC (Leicester: IVP; Grand Rapids: Eerdmans, 1988).

GUNDRY, R. H., *Mark: A Commentary on His Apology for the Cross* (Grand Rapids:
    Eerdmans, 1993).

—, *Matthew: A Commentary on his Literary and Theological Art* (Grand Rapids: Eerdmans,
    1982).

GUTHRIE, D., *Hebrews*, TNTC (Leicester: IVP; Grand Rapids: Eerdmans, 1983).

—, *New Testament Theology* (Leicester: IVP, 1981).

—, *The Pastoral Epistles*, TNTC (Leicester: IVP, 1990).

HAGNER, D. A., *Encountering the Book of Hebrews* (Grand Rapids: Baker Academic, 2002).

—, *Matthew 1–13*, WBC 33a (Dallas: Word, 1993).

—, 'The *Sitz im Leben* of the Gospel of Matthew', in D. R. Bauer and M. A. Powell (eds.),
    Treasures Old and New: Recent Contributions to Matthean Studies (Atlanta: Scholars Press,
    1996), pp. 27–68.

HARRINGTON, D. J., 'Matthew's Gospel: Pastoral Problems and Possibilities', in AUNE,
    Gospel of Matthew, pp. 62–73.

HARRIS, M. J., *The Second Epistle of the Corinthians*, NIGTC (Grand Rapids: Eerdmans;
    Milton Keynes: Paternoster, 2005).

—, *Slave of Christ: A New Testament Metaphor for Total Devotion to Christ*, NSBT 8 (Leicester:
    Apollos, 1999).

HARTIN, P. J., *James and the Q Sayings of Jesus*, JSNTSup 47 (Sheffield: JSOT Press, 1991).

HENGEL, M., *The Charismatic Leader and his Followers* (Edinburgh: T. & T. Clark, 1981).

HILL, D., 'Christian Prophets as Teachers and Instructors in the Church', in J.
    Panagopolous (ed.), *Prophetic Vocation in the New Testament and Today* (Leiden: Brill,
    1977), pp. 186–209.

—, *New Testament Prophecy* (London: Marshall, Morgan & Scott, 1979).

HILLYER, N., 'Scribe', *NIDNTT*, vol. 3, pp. 477–482.

HOCK, R. F., *The Social Context of Paul's Ministry: Tentmaking and Apostleship* (Philadelphia:
    Fortress, 1980).

HOOKER, M., 'A Partner in the Gospel: Paul's Understanding of his Ministry', in E. H.
    Lovering, Jr., and J. L. Sumney (eds.), *Theology and Ethics in Paul and His Interpreters*
    (Nashville: Abingdon, 1996), pp. 83–100.

HUGHES, P. E., *A Commentary on the Epistle to the Hebrews* (Grand Rapids: Eerdmans,
    1977).

JEREMIAS, J., *Jerusalem in the Time of Jesus* (London: SCM, 1967).

—, '*poimēn*', *TDNT*, vol. 6, pp. 485–502.

JOHNSON, L. T., *Decision Making in the Church* (Philadelphia: Fortress, 1983).

—, *The First and Second Letters to Timothy*, AB (New York: Doubleday, 2001).

—, 'Friendship with the World / Friendship with God: A Study in Discipleship in James', in F. F. Segovia (ed.), *Discipleship in the New Testament* (Philadelphia: Fortress, 1985), pp. 166–183.

—, *The Gospel of Luke*, SP 3 (Collegeville: Liturgical, 1991).

—, *The Letter to James*, AB (New York: Doubleday, 1995).

—, 'The Use of Leviticus 19 in the Letter of James', *JBL* 101 (1982), pp. 391–401.

KÄSEMANN, E., *Essays on New Testament Themes*, tr. W. J. Montague (London: SCM, 1964).

KEE, H. C., *The Community of the New Age* (London: SCM, 1977).

—, *Good News to the Ends of the Earth: The Theology of Acts* (Philadelphia: Trinity; London: SCM, 1990).

KELLY, J. N. D., *A Commentary on the Pastoral Epistles*, BNTC (London: A. & C. Black, 1963).

—, *The Epistles of Peter and of Jude*, BNTC (London: A. & C. Black, 1969).

KING, M. L., *A Testament of Hope: The Essential Writings of Martin Luther King Jr.*, ed. J. M. Washington (New York: HarperCollins, 1991).

KNIGHT III, G. W., *The Pastoral Epistles*, NIGTC (Grand Rapids: Eerdmans; Carlisle: Paternoster, 1992).

KRUSE, C. G., *The Letters of John*, PNTC (Grand Rapids: Eerdmans; Leicester: Apollos, 2000).

—, *New Testament Foundations of Ministry* (London: Marshall, Morgan & Scott, 1983).

KÜNG, H., *The Church*, tr. R. and R. Ockenden (London: Search, 1968).

LADD, G. E., 'Revelation and Tradition in Paul', in GASQUE and MARTIN, *Apostolic History*, pp. 223–230.

LANE, W. L., *The Gospel of Mark*, NICNT (London: Marshall, Morgan & Scott, 1974).

—, *Hebrews 1–8*, WBC 47a (Dallas: Word, 1991).

—, *Hebrews 9–13*, WBC 47b (Dallas: Word, 1991).

LANIAK, T. S., *Shepherds after My own Heart: Pastoral Traditions and Leadership in the Bible*, NSBT 20 (Downers Grove: IVP; Leicester: Apollos, 2006).

LIEU, J., *The Theology of the Johannine Epistles* (Cambridge: Cambridge University Press, 1991).

LINCOLN, A., *Ephesians*, WBC 42 (Dallas: Word, 1990).

—, *Truth on Trial: The Lawsuit Motif in the Fourth Gospel* (Peabody: Hendrickson, 2000).

LINDARS, B., *The Theology of the Letter to the Hebrews* (Cambridge: Cambridge University Press, 1991).

LITFIN, D., *St Paul's Theology of Proclamation: 1 Corinthians 1–4 and Greco-Roman Rhetoric*, SNTSMS 79 (Cambridge: Cambridge University Press, 1994).

LONG, T. G., *Hebrews*, Interpretation (Louisville: John Knox, 1997).

LUZ, U., 'The Disciples in the Gospel according to Matthew', in STANTON, *Interpretation of Matthew*, pp. 98–128.

MacDonald, M. Y., *The Pauline Churches: A Socio-Historical Study of Institutionalization in the Pauline and Deutero-Pauline Writings*, SNTSMS 60 (Cambridge: Cambridge University Press, 1988).

Malherbe, A. J., ' "Gentle as a Nurse": The Cynic Background to 1 Thess ii', *NovT* 12 (1970), pp. 205–210.

—, *Paul and the Thessalonians: The Philosophic Tradition of Pastoral Care* (Philadelphia: Fortress, 1987).

Marshall, I. H., *1 and 2 Thessalonians*, NCB (Grand Rapids: Eerdmans; London: Marshall, Morgan & Scott, 1983).

—, *1 Peter*, IVPNTC (Downers Grove: IVP; Leicester: IVP, 1991).

—, *Acts*, TNTC (Leicester: IVP, 1980).

—, *The Acts of the Apostles*, NTG (Sheffied: JSOT Press, 1982).

—, *The Epistles of John*, NICNT (Grand Rapids: Eerdmans, 1978).

—, *The Gospel of Luke*, NIGTC (Exeter: Paternoster, 1978).

—, *New Testament Theology* (Downers Grove: IVP; Leicester: Apollos, 2004).

—, *The Pastoral Epistles*, ICC (Edinburgh: T. & T. Clark, 1999).

Martin, R. P., *James*, WBC 48 (Waco: Word, 1988).

—, *Mark: Evangelist and Theologian* (Exeter: Paternoster, 1979).

—, *New Testament Foundations*, vols. 1–2 (Grand Rapids: Eerdmans, 1975, 1978).

Mead, L., *The Once and Future Church* (Herdon, Va.: St. Alban Institute, 1991).

Meeks, W., *The First Urban Christians* (New Haven: Yale University Press, 1983).

Messer, D., *Contemporary Images of Christian Ministry* (Nashville: Abingdon, 1989).

Michaels, J. R., *1 Peter*, WBC 49 (Waco: Word: 1988).

Minear, P. S., *Matthew: The Teacher's Gospel* (London: Darton Longman & Todd, 1984).

—, *To Heal and to Reveal: The Prophetic Vocation according to Luke* (New York: Crossroad, 1976).

Mitchell, M. M., 'New Testament Envoys in the Context of the Greco-Roman Diplomatic Epistolary Conventions: The Example of Timothy and Titus', *JBL* 111 (1992), pp. 641–662.

Moo, D. J., *The Epistle to the Romans*, NICNT (Grand Rapids: Eerdmans, 1996).

—, *The Letter of James*, PNTC (Grand Rapids: Eerdmans; Leicester: Apollos, 2000).

Moule, C. F. D., 'The Individualism of the Fourth Gospel', in *Essays in New Testament Interpretation* (Cambridge: Cambridge University Press, 1982), pp. 91–109.

Mounce, R. H., *The Book of Revelation*, NICNT (Grand Rapids: Eerdmans, 1977).

Mounce, W. D., *Pastoral Epistles*, WBC 46 (Nashville: Nelson, 2000).

Myers, C., *Binding the Strong Man: A Political Reading of Mark's Story of Jesus* (Maryknoll: Orbis, 1995).

Neale, D. A., *'None but the Sinners': Religious Categories in the Gospel of Luke*, JSNTSup 58 (Sheffield: JSOT Press, 1991).

Nolland, J., *Luke 1:1–9:20*, WBC 35a (Dallas: Word, 1989).

O'BRIEN, P. T., *The Letter to the Ephesians*, PNTC (Grand Rapids: Eerdmans; Leicester: Apollos, 1999).

—, 'Mystery', *DPL*, pp. 621–623.

ORTON, D. E., *The Understanding Scribe: Matthew and the Apocalyptic Ideal*, JSNTSup 25 (Sheffield: Sheffield Academic Press, 1989).

PETERSON, E. H., *The Contemplative Pastor: Returning to the Art of Spiritual Direction* (Grand Rapids: Eerdmans, 1989).

—, *Under the Unpredictable Plant: An Exploration in Vocational Holiness* (Grand Rapids: Eerdmans, 1992).

POWELL, M. A., *God with Us: A Pastoral Theology of Matthew's Gospel* (Minneapolis: Fortress, 1995).

QUAST, K., *Peter and the Beloved Disciple: Figures for a Community in Crisis*, JSNTSup 32 (Sheffield: Sheffield Academic Press, 1989).

QUICKE, M., *360-Degree Leadership: Preaching to Transform Congregations* (Grand Rapids: Baker, 2006).

—, *360-Degree Preaching: Hearing, Speaking and Living the Word* (Grand Rapids: Baker; Carlisle: Paternoster, 2003).

SCHLIER, H., '*bebaios*', *TDNT*, vol. 1, pp. 600–603.

SCHNABEL, E. J., *Early Christian Mission*. Vol. 1: *Jesus and the Twelve* (Downers Grove: IVP; Leicester: Apollos, 2004).

—, *Early Christian Mission*. Vol. 2: *Paul and the Early Church* (Downers Grove: IVP; Leicester: Apollos, 2004).

SCHROTENBOER, P., 'An Evangelical Response to BEM', *ERT* 13.4 (1989), pp. 291–313.

SELWYN, E. G., *The First Epistle of Peter*, 2nd ed. (Grand Rapids: Baker, 1982).

SENIOR, D., 'Directions in Matthean Studies', in AUNE, *Gospel of Matthew*, pp. 5–21.

SMITH, C., *American Evangelicalism: Embattled and Thriving* (Chicago: University of Chicago Press, 1988).

SMITH, D. M., 'Theology and Ministry in John', in E. E. Shelp and R. Sunderland (eds.), *A Biblical Basis for Ministry* (Philadelphia: Westminster, 1981), pp. 186–228.

—, *The Theology of the Gospel of John* (Cambridge: Cambridge University Press, 1995).

SPENCER, F. S., *The Portrait of Philip in Acts: A Study of Roles and Relations*, JSNTSup 67 (Sheffield: Sheffield Academic Press, 1982).

SPURGEON, C. H., *Lectures to My Students*, First Series (London: Passmore & Alabaster, 1900).

STANTON, G., *A Gospel for a New People: Studies in Matthew* (Edinburgh: T. & T. Clark, 1992).

— (ed.), *The Interpretation of Matthew* (London: SPCK, 1983).

STOTT, J. R. W., *Calling Christian Leaders: Biblical Models of Church, Gospel and Ministry* (Leicester: IVP, 2002).

—, *The Contemporary Christian* (Leicester: IVP, 1992).

STOTT, J. R. W., *The Epistles of John*, TNTC (London: Tyndale, 1964).

—, *The Message of Romans*, BST (Leicester: IVP, 1994).

STROM, M., *Reframing Paul: Conversations in Grace and Community* (Downers Grove: IVP, 2000).

TETLEY, J., 'Ordained Married Couples: A Theological Reflection', *Anvil* 9 (1992), pp. 149–156.

THIELICKE, H., *The Waiting Father* (Cambridge: James Clarke, 1960).

THISELTON, A. C., *The First Epistle to the Corinthians*, NIGTC (Grand Rapids: Eerdmans; Carlisle: Paternoster, 2000).

THOMPSON, J. W., *Pastoral Ministry according to Paul: A Biblical Vision* (Grand Rapids: Baker Academic, 2006).

THOMPSON, M. B., 'Tradition', *DPL*, pp. 943–945.

THURÉN, L., *Argument and Theology in 1 Peter: The Origins of Christian Paraenesis*, JSNTSup 114 (Sheffield: Sheffield Academic Press, 1995).

TIDBALL, D., *Builders and Fools: Leadership the Bible Way* (Leicester: IVP, 1999).

—, 'Practical and Pastoral Theology', *NDCEPT*, pp. 42–48.

—, *The Message of the Cross*, BST (Leicester: IVP, 2001).

—, *Skilful Shepherds: Explorations in Pastoral Theology*, 2nd ed. (Leicester: Apollos, 1997).

—, *The Social Context of the New Testament*, BCL 32 (Carlisle: Paternoster, 1997).

—, 'Social Setting of Mission Churches', *DPL*, pp. 883–892.

TILBORG, S. VAN, *The Jewish Leaders in Matthew* (Leiden: Brill, 1972).

TOON, P., 'Episcopalianism', in S. Cowan (ed.), *Who Runs the Church?* (Grand Rapids: Zondervan, 2004), pp. 21–48.

TOWNER, P. H., *The Goal of our Instruction: The Structure of Theology and Ethics in the Pastoral Epistles*, JSNTSup 34 (Sheffield: Sheffield Academic Press, 1989).

—, *The Letters to Timothy and Titus*, NICNT (Grand Rapids: Eerdmans, 2006).

TSANG, N. M., 'Paul as Teacher in 1 Thessalonians 1:2–2:12' (PhD diss., Brunel University, 2006).

TURNER, M., *Baptism in the Holy Spirit*, Renewal Series 2 (Cambridge: Grove, 2000).

—, *The Holy Spirit and Spiritual Gifts: Then and Now* (Carlisle: Paternoster, 1996).

—, *Power from on High: The Spirit in Israel's Restoration and Witness in Luke-Acts*, JPTSup 9 (Sheffield: Sheffield Academic Press, 1996).

TWELFTREE, G. H., *Jesus: The Miracle Worker* (Downers Grove: IVP, 1999).

—, 'Scribes', *DJG*, pp. 732–735.

WALTON, S., *Leadership and Lifestyle: The Portrait of Paul in the Miletus Speech and 1 Thessalonians*, SNTSMS 108 (Cambridge: Cambridge University Press, 2000).

WARRINGTON, K., *Jesus the Healer: Paradigm or Phenomenon?* (Carlisle: Paternoster, 2000).

WEBB, W. J., *Slaves, Women and Homosexuals: Exploring the Hermeneutics of Cultural Analysis* (Downers Grove: IVP, 2001).

WESTCOTT, B. F., *The Gospel according to St. John* (London: James Clarke, 1958).

WHITE, R. E. O., *An Open Letter to Evangelicals: A Devotional and Homiletic Commentary on the First Epistle of John* (Exeter: Paternoster, 1964).

WILLIMON, W., *Calling and Character: Virtues of the Ordained Life* (Nashville: Abingdon, 2000).

—, *Pastor: The Theology and Practice of Ordained Ministry* (Nashville: Abingdon, 2002).

WINTER, B. W., *After Paul Left Corinth: The Influence of Secular Ethics and Social Change* (Grand Rapids: Eerdmans, 2001).

WRIGHT, T., *Mark for Everyone* (London: SPCK, 2001).

YANCEY, P., *What's So Amazing About Grace?* (Grand Rapids: Zondervan, 1997).

YATES, T., 'The Importance of Repentance', *Care and Counsellor* 4.2 (1994), pp. 20–23.

YORK, J. O., *The Last Shall Be First: The Rhetoric of Reversal in Luke*, JSNTSup 46 (Sheffield: Sheffield Academic Press, 1991).

INDEX OF SCRIPTURE REFERENCES

INDEX OF NAMES AND SUBJECTS

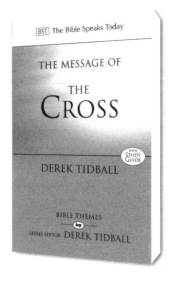
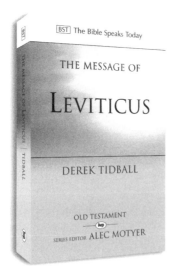

Shepherds after My own Heart

Pastoral traditions and leadership in the Bible

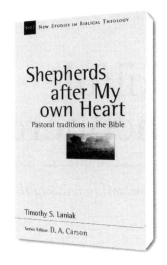

'I will give you shepherds after my own heart, who will lead you with knowledge and understanding' –Jeremiah 3:15

Most of the Bible's pastoral imagery is grounded in two traditions: Israel's 'wilderness drama', and the shepherd-king David and his dynasty, with its messianic promises. Old Testament prophets like Jeremiah made sustained use of pastoral imagery, seeing the LORD revealing himself as the ultimate Shepherd of his flock, and creating expectation of a new exodus and a unique shepherd king.

These traditions provided prototypes for leaders that followed, and formed the background for the ministry of Jesus – the 'good shepherd'. His disciples were sent as shepherds to feed his sheep – and as sheep among wolves. Today's pastors are still called to be shepherds after God's own heart, to lead his people, living on the margins of settled society, to their eternal home.

In this excellent study, Timothy Laniak draws on a wide range of Old and New Testament texts to develop a biblical theology of 'shepherd' imagery, and concludes with some principles and implications for contemporary 'pastoral' ministry.

Paperback 320 pages
ISBN: 978-1-84474-127-4

Available from your local Christian bookshop or via our website at **www.ivpbooks.com**

Skilful Shepherds

Explorations in pastoral theology

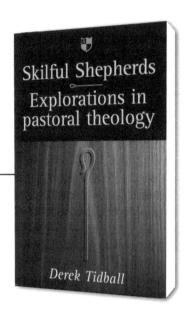

Pastoral theology is theology seen from the shepherding perspective. Relating to every aspect of church life – from leading congregations to counselling individuals – it calls for pastors with a good grasp of Christian doctrine and a wide range of skills.

Many books on this subject focus on the behavioural and social sciences. Others concentrate on management techniques. This book is different. The author seeks a biblical foundation for pastoral theology. He then surveys the various ways in which it has been understood in the history of the church. In his final section Dr Tidball considers five major themes – belief, forgiveness, suffering, unity and ministry – as examples of pastoral theology at work in the church today.

Since its first release in 1986, *Skilful Shepherds* has come to be seen as something of a classic in its field – the need for good pastoral theology has not diminished.

Paperback 368 pages
ISBN: 978-0-85111-454-5

Available from your local Christian bookshop or via our website at **www.ivpbooks.com**